Adobe Photoshop Elements 8

Unleash the hidden performance of Elements

Mark Galer

ELSEVIER

AMSTERDAM • BOSTON • HEIDELBERG • LONDON • NEW YORK • OXFORD
PARIS • SAN DIEGO • SAN FRANCISCO • SINGAPORE • SYDNEY • TOKYO
Focal Press is an imprint of Elsevier

Focal
Press

Focal Press is an imprint of Elsevier
The Boulevard, Langford Lane, Kidlington, Oxford OX5 1GB, UK
30 Corporate Drive, Suite 400, Burlington, MA 01803, USA

First edition 2010

Notices

Knowledge and best practice in this field are constantly changing. As new research and
experience broaden our understanding, changes in research methods, professional practices,
or medical treatment may become necessary.

Practitioners and researchers must always rely on their own experience and knowledge in
evaluating and using any information, methods, compounds, or experiments described herein.
In using such information or methods they should be mindful of their own safety and the safety
of others, including parties for whom they have a professional responsibility.

To the fullest extent of the law, neither the Publisher nor the authors, contributors, or editors,
assume any liability for any injury and/or damage to persons or property as a matter of
products liability, negligence or otherwise, or from any use or operation of any methods,
products, instructions, or ideas contained in the material herein.

British Library Cataloguing in Publication Data
A catalogue record for this book is available from the British Library

Library of Congress Control Number: 2009938288

ISBN: 978-0-2405-2183-1

For more information on all Focal Press publications
visit our website at: www.focalpress.com

Printed and bound in Canada

09 10 11 12 11 10 9 8 7 6 5 4 3 2 1

for Dorothy

Picture Credits

Contents - part 1

1

mize

optimize

Contents - part 2

2

enhance

Contents - part 3

3

montage

Contents - dvd

The DVD is a veritable treasure trove of supporting files for the projects in this book as well as a resource for your own creative projects. Just transfer the supporting files to your Photoshop Elements Organizer (see 'Getting Started'- page xiv) or Pictures folder for fast access to the images and movies. The movies are an invaluable resource, allowing you to start, stop and rewind so that the skills can be quickly and easily acquired at your own pace. The DVD also contains multilayered image files (PSDs) of the completed projects, uncompressed TIFF files with saved selections, Raw files and high-quality 16 Bits/Channel files. Loadable presets are also available to enhance your software together with a rich stock library of royalty-free images.

THE DVD PROVIDES EXTENSIVE SUPPORT IN THE FORM OF:

- Over seven hours of movie tutorials recorded using versions 7 and 8 of Photoshop Elements. These will support you through all of the projects in this book. You may need to install the QuickTime movie player from the supporting DVD to watch the movies from the Organizer or Bridge within Photoshop Elements 7 or 8.

- High-resolution, high-quality JPEG images to support all of the imaging projects.

- Full-resolution TIFF images with 'saved selections' for users interested in completing the projects in the least amount of time whilst achieving maximum quality.

- Camera Raw and 16 Bits/Channel files.

- Multilayered Photoshop documents (PSD files) of completed projects.

- A stock library of 100 high-resolution, royalty-free images for creative montage work.

- Adobe presets (layer styles and gradients) to enhance the performance capabilities of your Adobe Photoshop Elements software.

- Maximum Performance Action files to fast-track your workflows and editing tasks.

- Maximum Performance Smart Brushes to enhance your editing tasks.

- Printable PDF file of keyboard shortcuts to act as a quick and handy reference guide to speed up your image-editing tasks.

- Bonus project on DVD with supporting images and movie tutorial.

Preface

The creative projects in *Adobe Photoshop Elements 8 Maximum Performance* are designed to provide you with the essential techniques for professional quality editing – without the need to upgrade to the full version of Photoshop. The projects are designed to unleash the hidden potential of the budget software through a series of workarounds, advanced techniques and loadable presets. Each creative project is supported by a QuickTime movie tutorial and high-resolution images – all available on a supporting DVD. The DVD contains full and comprehensive movie support together with a library of royalty-free, high-resolution stock images for self-initiated creative projects. Each project is designed to build the skills required so that any photographer can attain the status of 'imaging guru'. The magic is deconstructed using a series of easy-to-follow step-by-step projects using large clear screen grabs and jargon-free explanations. Completed multilayered project files are also available on the DVD for those users who like to have access to the completed project for comparison and analysis.

This book will act as your guide to some of Elements' less well-known and more powerful post-production editing techniques. It will enable you to attain the same high-quality images as professionals using the full version of Photoshop. This book makes Elements a viable alternative to the full version of Photoshop for imaging professionals and enthusiasts looking to extract the maximum performance from their software.

This book is primarily concerned with the post-production stage of the creative process and demonstrates how this part of the creative process can optimize and enhance the original capture or create an entirely new image out of several images (the creation of a composite photograph or photomontage). Where appropriate the book will discuss measures that can be taken by the photographer in pre-production or production to enable the highest quality outcome as a result of the post-production stage. To ensure the best quality image from our sophisticated and professional post-production techniques we should make certain that we access quality raw materials whenever possible – 'quality in, quality out'. The vast majority of the JPEG images on the supporting DVD were processed from either Camera Raw files or high-quality 16 Bits/Channel scans. Many of the images featured in this book were captured using budget digital SLR and fixed-lens digital cameras, affordable cameras used to capture information-rich images.

The techniques used in this book promote a non-destructive approach to image editing wherever possible. The term 'non-destructive image editing' refers to the process of editing an image whilst retaining as much of the original information as possible and editing in such a way that any modifications can usually be undone or modified. Editing on the base layer of the image can often mean that modifications to the pixel information cannot be undone easily or at all, e.g. sharpening an image file cannot be undone once the file has been saved and flattened. It is, however, possible to sharpen non-destructively in post-production so that the amount of sharpening can be altered when the file is opened at a later date. This latter approach would be termed 'non-destructive'. When capturing images with a digital camera many users do not realize that if the JPEG file format is used image processing starts in the camera. Color correction, contrast adjustment, saturation levels and sharpening all take place in the camera. If maximum quality is to be realized the Raw format should be chosen in preference to the JPEG format, if possible. The post-production decisions can then be left to the Adobe software, allowing the user many more options.

Photoshop Elements replaced 'Photoshop LE' (limited edition – as in limited function and not availability); both of these software packages share something in common – they offer limited elements of the full version of Photoshop. Adobe strips out some of the features that would be the first port of call for some professional image editors and photographers, but this does not mean that the same level of control cannot be achieved when using the budget software. Professional post-production image editing does NOT have to be compromised by using Photoshop Elements. When editing images there is usually more than a single way to reach the destination or required outcome. With a good roadmap the Elements user can reach the same destination by taking a slightly different course. These roads are often poorly signposted, so are often inaccessible to the casual user of the software. This book will act as your guide to enable you to attain a broad range of sophisticated post-production image-editing skills through a series of creative projects designed to circumnavigate the missing features.

Photoshop Elements IS a viable alternative to the full version of Photoshop for most professional image-editing tasks. Many professionals may disagree with this statement, as a quick glance at the Elements package may result in a long list of the elements that are missing rather than taking a long hard look at the elements that remain (a case of 'the glass is half empty' rather than 'the glass is half full'). After a decade of professional image editing I have learnt that there is more than one way to create an image. There is no 'one way'. In short, it is possible to take a high-quality image file and work non-destructively to create an image which is indistinguishable from one that has been optimized using the full version of Photoshop. This book does not aim to outline every tool in your kit (a paintbrush doesn't really require an owner's manual and some of the automated features are sometimes more trouble than they are worth). It just deals with how to adapt the tools you do have to perform the tasks you didn't think you were able to. It aims to show you that Elements is better equipped than you were led to believe. Photoshop Elements really is the proverbial wolf in sheep's clothes.

mark galer

Location image by Dorothy Connop

Getting Started

Most users of this book will have some experience of digital imaging and Photoshop Elements, but just check the following to make sure all is in order before you start.

Following orders

The commands in Photoshop Elements allow the user to modify digital files and are accessed via menus and submenus. The commands used in the projects are listed as a hierarchy, with the main menu indicated first and the submenu or command second, e.g. Main Menu > Command. For example, the command for applying a Levels adjustment would be indicated as follows: Enhance > Adjust Lighting > Levels. If you get stuck or are unclear, watch the movie on the supporting DVD and follow my mouse cursor to help you find what you are looking for.

Calibrate your monitor

If your images are going to look good everywhere – not just on your own monitor – it is advised that you calibrate your monitor (set the optimum color, brightness and contrast). I recommend that you use a 'Hardware White Point' or 'Color Temperature' of 6500 °K (daylight) and a gamma of 2.2.

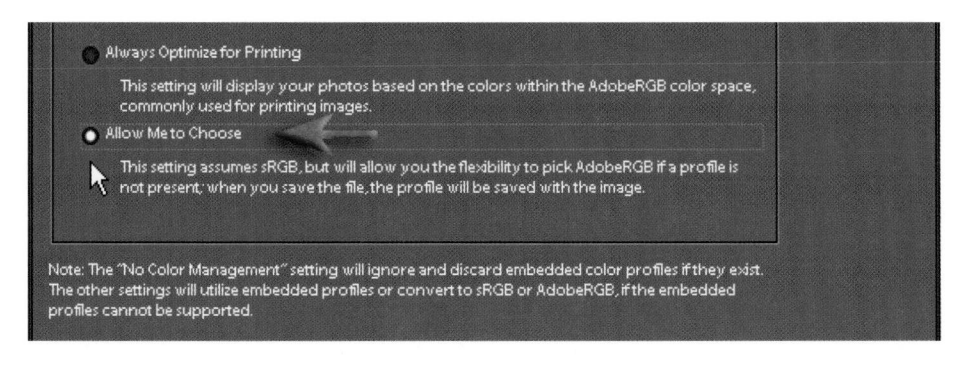

Color settings

The colors are kept consistent between devices such as cameras, computers and printers through the use of color profiles. If you intend to print your images you would be advised to go to Edit > Color Settings and then click on the radio button that says 'Always Optimize for Printing'. Elements will now use the larger Adobe RGB profile instead of the smaller sRGB profile.

Memory

You will be working on images in excess of six megapixels (the supporting DVD provides high-resolution images for ALL of the creative projects in this book). This professional level of image editing can place a strain on a computer's working memory or RAM. It is advised that you install at least one gigabyte of RAM (two gigabytes or more is not considered excessive when editing very large image files) so that the image editing you are about to undertake does not begin to crawl. Shut down any other applications that you are not using so that all of the available memory is made available to Photoshop Elements. Photoshop Elements keeps a memory of your image-editing process that it calls the 'History States'. The default setting in the General Preferences (Edit > Preferences > General) is 50 History States. Allowing the user to track back 50 commands, or clicks of the mouse, can again place an enormous strain on the working memory. I would recommend that you lower this figure to 20 for most editing work. This can be readjusted without restarting the software should you wish to increase Photoshop's memory for your editing actions. Just remember that the more memory you dedicate to what you have just done, the less you have available for what you are about to do. In Preferences > Performance you will see the Available RAM and the Ideal Range that can be assigned to Photoshop Elements. Adjust the slider so that you are using the top of the suggested range. Photoshop Elements will also be using your 'scratch disk' or hard drive in the image-editing process so be sure to keep plenty of gigabytes of free space available.

Give yourself some elbow room

I recommend that you keep the Photo Bin and Panel Bin closed until you need them (go to Window > Panel Bin). This will maximize the area on your screen for viewing the image you are editing. Only the Layers panel is used all of the time in advanced image editing. In the default mode it is stacked with the other panels in the Panel Bin. Locate the Layers panel and drag it out into the working area before closing the Bins. Similarly the Tools panel on the left side of the screen can be dragged to new locations so that it can be close to the action. I prefer to view the image in a window rather than in Maximize mode. This allows me to see the additional information that is displayed in the title bar together with the magnification. I like to view my images at 50% or 100% (Actual Pixels) to gain a more accurate idea of the image quality. This information is also available in the Navigator panel but, as I use keyboard shortcuts for moving and zooming in and out of images, I usually keep this panel closed as well.

Keyboard shortcuts

Many commands that can be accessed via the menus and submenus can also be accessed via keyboard shortcuts. A shortcut is the action of pressing keys on the keyboard to carry out a command (rather than clicking a command or option in a menu). Shortcuts speed up digital image processing enormously and it is worth learning the examples given in the study guides. If in doubt use the menu (the shortcut will be indicated next to the command) until you become more familiar with the key combinations. See the 'Shortcuts' sections at the end of the book for a list of the most frequently used shortcuts.

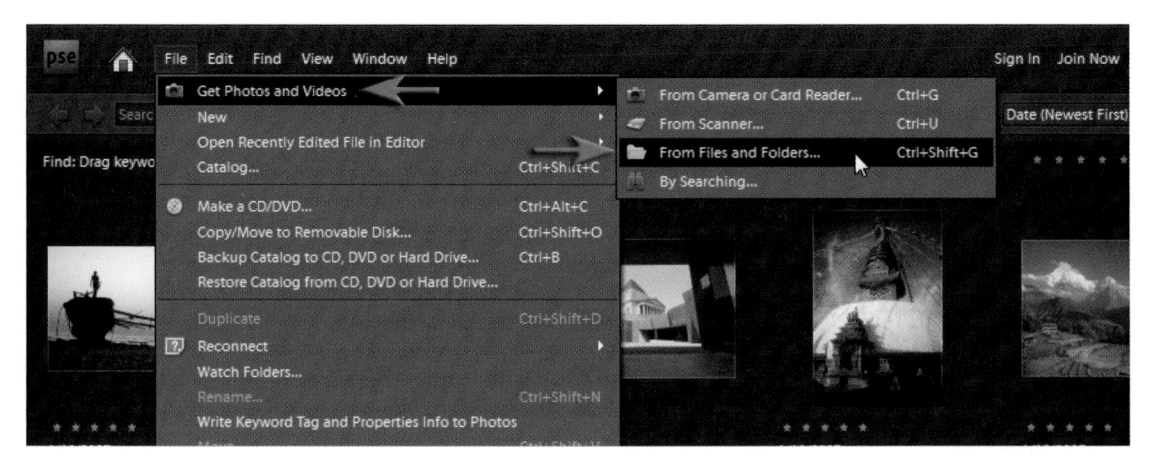

Accessing the support images and movies (Windows)

Open the Organizer from the Photoshop Elements welcome screen or click on the Organize icon directly above the Options bar in the Edit workspace. Install the DVD and click on the Organize and Edit option if asked. Alternatively, go to File > Get Photos and Videos in the Organizer workspace (the little camera) and choose the From Files and Folders option. Then locate the DVD (My Computer > MP8-DVD) and the resource folder you want to import. The JPEG files are high quality but will not take up much space on your hard drive. The TIFF files take up a little more room on your hard drive but have the advantage of containing saved selections that can be used to speed up the completion of the projects.

IMPORTANT: Download one folder of images or movies at a time so that they are separated in the Organizer space. **You may need to install the QuickTime movie player that is available on the DVD before watching the movies in the Organizer workspace.**

When the Get Photos and Videos dialog box opens make sure the Automatically fix Red Eye option in not checked and then click on the Get Photos button. Your images or movies will be imported and organized. Click on the Folder Location option from the Display menu in the Organizer window (top right-hand corner) to see the images as a collection. Use the keyboard shortcut Ctrl/Command + I to open any image in the Editor workspace. Double-click on any movie icon to watch the movie within the Organizer workspace.

Maximum Performance actions

On the DVD are two folders titled MP8_Photo-Effects and MP8_Action-Player in the MP8_Auto-Features folder. These folders contain files that may enable you to perform automated editing procedures for fast-tracking some of the skills presented in this book – a few clicks of the mouse that will then instruct Photoshop Elements to conduct an automated series of steps in just a few seconds. These actions may complete the editing task or just fast-track some of the repetitive editing procedures with the minimum of fuss. The actions may be installed using the Maximum Performance installer package (automated installation) on the DVD or manually by adding a series of action files and XML files that will help classify the new content for Elements 8. The actions can then be accessed via the Action Player in the Guided Edit space or from the Effects panel in the Full Edit space of Photoshop Elements.

Note > After installation restart Photoshop (the database may take several minutes to rebuild).

IMPORTANT: Some of the folders you need to find in order to add these files manually are 'hidden'. To find these folders you MUST select 'Show hidden files and folders' in the Folder Options > View advanced settings of your computer's operating system.

DISCLAIMER: The Maximum Performance actions will only work when using an English language version of Photoshop Elements 7 or 8 (and they may not work on previous versions). There is no guarantee that the actions will work on your computer. Every effort has been made to ensure that these actions can be implemented on standard systems running either Windows XP, Windows Vista or Apple OSX, but it is possible that a particular system setup or configuration may prevent these actions from working. Consult your local IT specialist if in doubt about any of these procedures.

Locating the folders in Windows XP for manual installation

The Action Player folder can be located by going to <windows volume>:\Documents and Settings\All Users\ApplicationData\Adobe\Photoshop Elements\<7.0 or 8.0>\Locale\<installed locale>\Workflow Panels\Actions. The adjustment layers, layer styles and photo effects folders are located in the Photo Creations folder, <windows volume (usually C:)> \Documents and Settings\All Users\Application Data\ Adobe\Photoshop Elements\<7.0 or 8.0>\Photo Creations\Photo Effects.

Important: Delete the MediaDatabase.db3 and ThumbDatabase.db3 files (see illustration above).
Note > After installation restart Photoshop (the database may take several minutes to rebuild).

Locating the folders in Windows Vista for manual installation

Like application data on XP, program data resides in a hidden folder, so the user will need to show hidden folders to find these folders. The Action Player files are placed in the Locale file: <windows volume (usually C:)>\Program Data\Adobe\Photoshop Elements\<7.0 or 8.0>\<installed locale>\ Workflow Panels\Actions. The Photo Creations folder for MP8_Photo-Effects in Vista is in <windows volume (usually C:)>\Program Data\Adobe\Photoshop Elements\7.0 or 8.0\Photo Creations.

Important: Delete the MediaDatabase.db3 and ThumbDatabase.db3 files (see illustration above).
Note > After installation restart Photoshop (the database may take several minutes to rebuild).

Locating the folders in Apple OSX for manual installation

The Action Player folder can be located by going to <Macintosh HD>:\Library\Application Support\ Adobe\Photoshop Elements\8.0\Locale\<installed locale>\Workflow Panels\Actions. The adjustment layers, layer styles and photo effects folders are located in the Photo Creations folder <Macintosh HD>:\Library\ Application Support\Adobe\Photoshop Elements\8.0\Photo Creations.

Important: Delete the MediaDatabase.db3 and ThumbDatabase.db3 files (see illustration above).
Note > After installation restart Photoshop (the database may take several minutes to rebuild).

When you see the Maximum Performance Action logo in Part 2 and Part 3 of this book, certain steps can be fast-tracked with just a few clicks of your mouse.

Actions from the Photo Effects panel

Actions can be accessed through the Effects panel or via the new Action Player in Photoshop Elements 8 (see page xxii). Click on the Photo Effects icon in this panel and choose Maximum Performance from the menu. Click on an action and then click the Apply button. Some of the actions may require opacity changes in the layers to fine-tune the effect or some further work as in the case of the Dodge and Burn action. Try combining various actions to create different effects.

Note > The masking actions are intended for the montage projects outlined in Part 3 of this book and will only work when a second layer named Layer 1 is sitting above the background layer.

BlackWhite and **BW_Luminosity** – converts color images into black and white using non-destructive adjustment layers or blend modes (see Part 2, Project 3 and Part 2, Project 8).

Channel_Blue, **Channel_Green** and **Channel_Blue** – extracts the red, green or blue channel information from a color image and places it as a gray layer above the background layer (see Part 2, Project 9).

Dodge-Burn – places a gray layer in the Overlay blend mode that can be used for non-destructive dodging and burning.

Mask_black and **Mask_white** – can be used to fast-track extracting a subject from a black or white background (see Part 3, Project 8).

Mask_HDR – fast-tracks the montage of two separate exposures to achieve an image with a higher dynamic range (see Part 3, Project 6).

Sharp_Print and **Sharp_Screen** – applies a composite layer and sharpens the image for screen or for print.

Softer_3-6MP and **Softer_6-12MP** – creates smooth tone images that are either three to six megapixels or six to twelve megapixels (see Part 2, Project 6).

Tone _1, **Tone_2** and **Tone_3** – creates split-tone images using non-destructive adjustment layers and gradient presets (see Part 2, Project 4).

Vignette_dark and **Vignette_light** – darkens or lightens the corners of an image using a non-destructive layer and blend mode.

iStock_000001683436 Headshot by aldra

USING THE ACTIONS FROM THE PHOTO EFFECTS PANEL

This stock image (courtesy of www.iStockphoto.com) was created using multiple actions. The Soft Focus effect was first applied and then followed by the Vignette, Dodge and Burn, Split Tone and Sharpen actions. A Transform command was used on the vignette and a little painting in the Dodge and Burn layer was needed to brighten the teeth and eyes in this three-minute makeover.

Maximum Performance actions via the Action Player

In Photoshop Elements 7 and 8 users can now play actions via the Guided Edit panel in addition to the Effects panel. The Action Player provides access to the Maximum Performance actions that can be used to fast-track or enhance your imaging projects. The additional actions that can be loaded into the Action Player include Black and White conversions, Channel Splitting, Smooth Tone effects, Surface Blur, Tone Mapping, Toning and Vignettes.

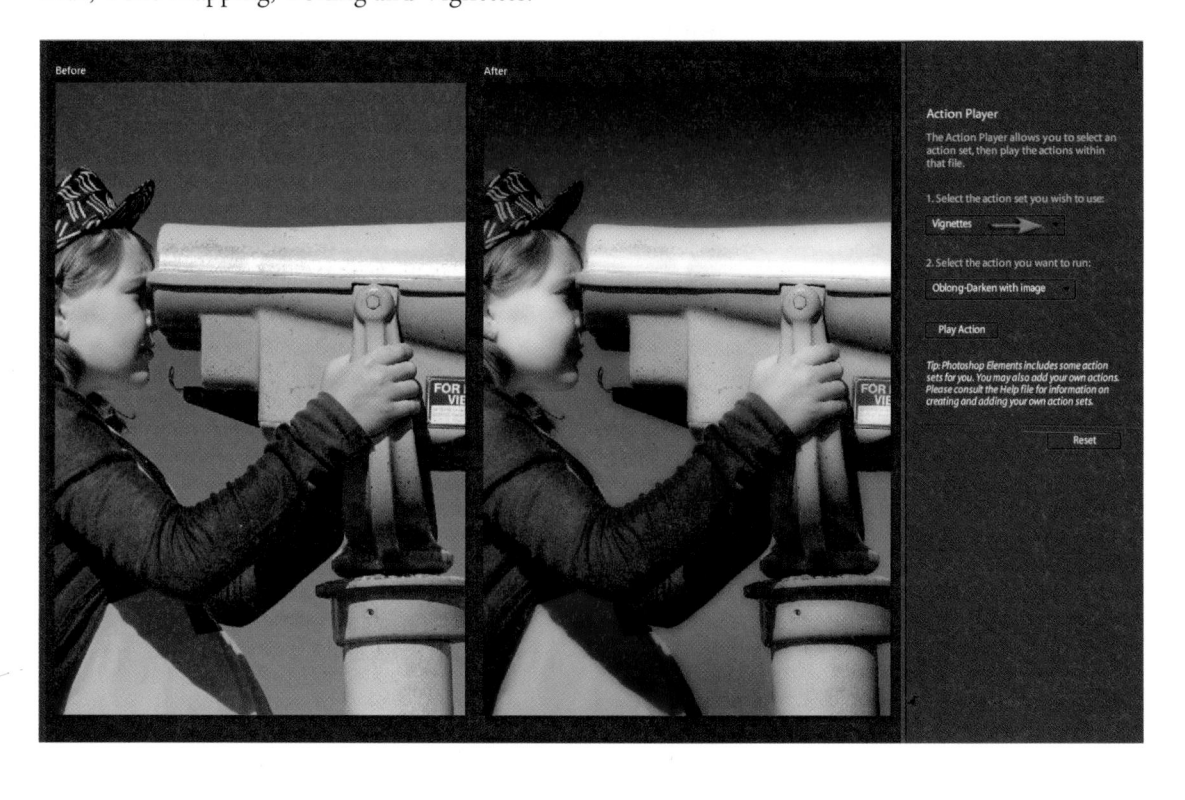

Advantages to using the Action Player

Although the user has to leave the Full Edit workspace to apply the action, the Action Player has the added flexibility of being able to preview a before and after view of the effect and allow you to reset the image to the step prior to applying the action using a single click.

Easier installation of actions

Unlike Photo Effects, actions created in the full version of Photoshop can be installed in Photoshop Elements 7 or 8 without the need for additional XML files to create listings for the new content. If you are installing actions manually rather than via an installer you can locate the Action Player folder by going to Photoshop Elements\7.0 or 8.0\Locale\<installed locale>\Workflow Panels\Actions. Close the software and then delete the MediaDatabase.db3 and ThumbDatabase.db3 files (see page xix).

Note > After installation you must restart Photoshop Elements. Photoshop may take more than 10 minutes to rebuild its database before the new content appears in the Effects panel or the Guided Edit Action Player.

Maximum Performance Smart Brushes (adjustment layers)

In Photoshop Elements 8 it is now possible to paint with adjustment presets using either the new Smart Brush tool or Detail Smart Brush tool. The Smart Brush tool creates its own mask as it applies the adjustment by looking for the edges of your subject matter. If the adjustment invades your subject you can hold down the Alt/Option key and then paint to remove the adjustment. Photoshop 7 and 8 come loaded with many 'interesting' presets that can be used to enhance or erode the quality of your photographic images. Most advanced users of Photoshop Elements will probably still prefer to make their own adjustments by applying adjustment layers via the Layers panel and then using the layer masks to hide or reveal their adjustments.

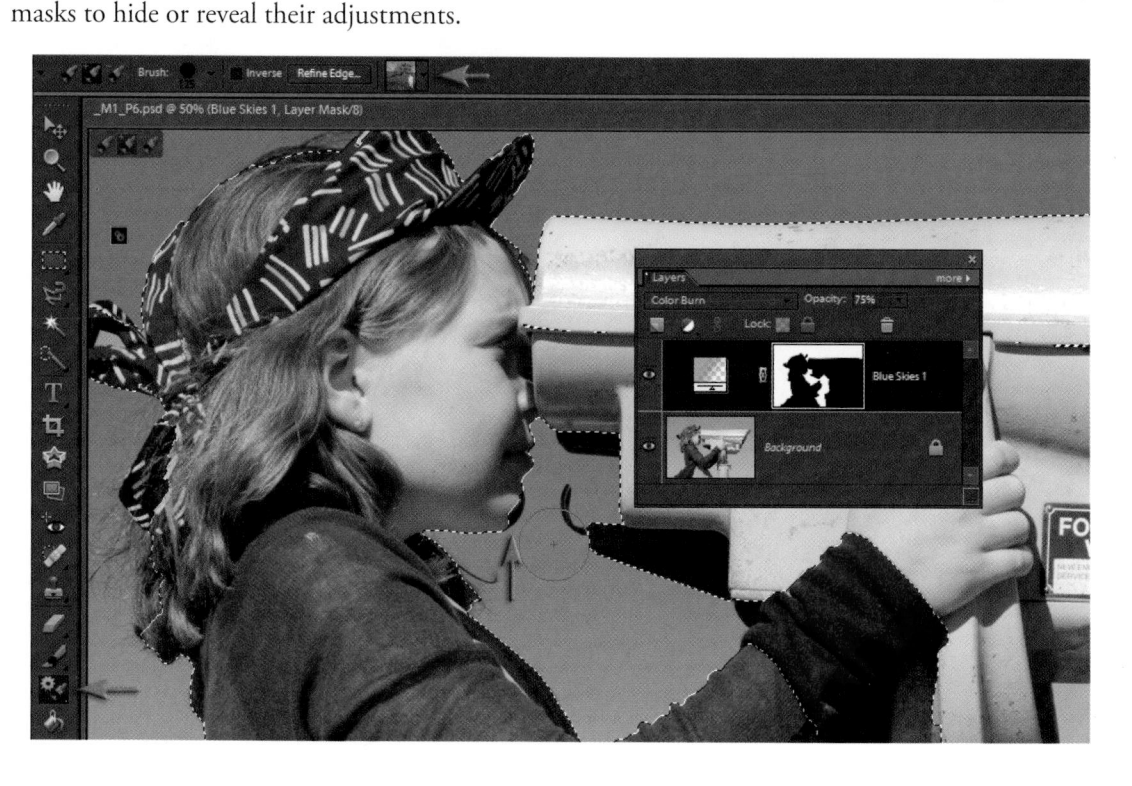

Luminosity brushes

Most of the projects in this book utilize this manual approach to making adjustments. There is one area, however, where adjustments are difficult to make using the limited range of adjustment layers afforded to users of Photoshop Elements. I have therefore decided to include a range of Maximum Performance Luminosity brushes that can be accessed from the MP8 menu in the Options bar (when the Smart Brush tool or Detail Smart Brush tool is selected) that will increase the performance of many of your retouching tasks. These Luminosity brushes allow the user to adjust the brightness of the color without upsetting its Saturation value (something the Lightness slider in the Hue/Saturation adjustment feature is unable to do). See Project 5 in Part 1 for a full step-by-step guide to applying these luminance adjustments using the new Detail Smart Brush in conjunction with the Maximum Performance Luminosity presets (MP8_Photo-Effects).

Note > There are also Smart Brush presets in the Maximum Performance collection to create high key, midtone contrast and cross process special effects (MP8-Effects).

part 1 optimize

Project 1

Adobe Camera Raw

Adobe Camera Raw (ACR) is the gateway for opening Raw images into the main editing space of Photoshop Elements, but ACR is also a great space for optimizing images quickly and easily. Many of the basic tasks such as straightening and cropping images, correcting exposure and color balance can all be achieved faster and more easily than by performing these same tasks in the main editing space of Photoshop Elements. One of the best-kept secrets of Photoshop Elements is that you can also open JPEGs into the ACR editing space to access these user-friendly editing tools. If you have not yet explored the ACR interface, or are having trouble breaking old habits, then the following project is designed to make you think again.

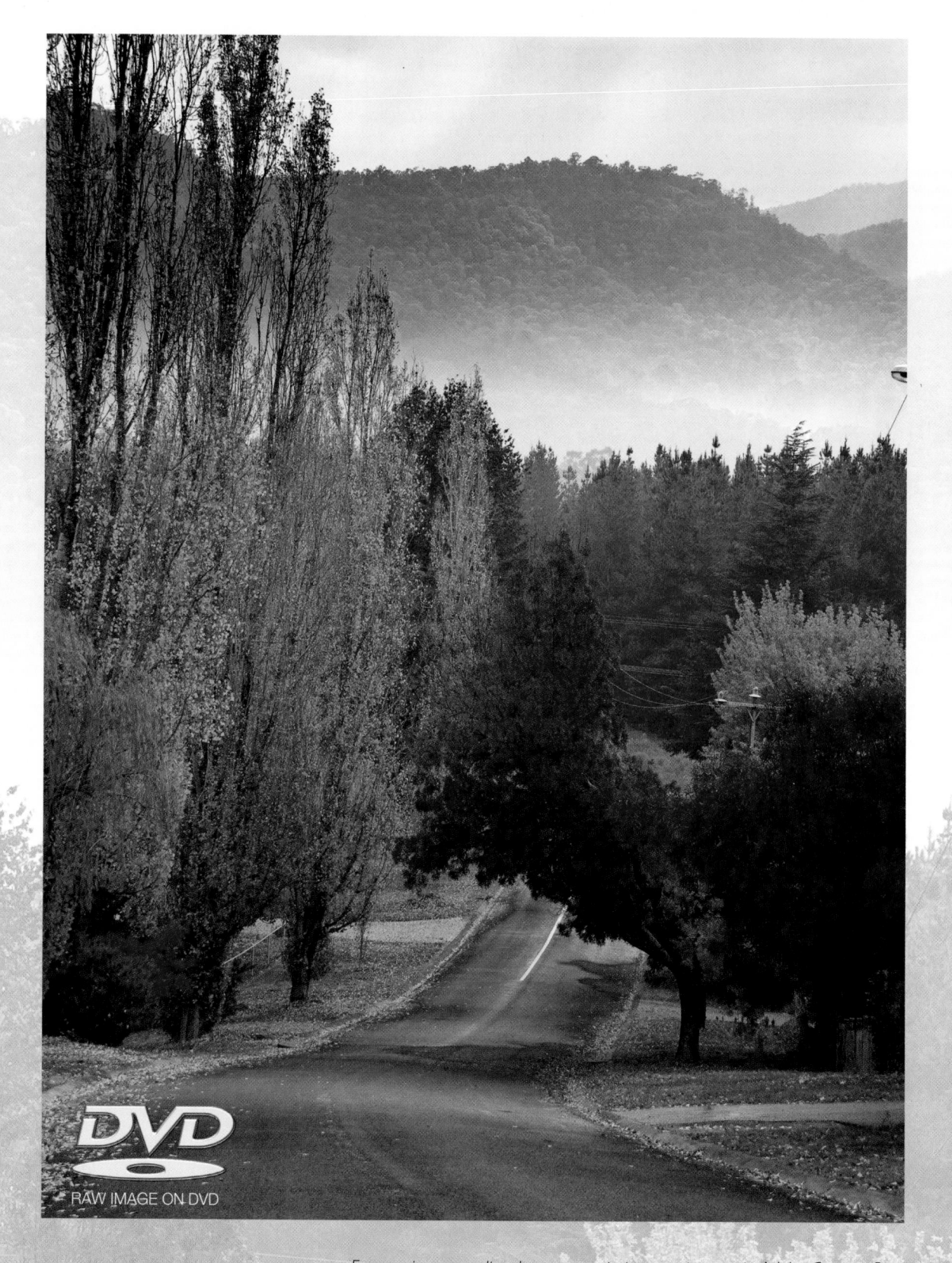

DVD

For maximum quality choose to optimize your images in Adobe Camera Raw

The Raw advantage

Most professional photographers capture images in the Raw format rather than the JPEG format. The Raw format offers greater flexibility in achieving different visual outcomes while ensuring a high-quality finished result. The JPEG file format can offer great quality so long as only minor editing is required after the image has been captured. A JPEG captured in-camera should be considered as a print ready file while a Camera Raw file is unprocessed data that can be edited extensively in Photoshop Elements. Most professional photographers have switched from JPEG capture to using the Camera Raw format for the following reasons:

1. Extended dynamic range (great for combating the photographer's worst enemy – subjects where the lighting contrast is high).
2. Higher bit depth: having access to 12, 14 or even 16 bits per channel instead of 8 results in higher quality if you have to 'fix' the image after capture.
3. Flexible editing (why worry about the correct camera settings before you shoot when you can set them after?). The processing, that is normally done by the camera (white balance, saturation, sharpening, etc.) can be carried out in Photoshop Elements after you have returned from your shoot.

Editing JPEGs in Adobe Camera Raw

For photographers who are choosing to work with JPEG images rather than using Raw images, the Adobe Camera Raw (ACR) space still offers an advantage over the main editing space of Photoshop Elements for quick and easy editing. Adobe Camera Raw can be considered as the 'Quick Fix' space for professionals and keen amateur photographers alike. You can open JPEG images in ACR from the Edit space of Photoshop Elements to take advantage of the powerful tools in this editing space. Just go to File > Open As (Windows) or File > Open (Mac). Browse to the JPEG you want to open and then in the Open As menu choose the Camera Raw option.

When the JPEG opens in Camera Raw you can utilize simple controls to optimize and enhance the color and tonality of your images. It is important to remember, however, that JPEGs are recorded by the camera at a lower 'bit depth' to Raw images so they are less able to withstand extreme adjustments before the quality becomes compromised. JPEG files also offer the photographer less chance of being able to recover highlights that were slightly overexposed in-camera.

Adobe Camera Raw – A non-destructive workspace

Adobe Camera Raw is a completely nondestructive workspace. Any changes that you make to your image in ACR can be completely undone, allowing the file you are working on to be returned to its original state (as recorded by the camera). Even if you crop your image in ACR, the pixels are never discarded – just temporarily hidden from view. Photoshop Elements simply records any change made in ACR as a list of processing instructions (XMP metadata) that is used to modify the preview. Every time a Raw image is displayed in ACR these processing instructions are applied to the image. Changes can only be permanently made to the actual pixels of the image file if the images are saved from the main editing space or processed (File > Process Multiple Images). When the user clicks 'Done' in the main editing space, Photoshop Elements will remember the changes you have made to the image. The changes are stored in a 'central cache' or memory bank that is, in turn, saved on your computer's hard drive. Adobe Camera Raw refers to this central cache to remember how you last processed the Raw file the next time you open it. If you want another computer running Photoshop Elements to be able to preview these changes you can hit the Save Image button in the ACR dialog and save your Raw file as a DNG file. Any changes you made in ACR will now be written directly to the file as well as the central cache.

Camera Raw defaults and image settings

You can choose to return to the Default preview (the original preview) at any time by clicking on the button in the top right-hand corner of the Basic tab in the ACR dialog and selecting Camera Raw Defaults from the drop-down menu. If you choose Image Settings in this menu the preview will revert to the version that started the current editing session. This will include any changes you made to the image the last time the Raw file was opened in ACR.

Done, Cancel or Open Image

Choosing Done in the bottom right-hand corner of the ACR dialog will save any changes you have made to the file or files open in ACR to the central cache and close or 'dismiss' the ACR dialog. If you choose Cancel the ACR space will close without modifying the previews, while choosing Open Image will open the selected image or images, with all of the changes you made in ACR, into the Edit space of Photoshop Elements. In addition to opening the image in the Edit space, this action also saves the ACR processing instructions to the central cache, so that the next time you open one of these images in ACR it looks just like it did when you clicked the Open Image button. Opening images into the Full Edit space will allow you to access all of the familiar features of the Edit workspace to continue the editing process.

File Naming

Example: Autumn_Leaves01.dng

| Autumn_Leaves | ∨ | + | 2 Digit Serial Number | ∨ | + |

| | ∨ | + | | ∨ |

Begin Numbering: 01

File Extension: .dng ∨

Format: Digital Negative

☑ Compressed (lossless)   JPEG Preview: Medium Size ∨
☐ Convert to Linear Image
☐ Embed Original Raw File

PERFORMANCE TIP

Adobe has created a universal Raw file format called 'DNG' (Digital Negative) in an attempt to ensure that all Camera Raw files (whichever camera they originate from) will be accessible in the future. The Save option in the Camera Raw dialog box gives you access to convert your camera's Raw file to the Adobe Digital Negative format with no loss of quality. The conversion will ensure that your files are archived in a format that will be understood in the future. Expect to see future models of many digital cameras using this DNG format as standard. One thing is for sure – Raw files are a valuable source of the rich visual data that many of us value, and so the format will be around for many years to come.

Thumbnails and previews of DNG files when not using Photoshop Elements

When using Photoshop Elements Organizer (Windows) or Bridge (Mac) you will probably not be surprised to find that you can see thumbnails and previews of all of your DNG Raw files before you open them in Photoshop Elements. If, however, you are using the Windows or Macintosh operating systems you may not see any thumbnail views or previews for these Raw files. Windows Vista users can download and install a 'DNG Codec' from the Adobe Labs website (http://labs.adobe.com) if they wish to view thumbnails when using the computer operating system to navigate and choose images instead of their Adobe software. Macintosh users are advised to keep their Preview and iPhoto Applications up to date if they are experiencing any problems viewing thumbnails and previews. Users of Windows XP will need to install the Microsoft RAW Image Thumbnailer and Viewer before they can view Raw images outside of the Adobe Photoshop Elements software.

A fast and efficient workspace for editing multiple Raw files

It is possible to open multiple images into the ACR dialog at the same time (just shift-click a range of Raw images in the Organizer workspace or in a folder of images in your Pictures folder and choose Open. If your computer's operating system does not recognize the Raw file format then drag the images on to the Photoshop Elements shortcut. Open all of the images from the Raw section of the supporting DVD to follow along with this project.

Note > Opening multiple images in ACR is less draining on your computer's working memory than opening the same number of images in the Edit workspace. Your computer just has to deal with the pixels that are on the screen rather than multiple megapixels of the files.

Managing your screen real-estate

Thumbnails of all the open files are displayed on the left side of the dialog – just click one of the thumbnails to display a large preview of the image. This column of thumbnails can be temporarily hidden from view by dragging the central divider to the left to increase the working area in the middle of the dialog. In the top-right corner of the dialog you can see a histogram that relates to the color and tone of the image you are viewing. This histogram is like the one you can access on the LCD screen of most good-quality cameras. This histogram has useful information about the color and tonality of your image. The beauty of the ACR space is that this is by far and away the best place to optimize the histogram to make each and every photograph you edit appear at its absolute best so that the world recognizes you for the wonderful photographer that you are. Click on the tiny icon just to the left of this histogram so that the ACR dialog goes full-screen. Professional photographers spend a lot of time in this dialog so make the most of this feature and give yourself some elbow room!

Checking exposure in Adobe Camera Raw

Above the histogram there are two triangles. These are the Shadow and Highlight clipping warning controls. The term 'clipping' is used by Adobe when the pixels in the red, green or blue channels, the three channels that make up an RGB image, are registering either level 0 or level 255 in one or more of the three channels. When there are pixels in the image that are registering level 0 in all three channels then the pixels in the image preview will appear as absolute black and the Shadow clipping warning triangle (the one on the left) will turn white. When there are pixels in the image that are registering level 255 in all three channels then the pixels in the image preview will appear as absolute white. The Highlight clipping warning triangle on the right will again appear white when this happens. When a shadow or highlight in the image is made up of pixels that are all level 0 or 255 then the surfaces will not have any detail. Shadows or highlights that do not have any surface texture or detail are referred to as being 'clipped' and this is usually regarded as a flaw by photographers, whose goal is generally to preserve as much detail as possible. Clipping may occur due to overexposure or underexposure in-camera or due to excessive contrast in the scene that was photographed. It is not uncommon for wedding photographers, for instance, to experience problems of clipping when photographing the bride and groom in sunny locations. They may review their images only to find that neither the bride's white dress nor the groom's dark suit has any detail. I often refer to level 0 and level 255 as the goal posts between which photographers must aim to squeeze all of their tonal information.

Activating the clipping warning in the image preview

If staring at the color of tiny triangles does not give you a lot of feedback about what is actually happening with the shadows and highlights within your image then try clicking the clipping warning triangles. Notice how the shadows or highlights in your image preview that are clipped are replaced with the color blue (for clipped shadows) or red (for clipped highlights). Click on either triangle to leave the warning on so that you can move your mouse cursor away and still retain warnings within the preview image.

1. Adjusting exposure in Adobe Camera Raw

In the Basic tabbed panel (below the histogram) is an Exposure slider. This slider can be used to control the brightest pixels in the image file. Moving the slider to the left will lower the exposure and quite often pixels in the image that were shown to be clipping can be brought back behind the 255 goal post so that the highlight tones are now filled with tone and texture. Notice in the image above how with a one stop (-1.00) lowering of exposure the fuel tank on the motorcycle is no longer clipped and the clipping warning triangle turns black. The highlights have effectively been restored to this image. This is usually only possible with files that were captured using the Raw file format or processed as a JPEG in-camera using a dynamic range optimizer setting if available. It may not always be possible to save overexposed highlights but Raw shooters may have one or two extra stops of highlight headroom compared to JPEG shooters. The image is now a little dark due to the one stop exposure adjustment but this can be fixed later using the Brightness slider.

Auto and Default

Click on the underlined blue Default option directly above the Exposure slider to return all the adjustments in the Basic tabbed panel back to their default settings or double-click on the slider control to return this single Exposure slider back to its default setting of 0.0. If you click on the Auto setting you will see that ACR tries to recover some (but not all) of the overexposed highlights using the Recovery slider instead (the one below the Exposure slider). We will look at this alternative approach to recovering highlight detail later.

Set the white point using the Exposure slider

Use the Exposure slider in ACR as a White Point slider. If you are used to using Levels in the main editing space of Photoshop Elements then this slider can be likened to the one under the extreme right-hand side of the histogram. It is used to ensure the brightest pixels in the image are touching, but not pushed beyond, the level 255 goal post.

Set the black point using the Blacks and/or Fill Light slider

We can restore the shadow detail in this image using the Fill Light and Blacks sliders (below the Exposure and Recovery sliders). Technically it is the Blacks slider that controls the black point in the image. We could drag this left so that the darkest tones do not clip to black. This approach, however, often leads to blacks with detail but that appear weak and without depth. If you move the Fill Light slider to the right to recover the shadow detail, instead of moving the Blacks slider to the left, the shadows will usually appear to have a lot more depth.

Note > You will notice that no matter how far you move the Fill Light slider to the right you will never be able to make the Shadow clipping warning triangle turn black. The clipping warning will remain blue from the time the slider is moved beyond +20, indicating that the blue channel will remain clipped no matter how far the slider is moved. You will, however, notice that there is no blue clipping warning in the preview image itself. The blue channel is not being clipped because of how dark the shadow tones are but because of how saturated or vibrant some of the leaves are in the background behind the motorcycle.

PERFORMANCE TIP

Excessive adjustment using the Fill Light slider can lighten the shadow but can also reveal the greater amounts of noise that lurk in the shadows. My advice would be to keep the Fill Light value below 35 and keep the camera's ISO setting low to avoid this problem. Keeping the camera's ISO low also keeps the noise in the image file low and the dynamic range of the sensor (the ability to record a range of brightness values) high.

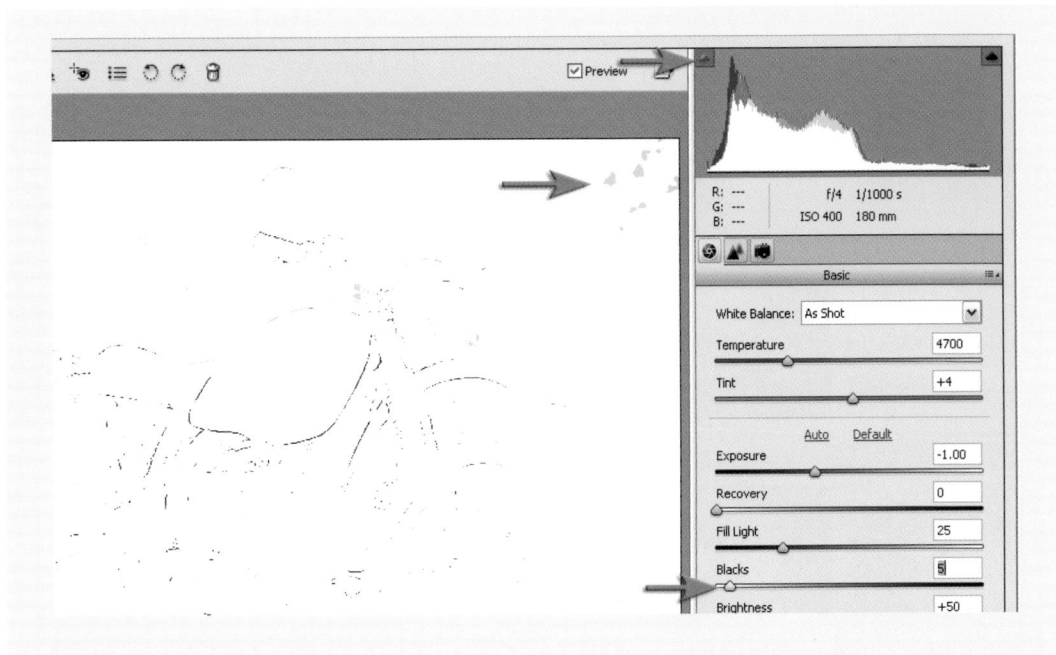

PERFORMANCE TIP

Hold down the Alt key (PC) or Option key (Mac) while clicking on the Blacks or Exposure sliders to give you a 'threshold' view in the preview window in order to obtain a more precise clipping warning. The threshold view will render the image preview entirely black or white except for where there is clipping. Instead of the regular blue and red clipping warnings you are now presented with a broader range of clipping colors to alert you to luminance clipping (all three channels) or whether the clipping is a result of very vibrant or saturated colors clipping. The issue of color saturation and clipping is dealt with later in this project.

Gamma adjustments

After setting the white and black points using the Exposure and Fill Light sliders you can then dial in your preferred brightness or 'gamma' value for the image. The Brightness and Contrast sliders will usually leave the black and white points where they are and so these adjustments can be considered non-destructive tonal controls, i.e. they are slow to clip tonality after first setting white and black points. If you see any highlight clipping warnings after raising the brightness, return to either the Exposure or Recovery slider to fine-tune the white point.

2. Correcting a low-contrast image

Select the Low-Contrast thumbnail from the column on the left. This image has the opposite tonal problems to the previous one. If you see a yellow warning triangle in the image preview window it is telling you that ACR is building a better preview from the data found in the Raw file. This time instead of having to recover shadow and highlight detail we have to expand the subject brightness range (SBR) or contrast. The original contrast was lost due to a combination of using a telephoto lens and the early morning mist.

Reestablish a white point by dragging the Exposure slider to a point just before the highlight clipping warning indicates that you have overcooked or clipped the brightest tones in the image (up to 1.5 stops brighter than the original in-camera exposure used to capture the image).

Reestablish a black point by dragging the Blacks slider to a point just before clipping occurs. You have now effectively expanded or stretched the histogram of the file to touch level 0 and level 255. The higher bit depth of the camera's sensor makes this possible without lowering the quality of the outcome (JPEGs are less forgiving).

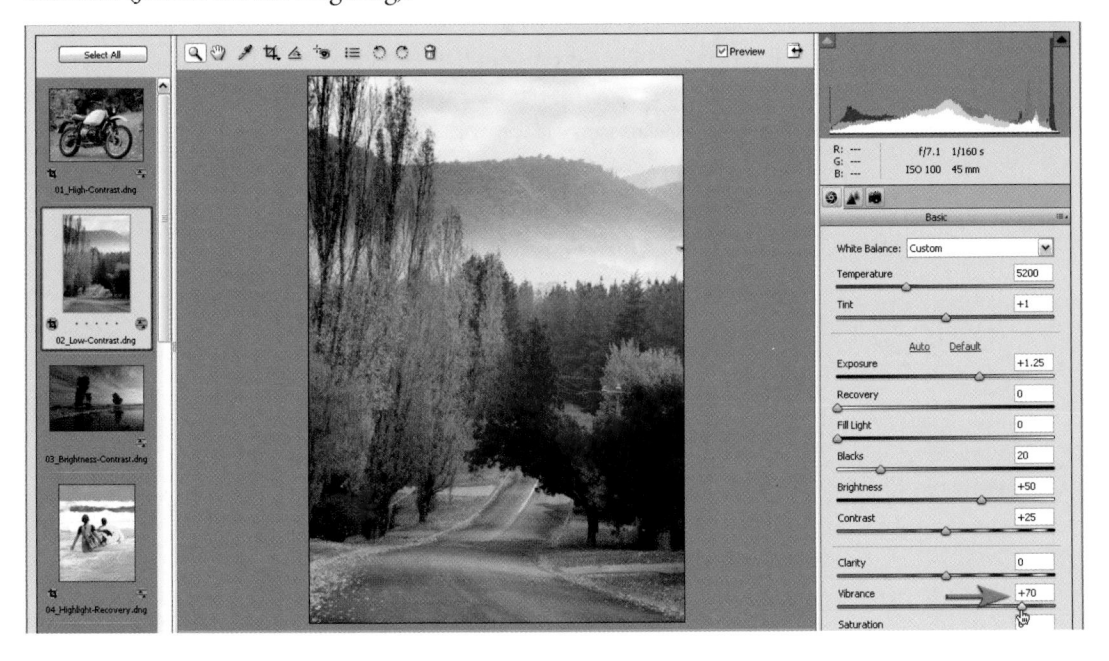

Drag the Vibrance slider to the right to increase the saturation of the colors. The Vibrance slider is less likely to cause saturation clipping compared to using the Saturation slider for this task. Compare the use of the Vibrance slider to the Saturation slider while observing the clipping warnings.

14

PERFORMANCE TIP

Is saturation clipping a bad thing? In this image I wanted the colors to reflect the strong vibrant autumn colors but saturation clipping seemed inevitable, even when using the Vibrance slider instead of the Saturation slider in order to achieve this effect. If we hold down the Alt key (PC) or Option key (Mac) and then click on the Blacks slider we can see the yellow and magenta colors are clipped. The reality is that when colors clip in one or two channels they will have slightly less texture than if they were processed to have information in all three channels. If, however, we value a vibrant appearance more than texture we must sacrifice texture for color. This is a subtle difference, so many viewers will fail to notice that the clipped colors they are looking at are slightly 'flat' (without a lot of texture) when compared to less vibrant colors that were not clipped. If we are printing to high-end print service providers or using high-quality inkjet printers then it is important to go to Edit > Color Settings in the main Edit space of Photoshop Elements before we open and process images in ACR. Choose Always Optimize for Printing in the Color Settings dialog. This informs ACR that you want to open files in the larger Adobe RGB color gamut rather than the smaller sRGB color gamut that is more suitable for most computer monitors and the cheap-and-cheerful print service providers (consult your own print service provider if you are not sure which yours fits into). If you choose to use the larger Adobe RGB color gamut you will have the advantage of being able to use more vibrant colors that clip less easily, i.e. you can enjoy vibrant colors with good detail and texture.

Note > If you choose the larger Adobe RGB color gamut then you must always remember to convert your images to the smaller sRGB color gamut (Image > Convert Color Profile) when uploading the files to web galleries and sharing the files with people who do not use Photoshop Elements to view their images.

3. Brightness and contrast

The Brightness-Contrast image can be optimized without the need to set a black or white point. The subject brightness range of the subject captured by the camera matches the dynamic range of the image sensor. In order to avoid overexposing the highlights in-camera, the exposure was reduced at the time of capture. This has led to an image that is slightly dark and also lacking in contrast and vibrancy. To correct these shortcomings the Brightness and Contrast sliders can be dragged to the right to bring this image back to life. These adjustments are largely 'subjective', i.e. there is no right or wrong.

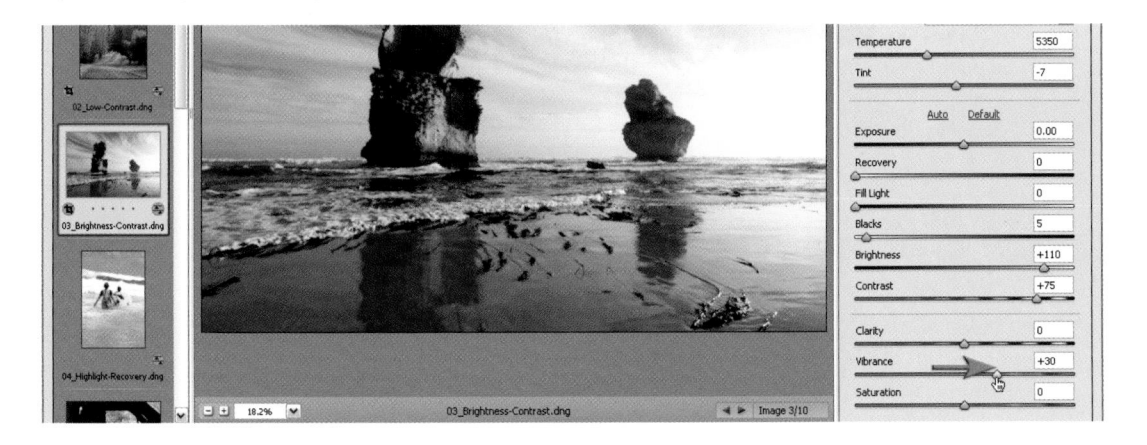

The Vibrance slider in this instance does not cause any saturation clipping when used to achieve the desired effect. If you require a brighter, more saturated outcome than the one shown you will need to raise the recovery slider slightly to ensure you don't lose some of the subtle highlight tones in the sky.

4. Straightening an image

Straightening an image in ACR is very easy. Open Image 04-5_Straighten-Highlight-Recovery, select the Straighten tool at the top of the ACR dialog and then find any horizontal line in the image (such as the horizon line as pictured in the illustration above). If you don't have a horizontal line in an image you are straightening you can select a vertical line so long as it is at, or near, the center of the image (so that you avoid using a vertical that is subject to perspective convergence). Then click and drag along the line while holding the mouse button down. When you let go of the mouse button the image is immediately rendered straight using the minimum amount of cropping.

Click on the Zoom or Hand tool to escape from the crop view so that you can see the image straightened in the ACR dialog. The cropped pixels that are hidden from view can be reclaimed at any time by going to the Crop tool and then selecting Clear Crop from the drop-down menu (this action also undoes the straightening effect, putting things back the way they were). You can also press the Enter key to escape from the crop view.

5. Highlight recovery

As discussed previously there are two workflows that can be employed for recovering highlight detail. The first option we looked at, where we lowered the exposure and increased the brightness, usually gives superior results to the single Recovery slider option. As we can observe in the examples above, the first option gives slightly better midtone contrast with slightly improved highlight detail. This workflow, however, is usually only superior when working with images that have the detail from the dynamic range headroom that Raw files possess. The Recovery slider really comes into its own when one or more channels are truly clipped, as would be the case with overexposed JPEGs.

6. Shadow recovery

Great care needs to be taken when using the Fill Light slider to rescue dark shadow tones. In Image 06_Shadow-Recovery an extreme adjustment is being made to rescue the shadow tones that have been accidentally underexposed due to the bright tones in the center of the viewfinder. Notice how the shadows are slow to clip in such an underexposed file. The shadow tones are moved away from the left hand wall of the histogram quite easily with the Fill Light slider. With such a heavy application of the Fill Light slider you may find the color saturation becomes excessive so this will need to be addressed using the Saturation or Vibrance sliders.

Note > Be careful with raising the Fill Light value too high, especially with photos taken with a high ISO setting. Fill Light will also brighten noise in the photo and make it more apparent. Photos taken at a lower ISO will be more forgiving to the Fill Light slider.

The brightness is raised and the vibrancy reduced to complete the editing of this underexposed file. If you take a look at the Highlight clipping warning there is an indication that there are overexposed highlights in the image. This DNG file, however, was converted from a JPEG file that was processed in-camera and would therefore require the recovery slider to be used to restore any detail in these brighter areas.

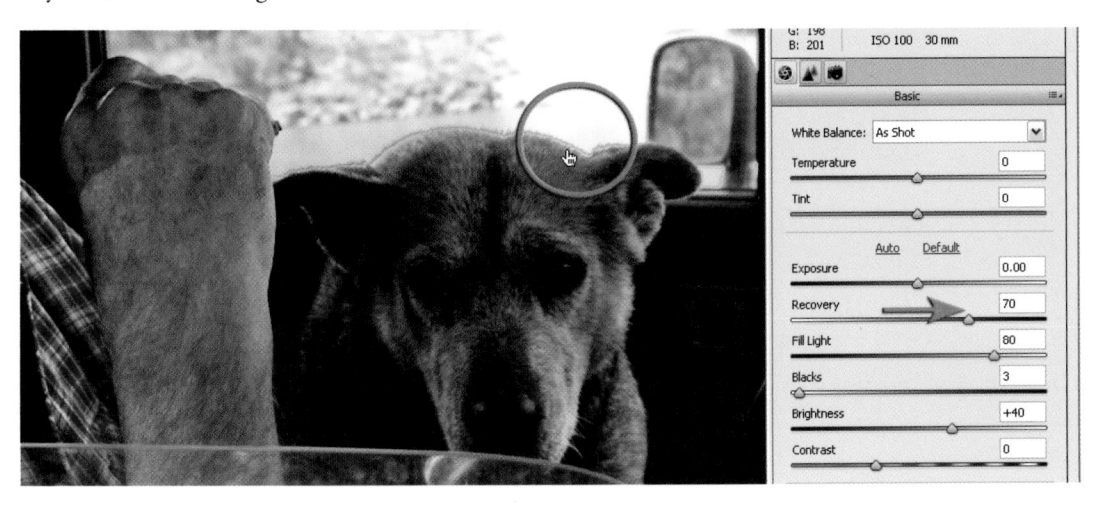

The problem with raising the Recovery slider and Fill Light sliders to high settings in the same image file is that high-contrast edges can acquire edge artifacts. In the image above a dark outline appears around the high-contrast edges in the image. A more pleasing result can be achieved in this instance if the file is opened in the main editing space and the Shadows/Highlights adjustment feature is used instead (go to Enhance > Adjust Lighting > Shadows/Highlights).

Image of Melissa Zappa courtesy of Victoria Verdon-Roe

7. Gamut control and white balance

In Image 07_Gamut much of the clipping warning you see when you first open the image is due to colors that are out-of-gamut rather than any luminance clipping. Many of the colors are simply too saturated to be contained by even the larger Adobe RGB gamut. It is, however, possible to put all of these colors back into the gamut with a little bit of care and attention. The first step is to ensure that these warm orange and yellow tones are no warmer than they really need to be (due to a slightly inaccurate Auto White Balance setting in-camera). Select the White Balance tool at the top of the ACR dialog and then click on the kitchen roll paper hanging on the wall to the right of the image.

Note > If you have not changed your Color Settings in the main Edit space of Photoshop Elements (Edit > Color Settings) to Always Optimize for Print then you will not be able to pull the colors back into the smaller sRGB color space.

The Recovery slider in this instance is useful for pulling the out-of-gamut colors at the 255 end of the histogram back into gamut, while moving the Blacks slider to 0 will take care of the out-of-gamut colors at the level 0 end of the histogram.

8. Correcting the white balance across a batch of images

As we have seen with editing the previous image, it is sometimes quicker to use the White Balance tool in the ACR interface to color-correct an image by simply clicking on a neutral tone within the image to set the correct color temperature and tint.

If the subject you wish to capture does not have an obvious neutral tone then you can introduce a neutral tone as a reference point in the first image of the shoot. This will enable you to measure the precise temperature and tint required to color-correct all the other images that share the same lighting conditions.

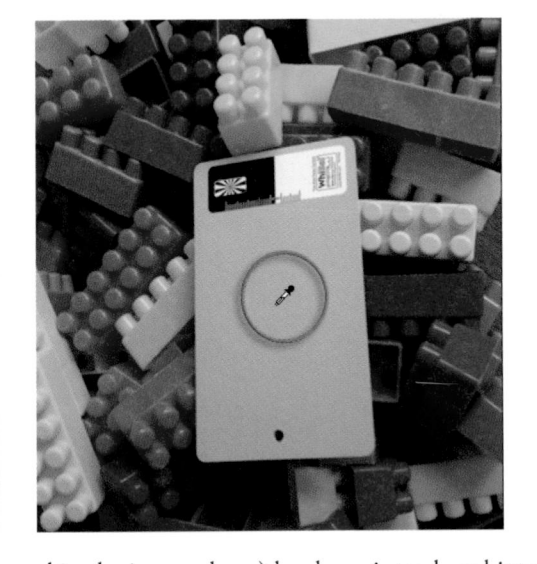

In this image a white balance card (a 'WhiBal' is used in the image above) has been introduced into the image; the White Balance tool is then used to set accurate temperature and tint settings.

In some scenes there may be no neutral tones to click on and no opportunity to include a white balance reference card in the scene. In these instances it is important to either create a custom white balance setting in the camera at the time of capture or capture a reference image using a product such as the 'Expodisc'. The Expodisc is placed in front of the lens and an image captured by pointing the camera back towards the light source (with the camera set to manual focus). The resulting image provides the photographer with a reference image that can be used to assign the correct white balance to all of the images captured in those lighting conditions.

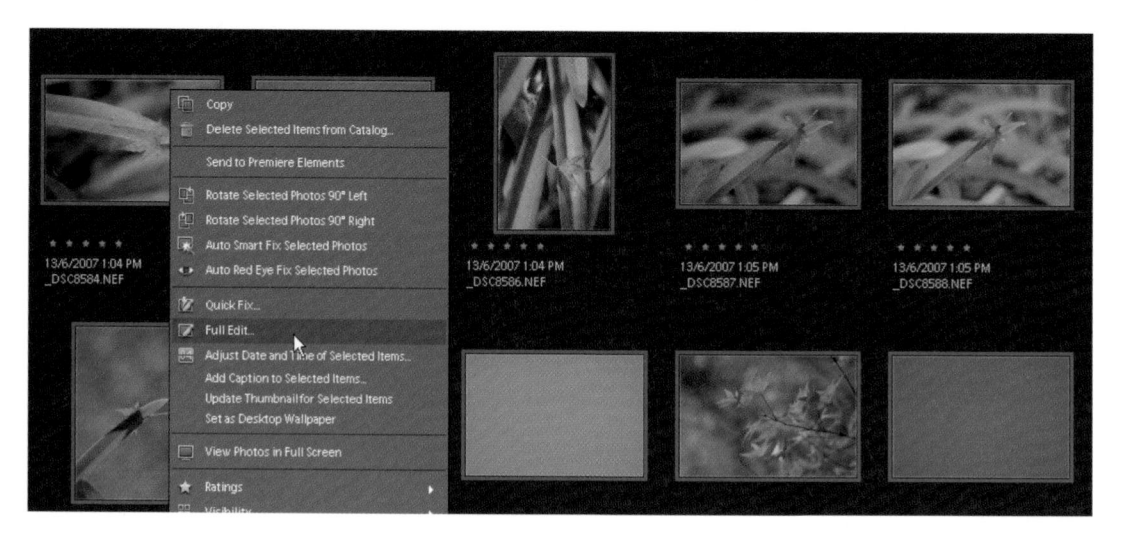

When you want to assign the correct white balance across a group of images, select multiple Raw files in the Organizer space (PC) or Bridge (Mac) and then open them in the ACR interface.

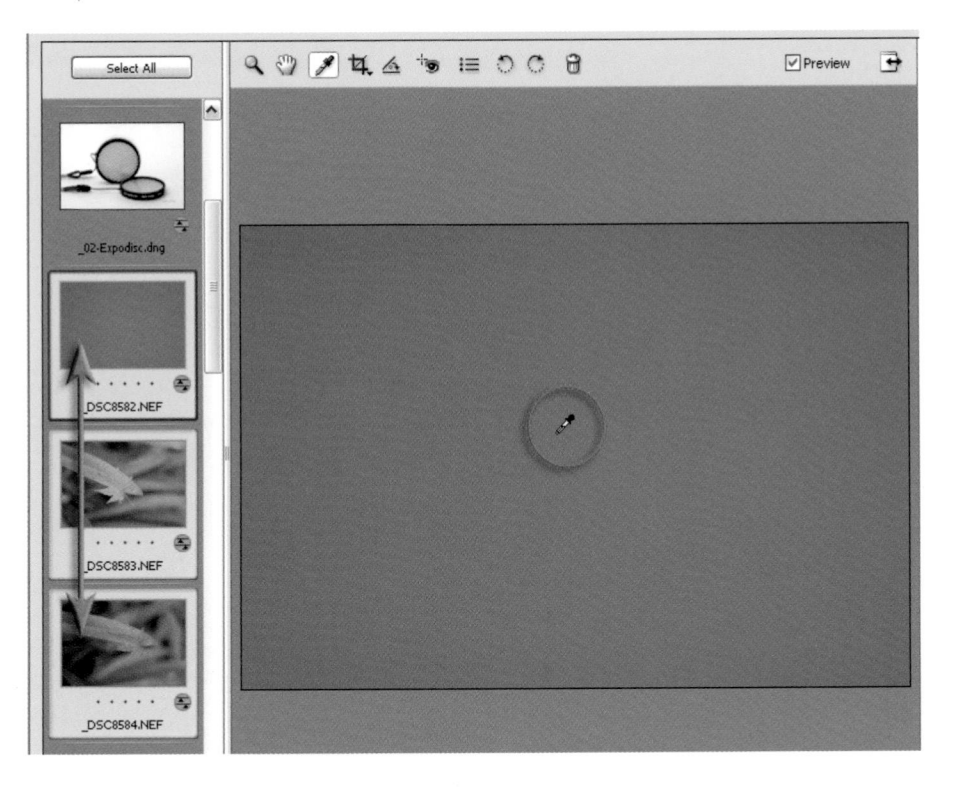

Click on the reference image thumbnail on the left-hand side of the ACR interface. Then hold down the Shift key and click on the last thumbnail in the group of images that share the same lighting conditions. Select the White Balance tool and click on the main reference image preview to assign the correct white balance to all of the images.

These before and after images of autumn leaves clearly demonstrate how the Auto White Balance setting in the camera has misjudged the correct white balance.

Note > The Expodisc can also be used to create custom white balance settings in the camera, to take accurate incident light meter readings and also to help locate any dust on the camera's sensor (go to www.expodisc.com for more details about this useful product).

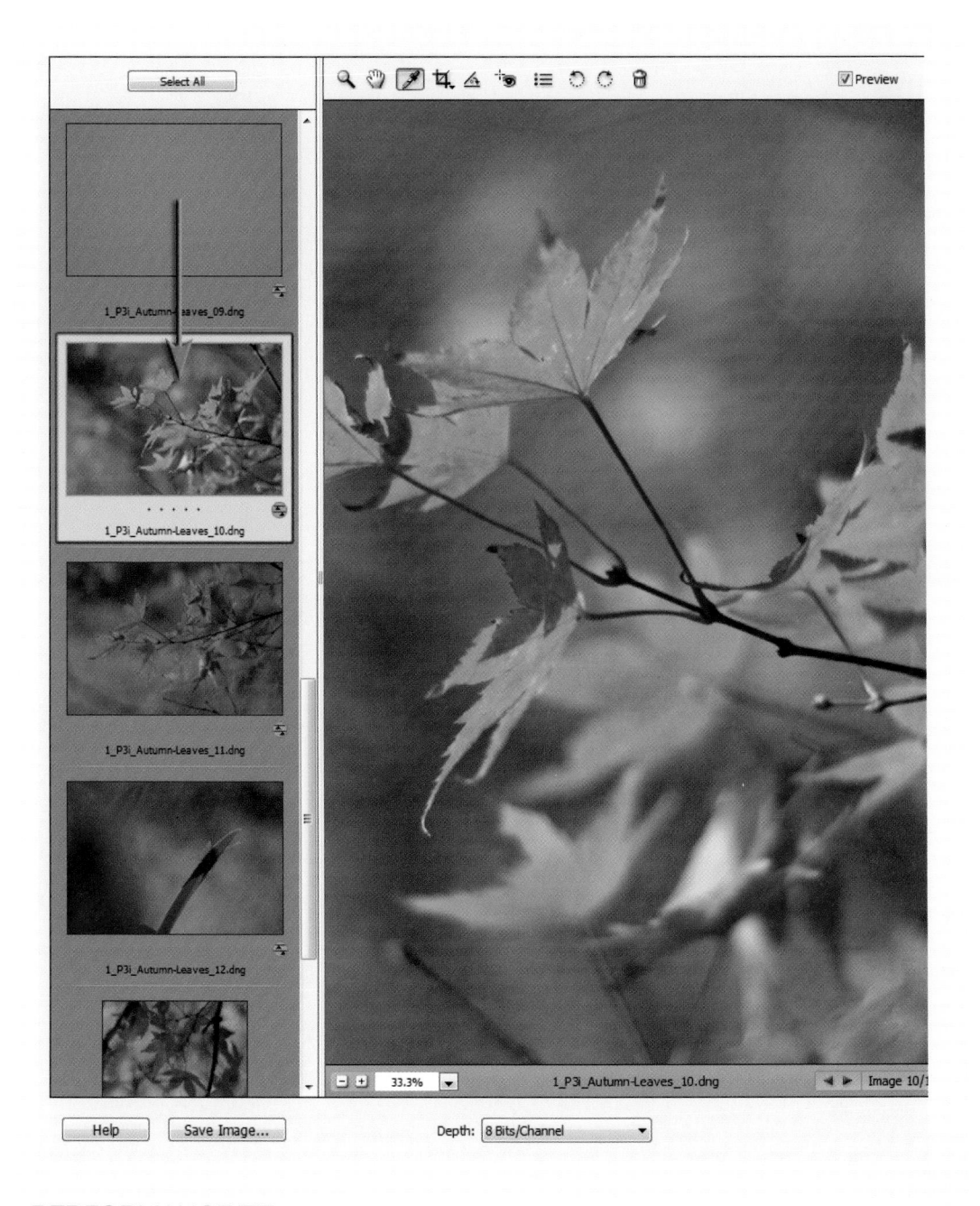

PERFORMANCE TIP

As long as the photographer takes frequent reference images as the lighting conditions (e.g. cloudy, sunny, time of day, etc.) change, color accuracy is assured with just a few clicks. Remember this color accuracy can only be fully appreciated if both computer monitor and printer are calibrated to display accurate color (see Project 7 – 'Printing').

9. Creative use of white balance to tone an image

In the illustration above the Crop tool has been used to crop into the most interesting aspect of this landscape. Even with this more dramatic crop the original white balance of the camera does not capture the mood of the cold winter morning in the valley. Instead of clicking on a neutral tone within the image with the White Balance tool (to create a neutral white balance) the Temperature slider has been lowered to something just above freezing by dragging it to the left! This had induced some extensive saturation clipping but now expresses the mood I am after.

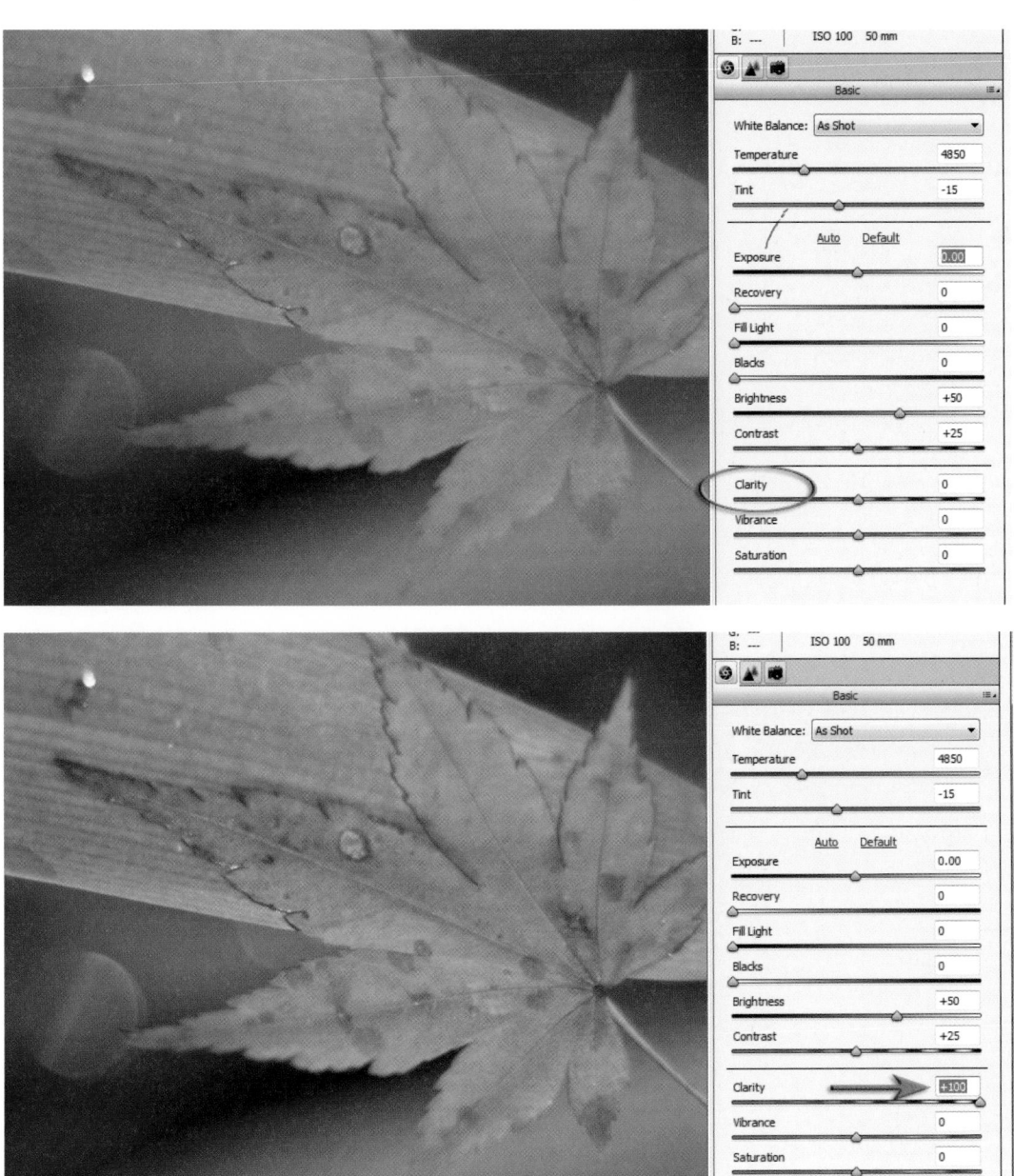

10. Clarity

The Clarity slider can be used to effectively increase localized contrast and give images more apparent depth (and sometimes make them a little sharper). Notice how contrast is raised both in the areas of fine detail and the broader areas of continuous tone. Unlike the Recovery and Fill Light sliders, which have to be used in moderation, this slider is slow to introduce unpleasant artifacts – especially in images where the light quality was soft and even.

11. Vibrance

Increasing saturation in ACR can lead to clipping in the color channels. Clipping saturated colors can cause a loss of fine detail and texture. The Vibrance slider applies a non-linear increase in saturation (primarily targeting pixels of lower saturation rather than colors that are already vibrant). The adjustment feature has also been designed to protect skin tones from becoming oversaturated and unnatural. The Vibrance adjustment feature should lead to fewer problems when compared to the Saturation control and should be used for most situations where increased color saturation is required.

Note > Choosing Adobe RGB in the Color Settings dialog box in the main editing space (Edit > Color Settings) will provide a working space with a larger color gamut than sRGB. This will allow saturation or vibrance to be increased to a greater degree before clipping occurs.

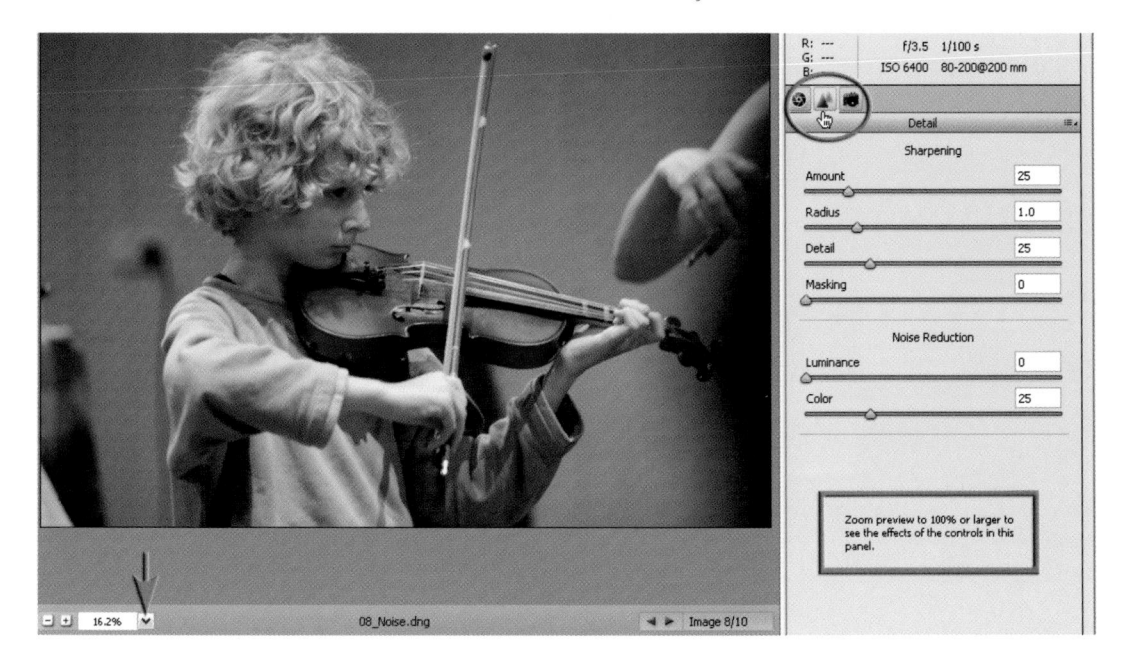

12. Detail tab (sharpening and noise reduction)

Zoom to 100% and click on the Detail tab (next to the Basic tab) to access the Sharpening and Noise Reduction controls. The Sharpening controls can be left at their default settings if you intend to implement the advanced sharpening techniques (see Project 6) or use the techniques outlined on page 32 (if you wish to apply sharpening settings to a batch of images). The Luminance Smoothing and Color Noise Reduction sliders are designed to tackle the camera noise that occurs when the image sensors' ISO is raised.

In the image above, the camera's ISO was set to 6400 (a Nikon D700 DSLR). Both luminance and color noise are evident when the image is viewed at 100% and the Color Noise slider is set to 0. When cameras are set to 100 or 200 ISO it may be possible to leave the Luminance slider at 0 as noise will be low or non-existent. Most files (even the ones captured at low ISO settings) benefit from a small amount of color noise reduction. Be careful not to apply too much, though, as this will steal color from the finer details within the image.

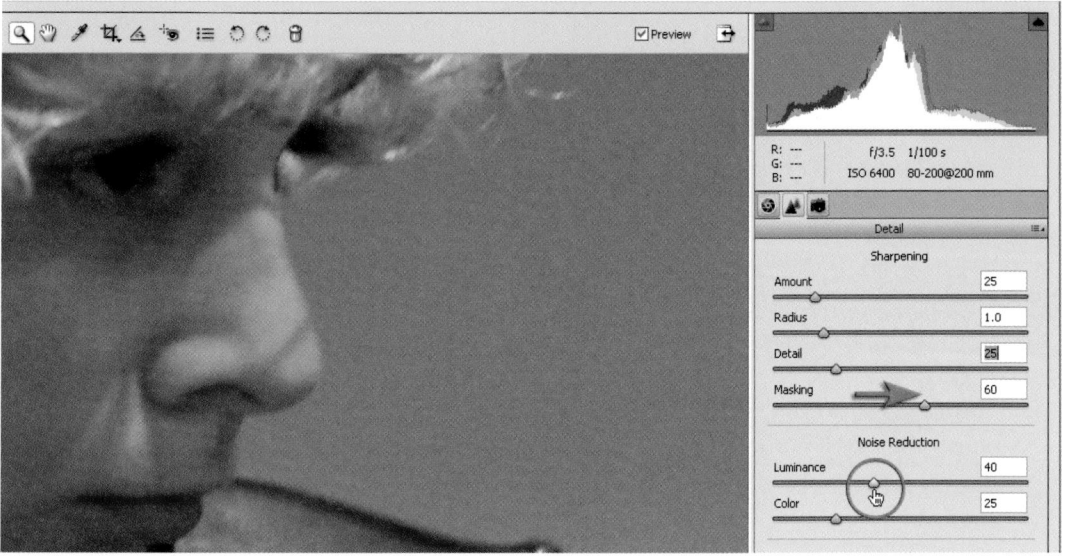

Luminance noise reduction

It is important to remember that the Noise Reduction controls are called 'noise reduction' and not 'noise elimination'. If we drag the Luminance Noise slider too far to the right we will take away too much detail from the image (see the illustration at the top of this page). It is also important to remember that the noise appears a lot bigger now that we are looking at the image at 100% (Actual Pixels) compared to how we will view the image in a screen presentation or a full page print. I am happy to just use a moderate amount of noise reduction (perhaps no more than 40) on my images captured at ISO 6400 in the full knowledge that the images will look reasonably detailed and smooth at 'normal' viewing sizes. So that we don't sharpen the areas of smooth tone, where the noise will be most visible, it is also advisable to drag the Masking slider (directly above the Luminance slider) to a value of around 60.

PERFORMANCE TIP

Hold down the Alt key (PC) or Option key (Mac) to see a Threshold view of the masking process. Any areas of the image that appear black will be shielded from the sharpening process

13. Sharpening multiple files

Just as a white balance setting can be applied across multiple images open in ACR, the same batch processing can be achieved when sharpening images. Although the sharpening controls have vastly improved in the ACR interface, it is still recommended that you sharpen in the main editing space to achieve maximum performance when sharpening (see Project 6 – 'Sharpening').

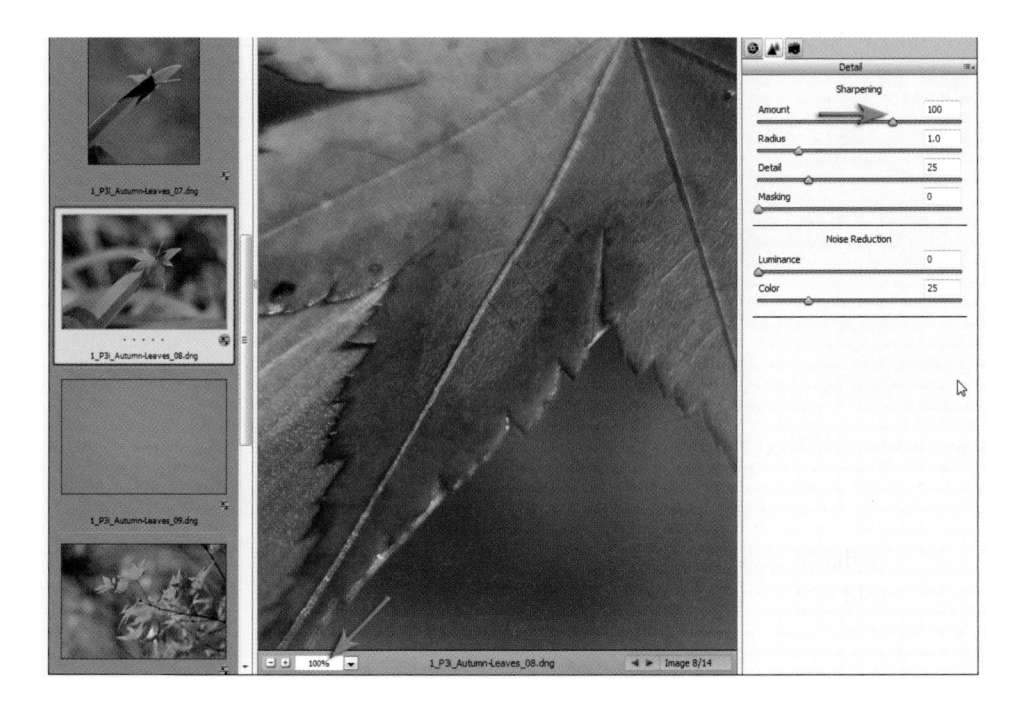

Set the magnification to 100% before sharpening any image in ACR as the results are not visible at smaller magnifications. Start by increasing the Amount slider until the edges that have the most contrast are suitably sharp. Amounts up to 100% are considered normal. If you hold down the Alt/Option key and click and drag the Amount slider the preview is displayed in black and white, which makes it easier to see the effects of the Amount slider. Generally it is recommended to leave the Radius slider at its default setting of 1.0.

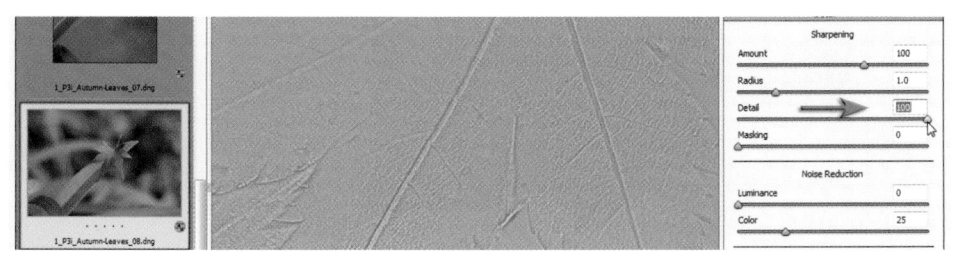

Hold down the Alt/Option key and drag the Detail slider to the left or right to observe the amount of detail that will be targeted for sharpening. Drag to the right to increase detail in the areas of continuous tone and to the left to decrease apparent detail. Let go of the Alt/Option key to observe the effect on the image.

To eliminate the sharpening process from areas of continuous tone we can drag the Masking slider to the right. Hold down the Alt/Option key as you drag this slider to observe the areas of the image that will not be sharpened (as indicated by the black mask).

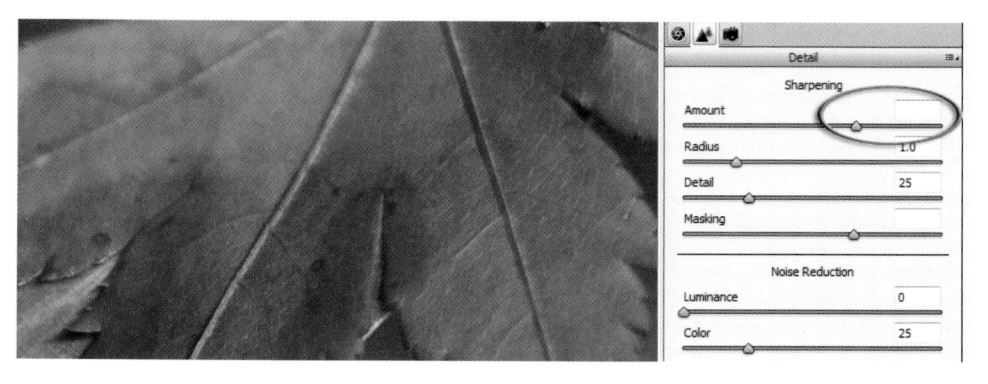

To apply these settings to the other images in the shoot simply choose the Select All option above the thumbnails on the left side of the ACR interface. The numbers for each slider will be blank if the settings are not the same for all of the selected images. Click on each slider in turn to sync the sharpening settings for all images. Click on Done to apply all of these changes and close the ACR dialog box. Select Save to process the files using the current Raw settings or select one or more images to open in the main editing space of Elements.

Note > Sharpening and other corrections applied over a batch of images may not always be desirable for every image. Check each image in turn to see if specific adjustments are required.

14. Cropping
Cropping an image to a specific output size

In step 4 ('Straightening an image') we saw how images can be cropped automatically in ACR using the Straighten tool. It is also possible to crop to a particular shape or 'aspect ratio' using one of the presets in the crop drop-down menu. If you select Custom you can also crop to a particular size as well as a particular shape. Select Custom in the Crop menu and then choose pixels, inches or cm from the Crop drop-down menu in the Custom Crop dialog. In the illustration above I have selected pixels and then entered 1920 by 1080 in the Width and Height fields (the dimensions of a wide-screen full-HD TV). Select OK and then click and drag the cropping marquee over the image to establish a cropping rectangle of the ratio of the two Pixel fields. You can then move the crop bounding box inside the image area to fine-tune the design. When you click on the Hand or Zoom tool the rest of the pixels will be hidden from view. You can also press the Enter key to execute the crop, while pressing the Esc key backs out of the crop altogether.

Cropping an image for print

If you return to the Highlight-Recovery image from step 4 and click on the Crop tool at the top of the ACR dialog you will see the pixels that were previously hidden from view. If you now select Custom from the crop Drop-down menu and choose inches from the Custom Crop dialog, you will be set to crop the image for a print output size rather than for the screen. I entered in 10 by 8 in the Width and Height fields to create a typical print size and then clicked and dragged inside the crop bounding box to perfect the composition. Note how the horizon line stays parallel to the top edge of the bounding box. The image can be rotated if required by moving your mouse cursor to a position just outside one of the corner handles of the crop bounding box and then clicking and dragging to rotate. Click on the Hand or Zoom tool in the ACR dialog to once again hide from view the pixels that lie outside the bounding box.

15. Processing files that have been optimized

If you click the Done button at the base of the ACR dialog, all of the changes you have been making to these files are saved. The Raw files cannot, however, be printed or displayed in web galleries or screen presentations unless the files are processed as TIFF, Photoshop or JPEG files. This process can be handled by going to the main Edit space in Photoshop Elements and then going to File > Process Multiple Files. In the Process Multiple Files dialog you can browse to your folder of Raw files and then process the files to any format of your choosing. The original Raw files will remain unchanged.

Note > Remember that the processed files will carry the profile as directed by the Color Settings dialog (Edit > Color Settings) at the time you process the files – either sRGB or Adobe RGB.

Project 2

Localized Adjustments

This project will show you how to create localized adjustments so that you can optimize different areas of an image using different adjustments. To achieve the optimum dynamic range possible from the information recorded by the image sensor (increased shadow detail and increased highlight detail), we can open two images from the same Raw file and optimize each for a different end of the exposure range.

DVD
CAMERA RAW
IMAGE ON DVD

Localized Levels – optimized quality starts here

We can then simply merge the two exposures together. Some would call this manipulation, but in reality all we are doing is restoring the tonality back to how our human vision first saw the scene rather than how the camera interpreted it. In this way we can create images with much more drama than by just setting the black and white points for the entire image. With localized adjustments we can have our cake and eat it!

1. Have I told you that contrast is the photographer's worst enemy? Contrast is the sneak thief that stole my shadow and highlight detail in this image. Just look at all that clipping warning that appears when I click on the two triangles above the histogram. I saw the detail with my own eyes but the camera saw something different. I want it back and in this project I will show you how to get it.

2. We need to do this in two stages because full detail can't be achieved in Adobe Camera Raw. Adobe Camera Raw is a 'global' editor and cannot localize its adjustments to specific areas of the image. First raise the Fill Light slider to +35 and reduce the Blacks to 2 to retrieve the shadow detail. Raising the Exposure to +1.5 stops and lowering the Brightness slider to +25 will improve the midtone contrast in the foreground. The sky will be hopelessly clipped by this stage but this is a recovery process in two stages and this is but the first. Select Open Image to open the processed raw data into the main Edit space of Photoshop Elements.

3. We do not need to edit the open image in the main Edit space just yet. First we must return to the same Raw file to process the data for the sky. From the File menu choose Place. When the Place dialog opens browse to the same Raw file you just processed.

4. The Raw file will open with the settings you used to process the file for the foreground rocks. We must now modify these settings to optimize the file for the sky. Start by dropping the Exposure to -1.75 stops and push the Recovery slider to +100. Raise the Brightness slider to +80 and the Contrast and Vibrance sliders to +50. Most of the highlight clipping you can see is either the sun or the very saturated colors in the sky. Select OK in the bottom right-hand corner of the dialog.

5. The new version of the processed file will be placed as a layer above the first version. There will be a big cross across the file, inviting you to scale the image. We just need to click on the green check in the bottom right-hand corner to commit the current size. You will now see a small icon in the bottom right-hand corner of the layer thumbnail. This indicates that the layer is a Smart Object. This can be resized multiple times without losing any of the quality. As we want both files pin-registered we do not need this ability. Right-click on the layer and select Simplify Layer from the context menu.

6. Select the Quick Selection tool in the Tools panel and check the Auto Enhance option in the Options bar. Click and drag the tool across the sky, being careful not to dip below the horizon line or rocks. The Quick Selection tool may not be that quick when working with high-resolution files but the quality is very good when it gets there.

8. The black areas of the adjustment layer mask can be used to hide the corresponding pixels on the layer above. This technique is called 'creating a clipping mask'. Hold down the Alt/Option key and click on the dividing line in between the top layer and the adjustment layer when you see the clipping mask icon appear (two crossing circles). Alternatively you can click on the top layer in the Layers panel and from the Layer menu choose Create Clipping Mask. We have now successfully combined the sky of the top layer with the foreground of the bottom layer.

7. With the selection active click on the background layer to make it the active layer. Click on the Create New Fill or Adjustment Layer icon and choose a Levels adjustment layer from the menu. The selection will automatically be turned into an adjustment layer mask. We do not need to make any adjustments in the Levels dialog as we are only going to use the accompanying layer mask for this exercise. Users of Photoshop Elements 7 will need to click OK to close the Levels dialog. Photoshop Elements 8 users do not have an OK button as their adjustments are 'non-modal' or always live (this is a good thing).

9. You are probably not that impressed at this stage as the two exposures need to sit a little more happily next to each other. Select the Gradient tool from the Tools panel. Click on the adjustment layer mask and check that black is the foreground color in the Tools panel. In the Options bar select the Foreground to Transparent Gradient, the Linear Gradient option and set the Opacity to 100%. Drag a short gradient from just below to just above the horizon line to create a smoother transition between the two exposures.

10. The exposure at the top of the rocks on the right-hand side of the image may need a little adjustment. We can adjust this without affecting the sky. Click on the background layer to make this the active layer and then from the Create New Fill or Adjustment Layer menu choose Levels. The Levels adjustment layer will appear above the background layer and any adjustment you now make will only affect the rocks and not the sky.

12. Select the Gradient tool from the Tools panel (or press the letter G). Check that black is the foreground color or you have selected the Black, White option in the Options bar. Drag another Linear gradient from the rocks on the beach almost to the top of the rocks near the sky. This will shield the foreground rocks from the darkening adjustment.

(that non-modal improvement once again).

Users of Elements 7 will need to click OK before they can work in the adjustment layer mask. Photoshop Elements 8 users can work directly in the layer mask with the Levels dialog still open

11. In the Levels dialog move the central Gamma slider, directly underneath the histogram, to the right to darken the rocks near the sky. The foreground rocks will also be affected by this adjustment but we can use the accompanying layer mask to shield this area of the adjustment.

13. To recover a little more detail in the water, select the Levels 1 adjustment layer mask. Select the Brush tool (press the letter B) and set white as the foreground color. Lower the opacity of the brush to around 30% and use a large soft-edged brush. Paint the water to reveal darker tones and more detail. The more you paint, the more detail you see, as you slowly remove the black mask in this area, allowing more of the top layer (the darker exposure) to be visible.

14. If any of the rocks need dodging (making lighter) or burning (making darker), click on the Create a New Layer icon in the Layers panel. Set the mode of this layer to Soft Light in the Layers panel. Again, with a white brush, but this time at an opacity of 20%, paint over the rocks to lighten them. Switch the foreground color to black and paint to darken them. Your localized adjustments are complete and the exposures successfully merged.

PERFORMANCE TIP

In the example some of the highlights (excluding the sun) are only just recoverable. If you are presented with a landscape with even more contrast, the only way of achieving additional information in the highlights or shadows is to bracket the exposures (covered in the 'High Dynamic Range' project in Part 3 of this book).

Project 3

Preparing for Print

Setting the levels in a digital image is only the first step to achieving optimized images. It is also necessary to optimize the image for the intended output device. To achieve optimum tonal quality in your digital images it is important to target both the highlight and shadow tones within each image. When using Photoshop Elements, the Eyedropper tool is a key to unlocking the quality that lies dormant in any one of your images which has been correctly exposed.

RAW IMAGE ON DVD

What you see is not always what you get — target your levels to your output device for predictable results

To achieve maximum quality, set the target levels in images that are in 16 Bits/Channel mode (accessed through the Camera Raw format or via 48-bit output scans from film). If you are optimizing your files in 8 Bits/Channel mode (via JPEG files) be sure to use an adjustment layer rather than an adjustment from the Enhance menu.

Ansel Adams was responsible for creating the famous/infamous 'Zone System' in order to precisely control the tonal range of each of his masterpieces. If you look carefully at one of his beautiful landscape photographs you will notice that only the light source (or its reflection – something termed a 'specular highlight') appears as paper white. All the rest of the bright highlights reveal tone or texture. Likewise, the shadows may appear very dark, but they are not devoid of detail. Ansel was careful only to render holes as black (the absence of a surface). Any surface, even those in shadow, would render glorious amounts of subtle detail.

Even though you may have set a black and a white point in Adobe Camera Raw (ACR), there is no guarantee that your shadow or highlight tones will be visible in the final print. To make sure the highlight detail does not 'blow out' (become white) and the shadow detail is not lost in a sea of black ink, it is possible to target the highlights and shadows in your image to the brightest and darkest tones that the printer can reproduce. The default settings of the eyedroppers to be found in the Levels dialog are 0 (black) and 255 (white). These settings are only useful for targeting the white overexposed areas or black underexposed areas; they can, however, be recalibrated to something much more useful, i.e. tones with detail. A typical photo quality inkjet printer printing on premium-grade photo paper will usually render detail between the levels 18 and 250. Precise values can be gained by printing a 'step wedge' of specific tones to evaluate the darkest tone that is not black and the brightest tone that is not paper white (see Project 7 – 'Printing' for more guidance on this subject).

PERFORMANCE TIP

The precise target values for images destined for the commercial printing industry are dependent on the inks, papers and processes in use. Images are sometimes optimized for press by skilled operatives during the conversion to CMYK and sometimes they are not. If in doubt you should check with the publication to get an idea of what you are expected to do and what you should be aiming for if the responsibility is yours.

1. Before we can set appropriate Shadow and Highlight values for the printer we must first optimize our file in ACR. The high-contrast project image shows that both the Shadow and Highlight values are 'clipped'. The darkest shadows are absolute black (level 0) and the brightest highlights are absolute white (level 255). Our first aim is to recover more appropriate black and white points and thereby attempt to recover lost detail in the shadows and highlights.

2. Click on the highlight clipping warning above the right-hand side of the histogram to locate the clipped highlights. Note how some of the clipping is due to saturated colors rather than overly bright highlights. Zoom in to 100% and focus your attention on the front of the tram (the brightest highlight in the image). Reduce the Exposure slider until most of the clipping has disappeared (between 0.5 and 1 stop). To remove all of the clipping you will need to employ the help of the Recovery slider.

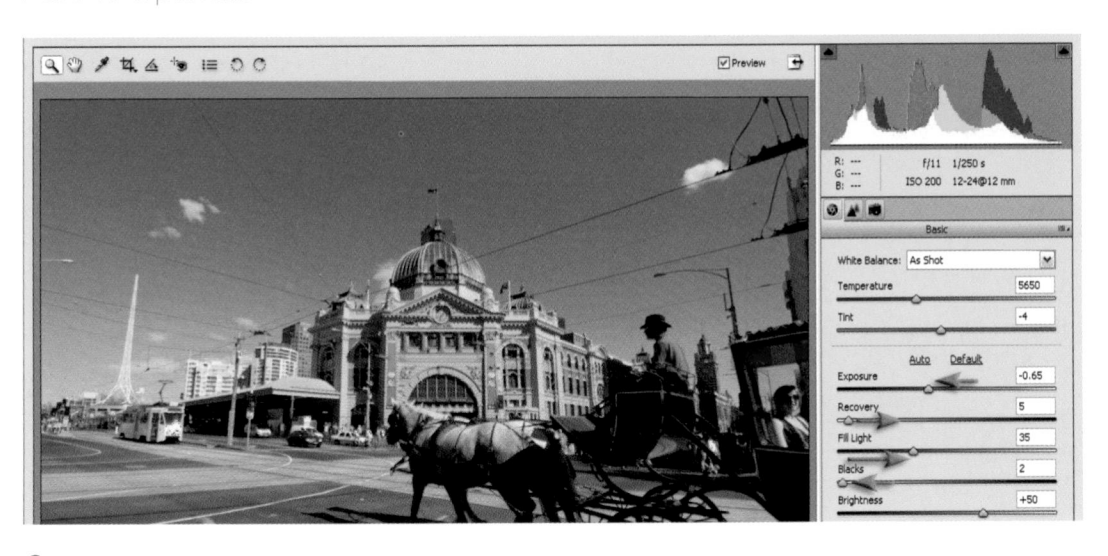

3. The shadow clipping can be removed by raising the Fill Light slider to +35 and lowering the Blacks slider to +2. Normally I would try to recover any shadow clipping using only the Fill Light slider (if the file was captured at low ISO) but raising the Fill Light slider too high can compromise the quality of the shadows (hence the limit of +35 Fill Light and the reduction of the Blacks slider).

4. The Brightness and Vibrance sliders have both been raised to give the image a summer feeling. In the illustration above you will notice the highlight clipping has turned red, indicating some saturation clipping is occurring due to the high vibrance of the colors. If there was luminance clipping (a loss of detail in all three channels) the highlight clipping warning triangle would be white.

Note > I have set the Color Settings in the Edit workspace to Always Optimize for Print so that I can preview the colors in the larger Adobe RGB gamut in ACR.

5. The Auto White Balance setting in-camera has rendered this file a little too warm. Assign a new white balance by selecting the White Balance tool at the top of the ACR dialog. Click to activate the tool and then click on something that should have a neutral tone in the image preview. I have selected the side of the building on the extreme right-hand side of the image. Now that the image has been optimized in ACR we can choose Open Image in the bottom right-hand corner of the dialog so that we can complete the editing process in the main Edit space of Photoshop Elements.

6. Click on the Create New Fill or Adjustment Layer icon in the Layers panel and select a Levels adjustment. There have been some subtle changes to the adjustment layers for Photoshop Elements 8 users. There is no OK button as the adjustments are always live (what Adobe describes as being 'non-modal'). There are new icons at the base of the Adjustment dialog that allow you to switch off the visibility of the adjustment or reset it to its default settings. There have also been some subtle but powerful changes to the performance of the Eyedropper tools that will allow us to optimize the shadow and highlight tones of this image for printing much more easily than in previous versions of the software.

7. Before we start to locate and adjust the shadow and highlight tones within this image we should optimize the performance of the Eyedropper tool in the tools panel and the second readout values in the Info panel. Elements 7 users will have to close the Levels panel they have just opened in order to do this by selecting OK in the Levels dialog, but Photoshop Elements 8 users are not troubled by this 'modal' way of working. This is the beauty of non-modal editing. Non-modal editing gives the user the freedom to work on other aspects of the image controls and adjustment features without having to close and reopen adjustment dialogs. Select the Eyedropper tool in the Tools panel and in the Options bar set the Sample Size to a 5 by 5 average. This will give us a much more representative sample of the area we are monitoring than a single pixel from that area. From the Window menu choose Info to open the Info panel. Click on the second mini eyedropper in the Info panel to access the sample options. Choose HSB so that we can monitor the brightness of the shadows and highlights rather than the RGB levels.

8. In this step we will locate the darkest area of the image that has shadow detail. Double-click on the Black eyedropper in the Levels dialog to open the Select target shadow color dialog. Enter a value of 7 or 8% into the 'B' field (the actual value depends on the shadow performance of your printer – see the 'Printing' project, page 92). Select OK and then Yes when you see the 'Save new target colors as defaults?' dialog.

9. With the Black eyedropper still selected, hold down the Alt/Option key and drag the shadow slider to the right slightly. The image will now appear in threshold view. Only the shadows that are clipping will be visible against a white background. Locate an area of black rather than a color and zoom in on this region until you are at 100%, or Actual Pixels (Ctrl/Command + Spacebar will access the Zoom tool for Elements 7 users). Hold down the Alt/Option key and move your cursor into the image preview and click on this region (users of version 7 will have to remember where the dark tone was as they will not be able to see the Threshold view when they move into the image preview).

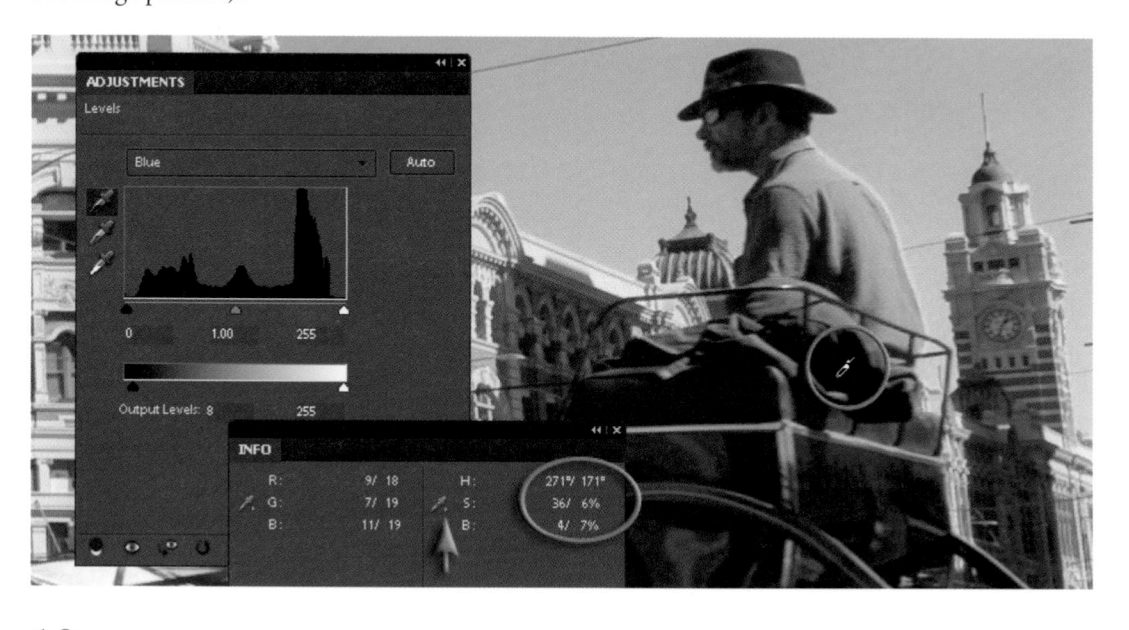

10. Clicking on this darkest area of the image will render your shadow detail lighter so that it will not appear as absolute black in the final print. If you observe the readout in the Info panel you will see before and after sets of numbers. As you move your mouse cursor over the darkest shadow again you will notice that the darkest tones now read the 7 or 8% Brightness value that you assigned to them.

11. In this step we will locate the lightest area of the image in which we want to see highlight detail in the print. Double-click the Set White Point eyedropper to display the Select target highlight color dialog. This time enter a value of 98 in the Brightness field and select OK. Choose Yes when the info dialog appears asking you if you want to 'Save the new target colors as defaults'.

Note > Most printers are much better at handling bright highlight detail than they are at rendering good shadow detail.

12. Hold down the Alt/Option key and drag the white Input slider (underneath the histogram) in the Levels dialog to the left so that you can see the highlights clipping in the Threshold view. You will notice that the front of the tram is the brightest part of this image. Zoom in to 100% (Actual Pixels) to take a closer look at this area of the image.

13. Hold down the Alt/Option key, move your mouse cursor into the image preview and click on this clipped tone. When you click you will see the clipping disappear. The highlight tones will be made a little less bright so that they conform to the values you set in the Color Picker.

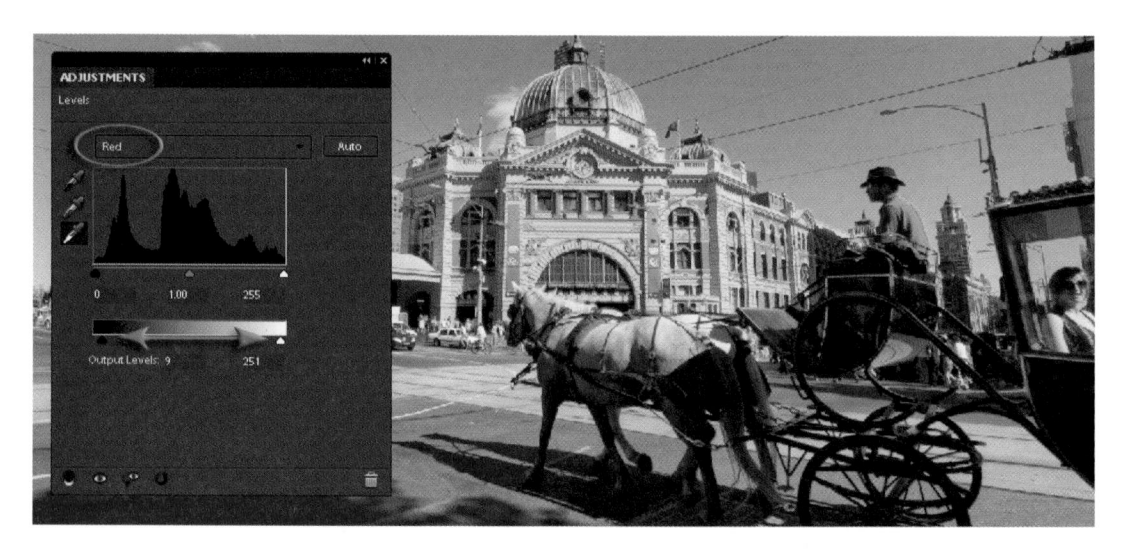

14. If you notice that a color cast has been introduced by setting new Shadow and Highlight values, select the Set Gray Point eyedropper (between the Black and White eyedroppers) and then click on the building you first clicked on in ACR to reestablish the correct white balance. The neutral tone selected to be the 'Gray Point' can be a dark or light tone within the image.

Note > If you look at the individual Red, Green and Blue channels in the Levels dialog, you will be able to see how the shadows and highlights have been optimized for the printer targets. The Output values have been increased to encourage either more or less ink to be applied to highlights or shadows so that they are information-rich in print and not clipped by excessive contrast.

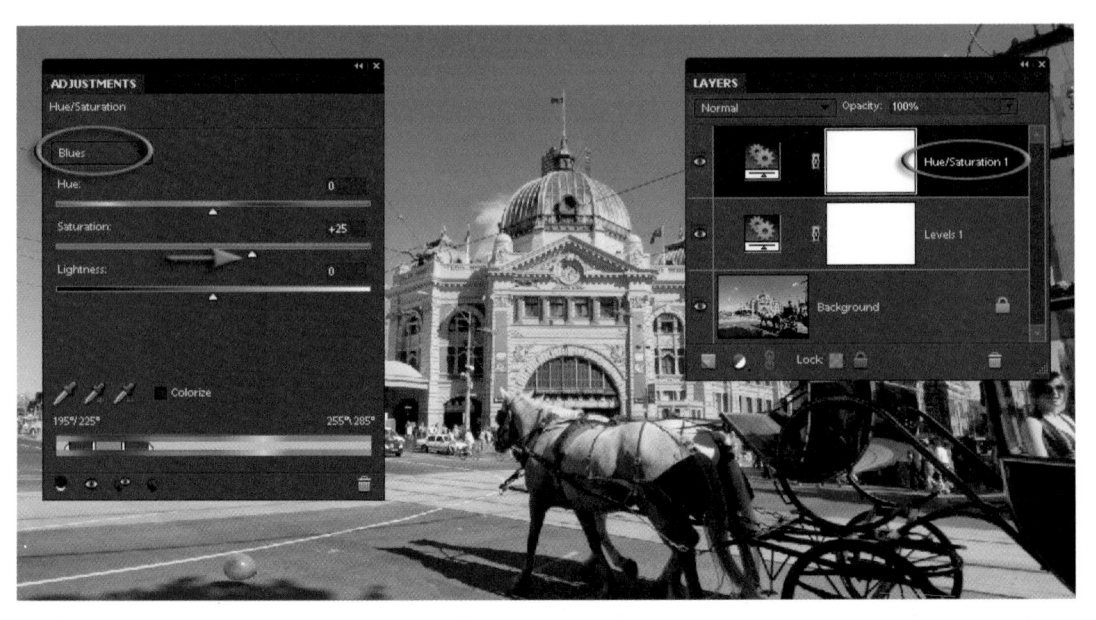

15. We can target specific colors within an image and adjust either their hue or saturation using a Hue/Saturation adjustment layer. In the illustration above I have selected the Blues and increased the saturation. I have then selected the Yellows and again increased the saturation. These are called targeted adjustments as they do not affect all colors.

16. At the moment the adjustment layers give me the flexibility to make any changes I want by simply selecting the adjustment layer and making further changes (Elements 7 users will have to double-click the Adjustment Layer icon to open the Adjustment dialog). If I want to discard the adjustment I can simply drag it to the trash in the Layers panel. If I want to 'bake in' the changes to the pixels I can either flatten the file (select Flatten Image from the Layer menu) or 'stamp' the visible layers into a new layer. Windows users can do this by first selecting the top layer and then, while holding down the Ctrl, Alt and Shift keys, typing the letter E. Mac users must hold down the Command, Option and Shift keys and then type the letter E. This keyboard shortcut is unlisted by Adobe and is called 'stamp visible' by those 'in-the-know'.

17. If you notice that your image is a little crooked (perhaps you forgot to straighten it in ACR) then you can straighten it now using the Straighten tool from the Tools panel. Select the tool and then click and drag over something that you know or feel to be horizontal. The image will automatically straighten itself based on the line that you draw.

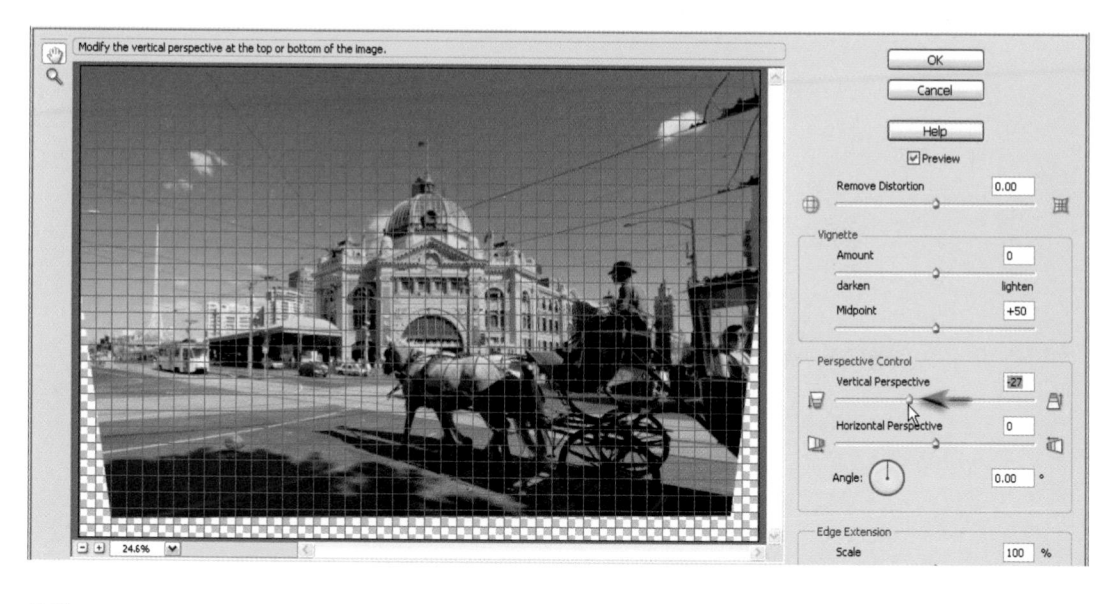

18. When a camera is tilted up or down with a short focal length lens (wide angle) the verticals within the image can lean excessively inwards or outwards (converging verticals). Professional architectural photographers use cameras with movements or special lenses to remove this excessive distortion. To correct perspective in Photoshop Elements 7 or 8 use the Correct Camera Distortion filter. The process of correcting the verticals in an image is often referred to as 'keystoning'. To start the process go to Filter > Correct Camera Distortion. The top slider in this dialog corrects either barrel distortion or pincushion distortion, which sometimes result when using the extreme focal lengths of the zoom lens. Both result in curved straight lines which are usually most noticeable with the curvature of a horizon line when using a short focal length (wide angle) lens. In this image we just need to move the Vertical Perspective slider so that the buildings are not leaning inwards. You will notice that the image gets smaller at the bottom of the dialog and transparency appears around the image.

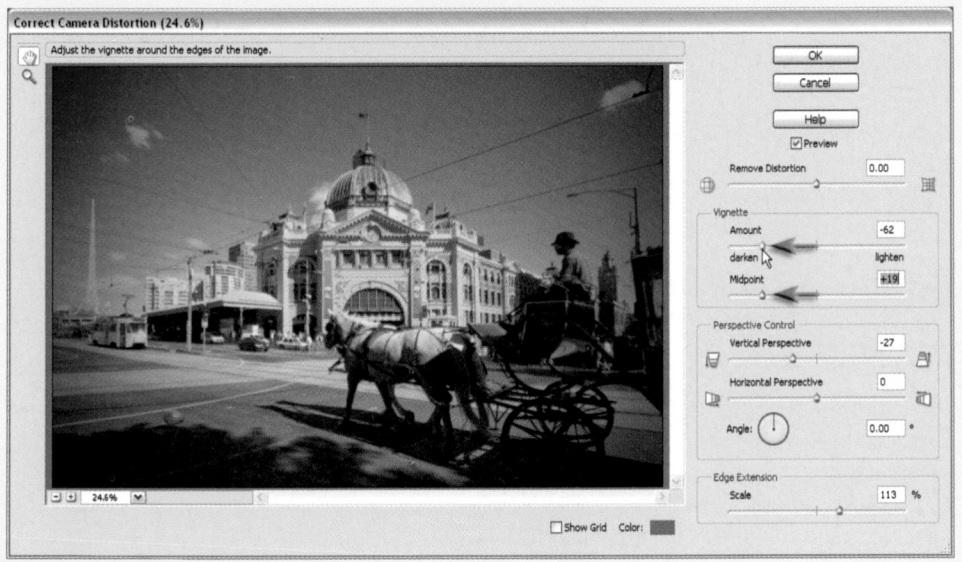

PERFORMANCE TIP

It is possible to remove transparency in the Correct Camera Distortion dialog by increasing the scale of the image. This will, however, result in 'bicubic interpolation', i.e. Photoshop Elements will add new pixels to grow the image. A small amount of scaling will probably go unnoticed but it is actually kinder to the file to first select OK and then crop the transparency away using the Crop tool in the main Edit space. This may, however, not be an option if you first cropped the image to your output size in ACR. It is also possible to either correct lens vignetting (images where the corners appear darker or lighter than the rest of the image) or add creative vignettes for effect in the Correct Camera Distortion dialog. There is a more effective way of darkening the corners of an image for effect that is outlined in the following steps.

19. If you have not scaled the image in the Correct Camera Distortion dialog to remove the transparency then hold down the Alt/Option key and click on the Visibility icon of the Stamp Visible layer (I have renamed mine by double-clicking on the name of the layer). This action will switch the visibility of the other layers off so that you can see the transparency once again.

20. Select the Crop tool in the Tools panel and then click and drag over the image to select the area to be cropped. While still holding down the mouse button press and hold the spacebar as well to float the crop bounding box so that you can move it into position. I have selected white as my mask color rather than black, which I find makes it easier to compose my shot. Press the Return/Enter key to commit the crop.

21. Open the Layers flyout menu and choose Flatten Image. If the visibility of the other layers is still turned off you will see a warning dialog that asks you if you want to 'Discard hidden layers'. Select Yes and the other layers will be removed from the file.

22. A superior way to add a vignette (compared to the adjustment in the Correct Camera Distortion dialog) is to first duplicate the background layer (formerly the Stamp Visible layer). Duplicate the background layer using the keyboard shortcut Ctrl/Command + J. Select the Rectangular Marquee tool from the Tools panel and set a 150 to 250 pixel feather in the Options bar (you will need to use a lower amount for low-resolution images). Click and drag over the central portion of the image to make a selection. Photoshop Elements may take a while to make this selection with such a large feather radius. Hit the Backspace/Delete key to remove the central portion of this layer. Set the mode of the layer to Multiply (which is one of the darkening modes) and then lower the opacity of the layer until you achieve a subtle effect. From the Select menu choose Deselect. This technique is superior for creating a vignette because it does not unnaturally darken any bright highlights that are sitting at the edge of the frame.

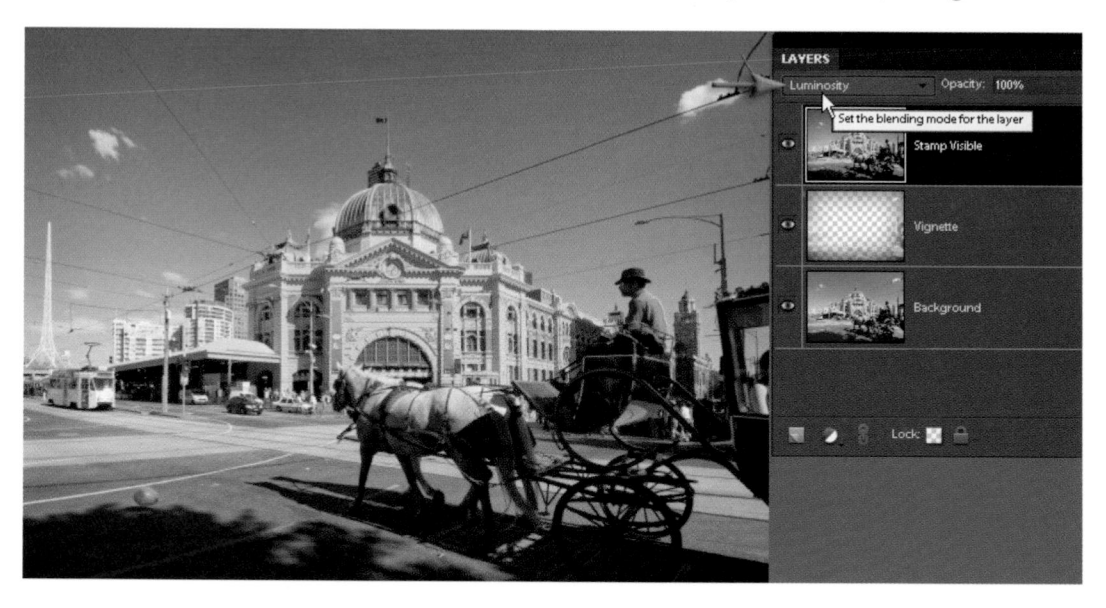

23. Before printing any file it is advisable to stamp the visible layers to a new layer (remember that 'stamp visible' keyboard shortcut from step 16) and sharpen the file. Printed images always look a little softer than the screen files they were printed from. This type of sharpening is called Output sharpening. Set the mode of this Stamp Visible layer to Luminosity in the Layers panel.

Note > Sharpening on a separate layer will give us the flexibility to adjust the opacity of the Sharpening layer and thereby adjust the sharpening of the file to suit the printer and paper we are printing to, i.e. there will be no need to go back to an unsharpened file and repeat the sharpening process.

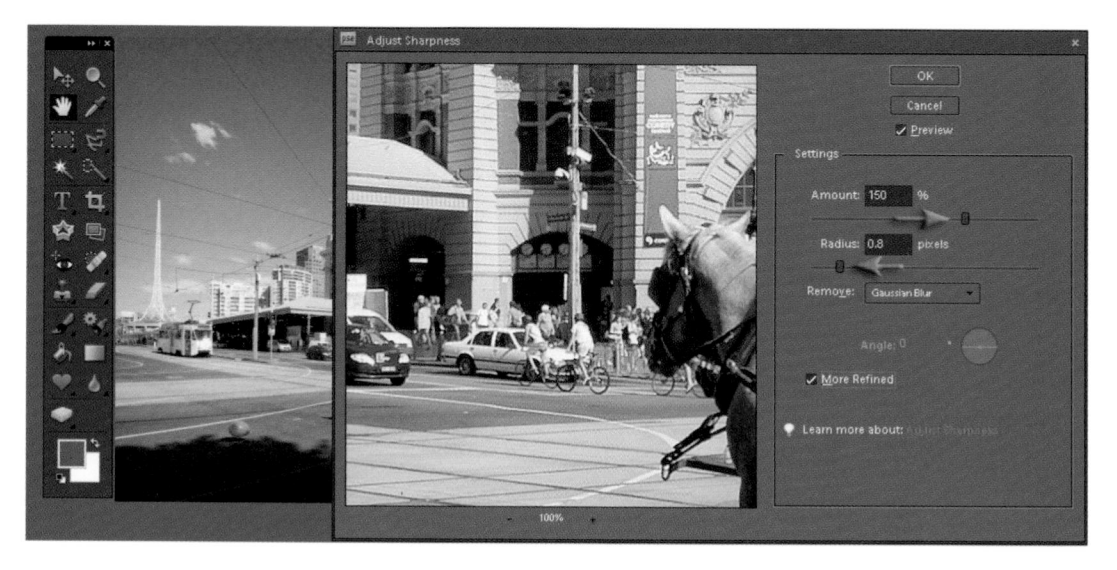

24. From the Enhance menu choose Adjust Sharpness. I typically use a high Amount (between 100 and 300%) and a low Radius setting (between 0.5 and 1.0 pixel) for print images. My image is now ready for print!

Project 4

Curves

One of the most important image adjustment features in a professional photographer's workflow is Curves (a sort of Levels command on steroids). Adobe, in their wisdom, decided to include this feature in Photoshop Elements 5.0. Color Curves now makes a welcome appearance in the Enhance menu but it is still not available as an adjustment layer. This project shows you several ways to control contrast using adjustment layers to increase your post-production editing power to maximum performance.

DVD
RAW IMAGE ON DVD

Create dramatic images by building in some non-destructive contrast

The revised Brightness/Contrast adjustment feature

If you have been image editing for some time you will know that 'Levels' has always been a superior option for enhancing the brightness and contrast of your image to the Brightness/Contrast feature. Adjusting the brightness or contrast of an image using the Brightness/Contrast adjustment used to be very destructive. For example if you wanted to make the shadows brighter and elected to use the Brightness/Contrast control, all of the pixels in the image were made brighter (not just the shadows), causing the pixels that were already bright to fall off the end of the histogram and lose their detail or become white (level 255). The Brightness/Contrast adjustment feature was fully revised with version 7 so that its behavior now falls in line with the non-destructive nature of the Brightness and Contrast sliders in Adobe Camera Raw (ACR).

Using the Brightness slider is now like moving the center (Gamma) slider in the Levels adjustment feature, i.e. the image is made brighter whilst preserving the black and white points within the image. The Contrast slider, on the other hand, makes the shadows darker and the highlights brighter but not at the expense of the black and white points of the image. The only problem with new Brightness/Contrast adjustment feature is that it cannot focus its attention on a limited range of tones, e.g. make the shadows darker or lighter but leave the midtones and highlights as they are.

The Curves adjustment feature as seen in the full version of Photoshop

The Curves adjustment feature allows the user to target tones within the image and move them independently, e.g. the user can decide to make only the darker tones lighter whilst preserving the value of both the midtones and the highlights. It is also possible to move the shadows in one direction and the highlights in another. In this way the midtone contrast of the image can be increased with a great deal more control than the new Brightness/Contrast adjustment feature.

Resolving the problem

Now there are three ways to enable you to harness the power of Curves in Adobe Elements 7 or 8.

Method 1 – Color Curves

Adjust Color Curves is a user-friendly version of the Curves adjustment feature found in the full version of Photoshop and can be accessed from the Enhance menu (Enhance > Adjust Color > Adjust Color Curves). The user should first set the levels of the image file by using the techniques outlined in Projects 1 and 2. Unfortunately, Adjust Color Curves is not available as an adjustment layer so it would be advisable to first duplicate the background layer and then apply the changes to this duplicate layer. Start by clicking on the thumbnail of your choice and then click on the advanced options to access the sliders that are required to fine-tune the tonality of your image. It may be necessary to add a Hue/Saturation adjustment layer to modify any changes in the color saturation that may have occurred as a result of the Color Curves adjustment.

Accessing curves as an adjustment layer

The second way of using curves, this time as an adjustment layer, is a bit cheeky and is possible if you have access to a multilayered file created in the full version of Photoshop (check out the supporting DVD to download the file used in the example below).

A Photoshop file opened in Elements will allow the user limited functionality to modify the adjustments

Method 2 – Grand theft

One of the great mysteries of life is that although you can't create a Curves adjustment layer in Photoshop Elements you can open an image that already has one. Photoshop Elements allows you to see the effects of the Curves adjustment layer (that was created in the full version of Photoshop), to switch it off and on, and to lower the opacity of the Curves adjustment layer (enabling you to lower the effect of the adjustment layer gradually). You can also drag this Curves adjustment layer into any other image file that is open in Elements (just click on the adjustment layer thumbnail in the Layers panel and drag it into another image window). Theoretically this means that, if you had a single file that was created in Photoshop with a wide range of Curves adjustment layers to suit your everyday image-editing tasks, you could use this as a 'Curves resource' – just drag, drop and adjust the opacity to suit the needs of each image you are editing. The sort of adjustment layers that would be particularly useful would be those that enabled the Photoshop Elements user to increase and decrease image contrast, raise or lower shadow brightness independently, and raise or lower highlight brightness independently. If the adjustment layers contained generous adjustments they could be simply tailored to suit each new image-editing task by just lowering or increasing the layer opacity. The adjustment layers are resolution-independent, which is another way of saying that they will fit any image, big or small – naughty but very nice!

Method 3 – Gradients

The third version is for users of Elements who want a little more control, have a guilty conscience or prefer to explore the advanced features of the package they have purchased rather than the one they have not. This method allows you to access the ultimate tonal control that Curves has to offer using a different adjustment feature not really designed for the job but which, when push comes to shove, can be adapted to fit the needs of the cash-strapped image editor seeking quality and control.

1. The first step is to hold down the Alt/Option key while selecting the Gradient Map adjustment layer from the Create Adjustment Layer menu in the Layers panel. This will open the New Layer dialog box. Select Luminosity from the Mode menu and click OK.

2. In the Adjustments panel click to open the drop-down menu and then select the third gradient swatch in the presets menu (Black, White). Click on the gradient above the presets to open the Gradient Editor.

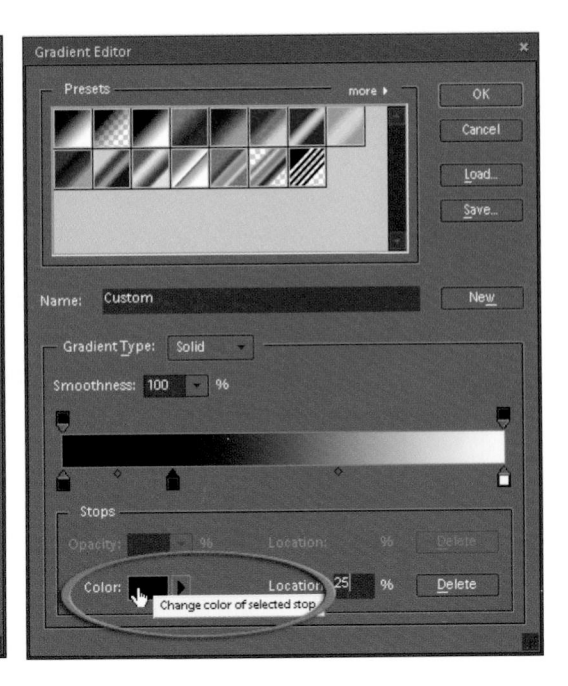

3. Move the cursor to just below the gray ramp and click to add a 'stop' slightly left of center. Type in 25% as the location and click on the color swatch to open the Color Picker.

4. Choose a Brightness value of 25% and click OK (ensure a value of 0 is entered in the other two fields of the HSB radio buttons). Add another stop right of center (at a location of approximately 75%) and again click on the color swatch to open the Color Picker. This time choose a Brightness value of 75% and again click OK.

5. The Black/White gradient map in Luminosity mode will leave the existing tonal values of your image the same as before. The magic starts when you start to drag the stops you created to new positions on the gray ramp. Moving the two sliders further apart will lower the contrast whilst dragging them closer together will increase it. A 'color midpoint' also appears between the two stops that you are adjusting to allow you to fine-tune your adjustment. In this project drag the two sliders together to increase the contrast but move the color midpoint to the left so that deep shadows do not become too dark. Be amazed – you are exercising absolute control over the brightness values of your image! This technique allows all of the versatility of a Curves adjustment layer when editing the luminosity of your image.

GRADIENT PRESETS ON DVD

PERFORMANCE TIP

When you have created a modified gradient map you can name the map and add it to the list of presets for future use. Download the Gradient presets file (Tonal_Gradients.grd) from the supporting DVD and use either your Preset Manager from the Edit menu to add them to your gradient library or load them directly using the Gradient Editor by clicking on the Load button.

Note > Moving stops too close together can create steps or bands in the tonality of your image, producing an effect that is posterized and unnatural. It is important to realize there are limits to how much tonal manipulation an image is capable of handling before the quality suffers.

The Gradient Map adjustment layer set to Luminosity mode acts like a 'hot-wired' Levels adjustment layer. Its advantage is that you can set as many stops or sliders as you like, giving you total control. Any localized areas that require further attention can simply be masked on the adjacent layer mask and tackled separately on a second Gradient Map layer.

Note > If you have a selection active when you choose the Gradient Map adjustment layer, it automatically translates the selection into a layer mask, restricting any adjustments to the selected area.

6. If you are looking to achieve a simple global contrast adjustment the project is complete. If, however, you want to enhance the image further using more gradients, try the following techniques. Select the Gradient Map adjustment layer and choose the Gradient tool from the Tools panel (or type the letter G on the keyboard). Choose the Black/White and Linear options and then drag a gradient from the top of the image window to just below the horizon line. This will shield the sky from the contrast adjustment applied by the Gradient Map adjustment layer.

7. We will now balance the tonality in the image by darkening the sky. Click on the Create a New Layer icon in the Layers panel and set the blending mode of this new layer to Soft Light.

8. Ensure that black is the foreground default color (type the letter D on the keyboard) and then choose the Foreground to Transparent gradient. Drag a gradient from the top of the image to a position just below the horizon line. Holding down the Shift key as you drag a gradient will 'constrain' the gradient to ensure that it is absolutely straight. Try changing the blend mode of this gradient layer to Overlay and Multiply to see the variations of tonality that can be achieved.

9. Yet another way of targeting tones for adjustment is using the Shadows/Highlights adjustment feature. This very useful adjustment feature is not available as an adjustment layer so you will need to create a 'composite' layer of the work carried out so far before you can apply it, by using the unofficial Stamp Visible technique we learnt in Project 3 (page 56). Select the top layer in the Layers panel and then hold down the Shift + Alt/Option + Ctrl/Command keys whilst you type the letter E on the keyboard. The new layer should appear on top of the layers stack. Double-click the name of the layer to rename it 'Stamp Visible'. Now choose Shadows/Highlights from the Enhance > Adjust Lighting submenu. Set the Lighten Shadows and Darken Highlights sliders to 0 and raise the Midtone Contrast to +30. You can watch the effects of raising this slider by clicking on the Preview box and by viewing the histogram in the Histogram panel.

10. Create another new layer and this time set the blend mode to Multiply. As with the previous gradient you can experiment with alternative blend modes after you have finished creating this second gradient.

Note > You can also set the blend mode for a new layer in the New Layer dialog box.

11. Choose the Elliptical Marquee tool from the Tools panel and choose a large amount of feather (increase the amount of feather as the resolution of the file gets bigger). Draw an elliptical selection in the image window.

Note > You can check how soft this edge is by using the Selection Brush tool. Choose Mask from the Mode drop-down menu in the Options bar.

12. From the Select menu choose Inverse (Shift + Ctrl/Command + I) and then from the Edit menu choose the command Fill Selection. From the Contents section of the dialog box choose Foreground Color. Move the mouse cursor into the image, choose a deep blue color from the image window and then click OK. Lower the opacity of the layer until the vignette is subtle.

PERFORMANCE TIP

Use the Shadows/Highlights adjustment feature on the Stamp Visible layer if the darkening of the shadows becomes excessive as a result of the vignette.

Project 5

Hue/Saturation & Luminance

Levels is a powerful adjustment feature for controlling tonality and overall color balance. It cannot, however, target and control the hue of specific color values or the saturation of color in general. For this final level of control we need to master the powerful Hue/Saturation adjustment feature. In this project we will target specific colors and then change the hue and saturation of these targeted colors to creatively enhance an image.

RAW IMAGE ON DVD

Target and adjust the hue, saturation and luminance of selected colors within the image — the blues are made darker and the magentas are moved towards blue. The image is then completed using two of the Maximum Performance actions

The third slider in the Hue/Saturation dialog is the Lightness slider and this is so useful (not), that Adobe decided to leave its name off the name of the adjustment layer. It doesn't matter whether you decide to make the selected color lighter or darker, the slider always desaturates the target color. In this project we will explore how to adjust how bright the color appears without desaturating it. This is all made possible with the new Smart Brushes that come with the DVD and some very clever Maximum Performance know-how.

1. In Photoshop Elements it is possible to paint with adjustment presets using either the new Smart Brush tool or Detail Smart Brush tool. The Smart Brush tool creates its own mask as it paints the adjustment by looking for the edges of your subject matter. In the example above the Smart Brush tool is used in conjunction with the Blue Skies preset to increase the vibrancy of the existing sky. If the adjustment invades your subject you can hold down the Alt/Option key and then paint to remove the adjustment in this area. In areas where there is low edge contrast this preset can be difficult to apply. A Hue/Saturation adjustment can also be used to target colors and adjust them without upsetting other colors in the image.

2. Although a Hue/Saturation adjustment layer can be used to effectively adjust the hue or saturation of a selected color (Blues have been selected in the image above), it is less than effective for controlling the brightness of the target color. Note how the blue appears desaturated when the Lightness slider is moved to -100.

3. Switching the mode of the Hue/Saturation layer to Luminosity will help to restore the saturation levels of the adjusted color but the darkening or lightening effects are limited when using this technique and any hue or saturation adjustments that have been made using this adjustment layer are also removed. A better way to adjust the brightness of a target color is to emulate the powerful and superior Luminance sliders that can be found in Photoshop Lightroom. If you have installed the Maximum Performance actions and presets from the supporting DVD you will be able to create a much darker sky by adjusting the existing colors using the power of my MP8 Luminance presets.

4. The MP8 Luminance presets (designed to make a target color lighter or darker) can be selected from the Options bar after first selecting the Smart Brush tool or Detail Smart Brush tool. The Detail Smart Brush tool does not have the edge detection capability of the Smart Brush tool but is quicker to use when there is no need for edge detection, i.e. the neighboring colors surrounding the area you want to adjust are a different hue. Select the Darker Blues 3 preset in the Options bar and then paint over the sky with large soft brush (the presets come in three strengths, mild, medium and extra strong, with 3 being the strongest adjustment).

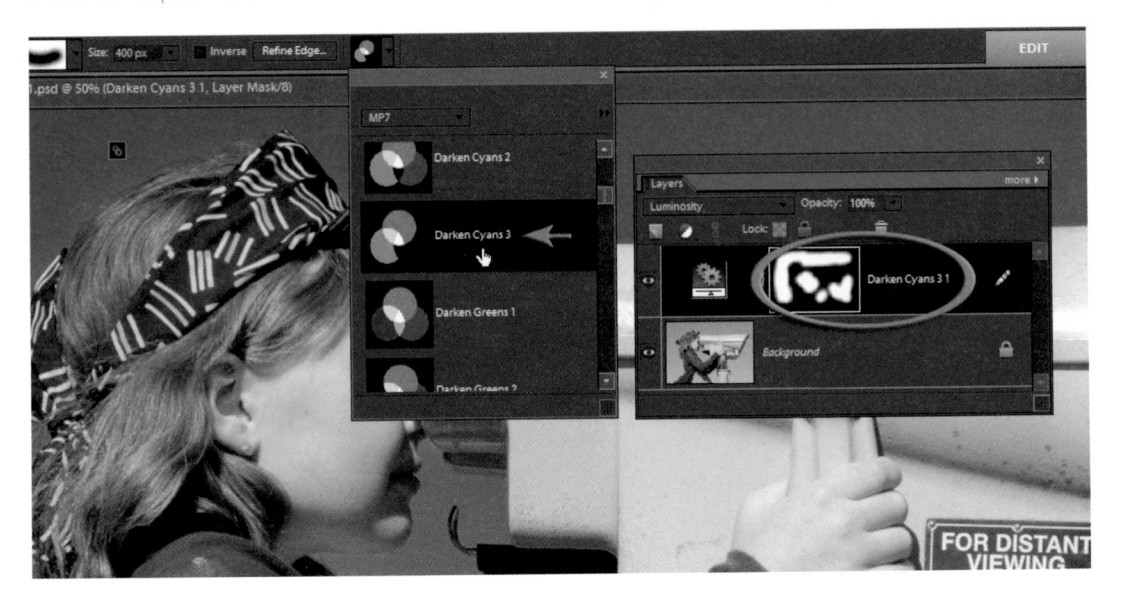

5. In the Layers panel you will see that an adjustment layer has been created. You cannot edit this preset by double-clicking on the layer thumbnail but you can lower the opacity or click on an alternative color in the Preset options. In the illustration above I have clicked on the Darker Cyans 3 preset to more effectively target the sky in this image (the hue of the sky is closer to cyan than blue).

6. To adjust another color you must first click on the background layer so that when you click on a new preset it does not change the first adjustment. In the illustration above I have selected the Darker Yellows 3 preset and then painted over the bright yellow tones in the image to lower their Luminance value.

7. The third color adjustment in this project does not need to use the luminance presets. Select a Hue/Saturation adjustment from the Create New Adjustment menu in the Layers panel and select Magentas from the Edit drop-down menu. Move the Hue and Saturation sliders to the left to adjust the magenta to a desaturated blue color. Select OK to apply the changes.

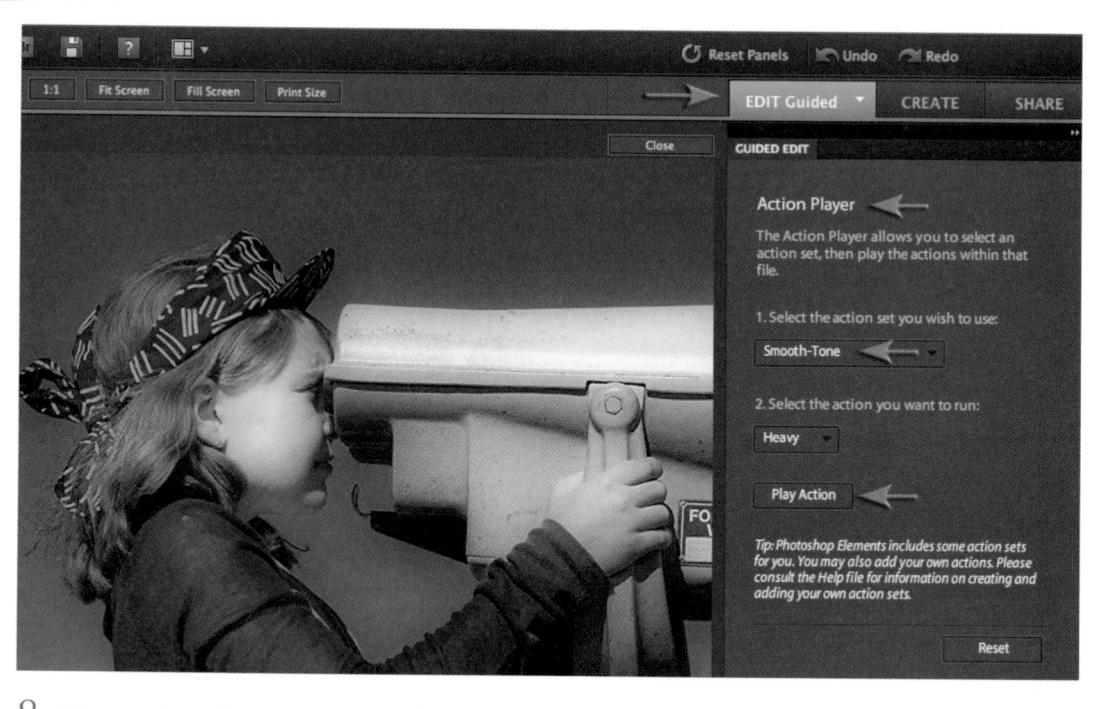

8. To complete this project we will use two of the Maximum Performance actions that come with the supporting DVD. First you will need to flatten the image (Layer > Flatten Image) or stamp the visible elements of all four layers in the Layers panel into a single new layer (hold down the Shift + Ctrl/Command + Alt/Option keys and press the E key). To access these actions click on the Guided Edit option and select the new Action Player from the Automated Actions section. Select the Smooth Tone action set (you will need to scroll down to find it) and then select the Heavy option. Click on the Play Action button to run the action and give the image smoother tones.

Action Player

The Action Player allows you to select an action set, then play the actions within that file.

1. Select the action set you wish to use:

Vignettes

2. Select the action you want to run:

Oblong-Darken with image

Play Action

Tip: Photoshop Elements includes some action sets for you. You may also add your own actions. Please consult the Help file for information on creating and adding your own action sets.

Reset

Done   Cancel

Before & After - Horizontal

9. We can use the Action Player to apply a Maximum Performance vignette to the image. The Oblong-Darken with image vignette has been optimized to darken the edges of the image without excessively darkening any highlight details at the edge of the frame. In the bottom right-hand corner of the panel you can access a before and after button. Pick Edit Full from the Edit tab drop-down list to return to the main editing space (Elements 7 users need to click on the Full button at the top of the panel to return to the main editing space).

Layers

Multiply   Opacity: 60%

more ▶

Lock:

Layer 1

Sharpen_50%

FOR DISTANT

10. In the Layers panel you can observe all of the layers that have been used to create these two effects. If you want to decrease the strength of the vignette simply lower the opacity of the layer in the Layers panel until the appropriate level of darkening is achieved.

11. In the final step we can digitally darn a couple of annoying holes in the top the girl is wearing. Click on the Create a New Layer icon in the Layers panel and then select the Spot Healing Brush tool in the Tools panel. Select the All Layers option in the Options bar. Adjust the size of the brush in the Options bar until the brush cursor is slightly larger than the hole in the fabric at the top of the arm. Click once to heal this area (replacing the offending pixels with color and texture from the surrounding area).

Note > The Maximum Performance DVD comes with dozens of useful actions that will help you to create visually stunning images and enhance your editing workflows. They turn lengthy, and often complex, editing procedures into simple-to-apply effects that are non-destructive to your background image. All layers used to create the effect are left so that you can adjust the technique to fit your own imaging needs.

PERFORMANCE TIP

The Hue/Saturation technique has many applications – from changing one odd bloom in a bouquet of flowers to color coordinating a background color with your subject. If you can't capture your subject against the perfect color backdrop it is usually an option to capture it against a color that has nothing in common with its general skin tones and hair color, e.g. blue sky or green foliage – just remember to mask the blue or green eyes.

Note > It is possible to increase or restrict the range of colors that are targeted by adjusting the sliders on the color ramp at the base of the dialog.

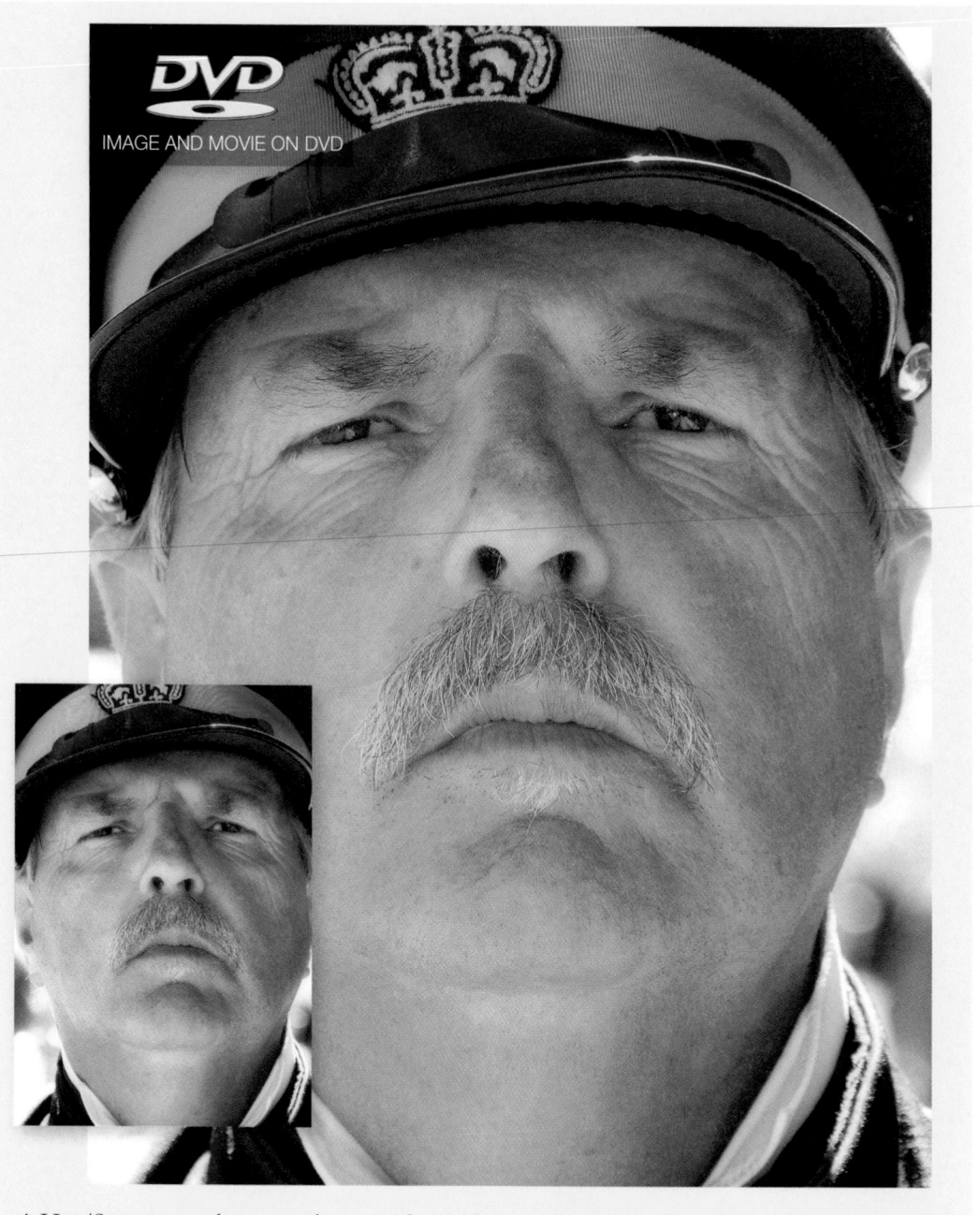

IMAGE AND MOVIE ON DVD

A Hue/Saturation adjustment layer can be used to accurately target an extremely narrow range of colors. In the example above the sunburnt colors on the man's face have been targeted and then adjusted to match the surrounding skin colors. The movie and image used to demonstrate this advanced technique are available on the supporting DVD.

Note > This technique is not recommended as an alternative to an effective sunscreen or a good broad-rimmed hat!

Project 6

Unsharpened

Sharpening

All digital images require sharpening – even if shot on a state-of-the-art digital SLR in focus. Most cameras can sharpen in-camera but the highest quality sharpening is achieved in post-production. Photoshop Elements will allow you to select the amount of sharpening and the areas that require it the most. For images destined for print, the monitor preview is just that – a preview. The actual amount of sharpening required for optimum image quality is usually a little more than looks comfortable on screen – especially when using an LCD/TFT monitor (flat panel).

RAW IMAGE ON DVD

Advanced sharpening – targeted for maximum impact

The basic concept of sharpening is to send the Unsharp Mask filter on a 'seek and manipulate' mission. The filter is programmed to make the pixels on the lighter side of any edge it finds lighter still, and the pixels on the darker side of the edge darker. Think of it as a localized contrast control. Too much and people in your images start to look radioactive (they glow); not enough and the viewers of your images start reaching for the reading glasses they don't own.

The art of advanced sharpening

The best sharpening techniques are those that prioritize the important areas for sharpening and leave the smoother areas of the image well alone, e.g. sharpening the eyes of a portrait but avoiding the skin texture. These advanced techniques are essential when sharpening images that have been scanned from film or have excessive noise, neither of which needs accentuating by the Unsharp Mask. So, let the project begin.

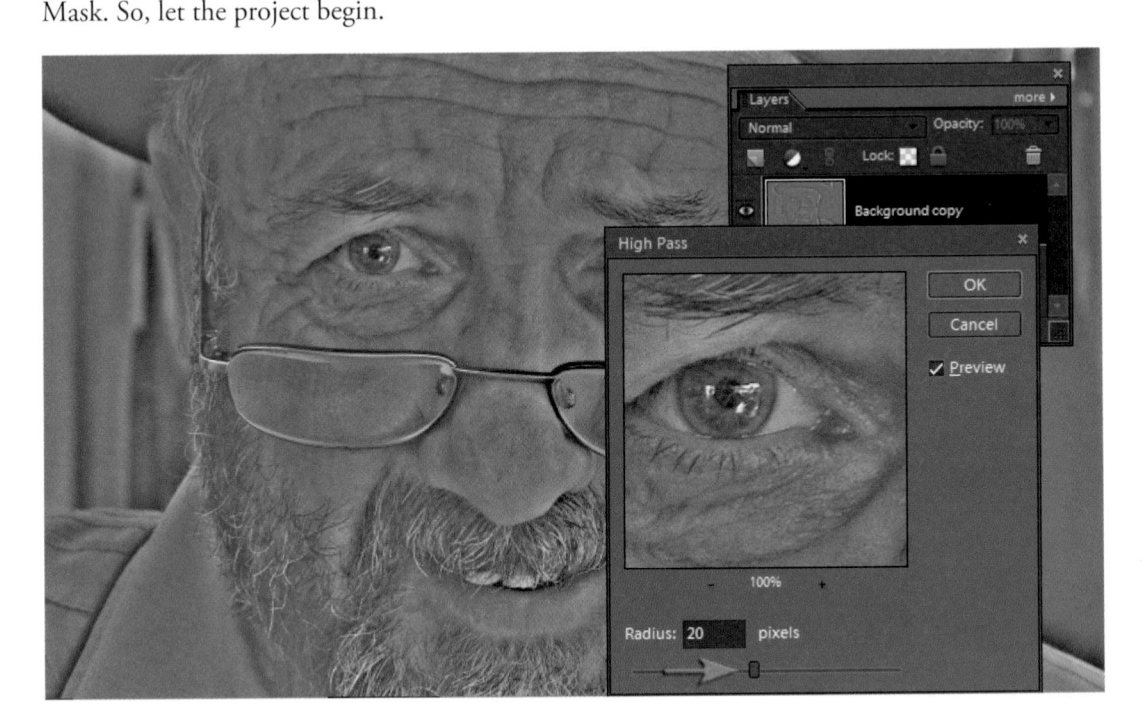

1. Duplicate the background layer by dragging it to the New Layer icon in the Layers panel. Go to Filter > Other > High Pass. Increase the pixel radius to around 20 to 30 pixels for a 6 to 12 megapixel image. Select OK. Apply the Despeckle filter (Filter > Noise > Despeckle) and also the Dust and Scratches filter (Filter > Noise > Dust and Scratches) using a Radius value of 1 pixel and setting the Threshold slider to 0 Levels.

Note > The High Pass filter is sometimes used as an alternative to the Unsharp Mask if the duplicate layer is set to Overlay or Soft Light mode. In this project, however, we are using the High Pass filter to locate the edges within the image only.

PERFORMANCE TIP

If you have any sharpening options in your camera or scanner it is important to switch them off or set them to minimum or low. The sharpening features found in most capture devices are often very crude when compared to the following advanced technique. It is also not advisable to sharpen images that have been saved as JPEG files using high-compression/low-quality settings. The sharpening process that follows should also come at the end of the editing process, i.e. after adjusting the color and tonality of the image.

2. Apply a Threshold filter to the High Pass layer from the Filter > Adjustments submenu. The threshold will reduce this layer to two levels – black and white.

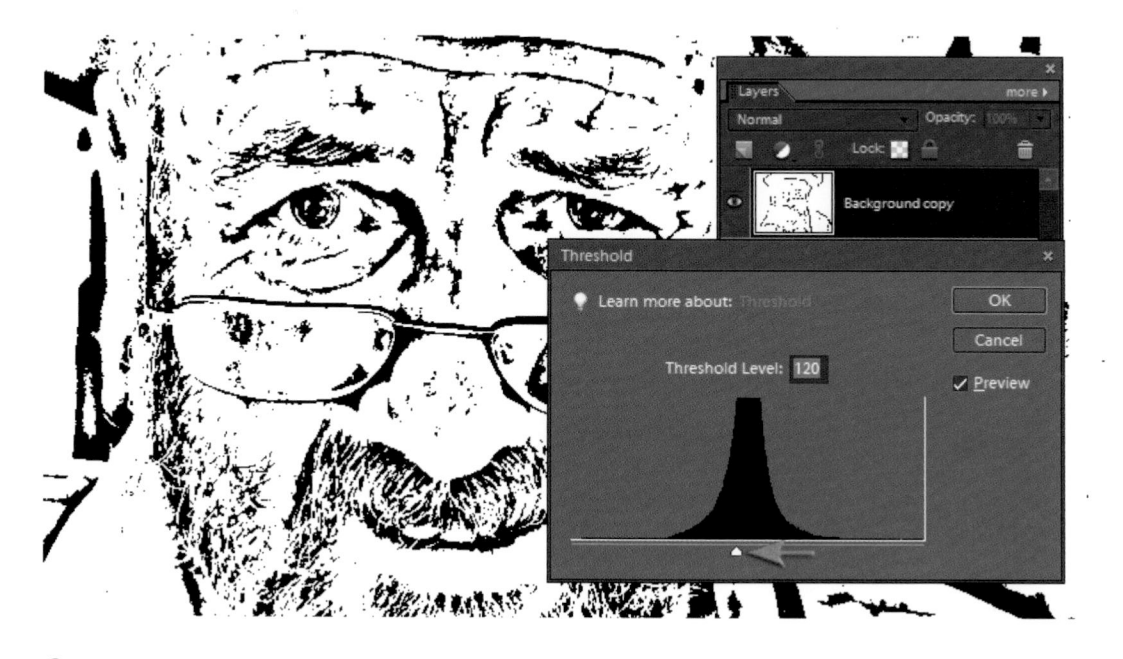

3. Drag the slider just below the histogram to isolate the edges that require sharpening. The aim of moving these sliders is to render all of those areas you do not want to sharpen white (or nearly white). Select OK when you are done. You are halfway to creating a sharpening mask. The mask will restrict the sharpening process to the edges only (the edges that you have just defined). Increasing or decreasing the radius in the High Pass filter will render the lines thicker or thinner.

4. Paint out any areas that were not rendered white by the Threshold adjustment but that you do not want to be sharpened. For example in the portrait used in this example any pixels remaining in the skin away from the eyes, mouth, nose and background were painted over using the Brush tool with white selected as the foreground color.

5. Go to Filter > Blur > Gaussian Blur and apply a 4-pixel radius to blur this layer. This step will ensure that the sharpening process will fade in slowly rather than have an abrupt edge.

6. Select the Magic Eraser tool in the Tools panel (behind the Eraser tool). Deselect the Contiguous option in the Options bar and then click on any white area within the image. You should be left with only the edge detail on this layer and none of the white areas. The image will appear a little strange until we complete the next couple of steps.

7. Duplicate the background layer and drag this duplicate layer to the top of the layers stack. Ensure the image is zoomed in to 100% for a small image or 50% for a larger print resolution image. From the Layer menu select Create Clipping Mask (previously called Group With Previous Layer) or position the mouse cursor between the two layers in the Layers panel, hold down the Alt/Option key and then click when the Create Clipping Mask icon appears. The transparent areas on the Threshold layer will act as a mask so only the important areas of the image will appear sharpened.

8. Go to Enhance > Unsharp Mask. Adjust the Amount slider to between 80 and 150%. This controls how much darker or lighter the pixels at the edges are rendered. Choose an amount slightly more than what looks comfortable on screen if the image is destined for print rather than screen. The Radius slider should be set to 0.5 pixels for screen images and between 0.8 and 1.5 for print resolution images. The Radius slider controls the width of the edge that is affected by the Amount slider. Raising the Threshold slider to 5 will prevent the Unsharp Mask from sharpening the noise within the image. If the Threshold slider is raised too high the Unsharp Mask will not sharpen the lower contrast edges.

Note > For low noise images (DSLR images where the ISO setting is low) you may get a superior result by using the Adjust Sharpness rather than the Unsharp Mask.

PERFORMANCE TIP

If you are sharpening an excessively 'noisy' or 'grainy' image the Threshold slider is moved progressively higher to avoid sharpening non-image data. The exact Threshold setting is not so critical for this advanced technique.

DVD
IMAGE ON DVD

Create this image using the sharpening techniques from Project 6 in this section

Project 7

0	3	5	8	10	13	15	18	20	23	26	229	232	235	237	240	242	245	247	250	252	255

Printing

The secret to successful printing is to adopt a professional print workflow that takes the frustration out of seeing the colors shift as your image moves from camera to monitor and from monitor to print. Color consistency has never been more easy and affordable to implement for keen amateurs and professional photographers. This project guides you along the path to ultimate print satisfaction, so that you will never again say those often-heard words – 'why do the colors of my print look different to my monitor?'

DVD

PRINT RESOLUTION IMAGE ON DVD

Adopt a color management workflow that delivers predictable prints every time

The reward for your effort (a small capital outlay and a little button pushing) is perfect pixels – color consistency from camera to screen to print. Once the initial work has been carried out, predictable color is a real 'no-brainer', as all of the settings can be saved as presets. As soon as you start printing using your new color-managed workflow you will not only enjoy superior and predictable prints, but will also quickly recover the money outlaid to implement this workflow (no more second and third attempts).

The problem and the solution

Have you ever walked into a TV shop or the cabin of an aircraft and noticed that, although the TVs are all showing exactly the same TV program, no two pictures are the same color? All of the TVs are receiving exactly the same signal but each has its own unique way of displaying color (its 'color characteristics'). Different settings on each TV for brightness, contrast and color only make the problem worse.

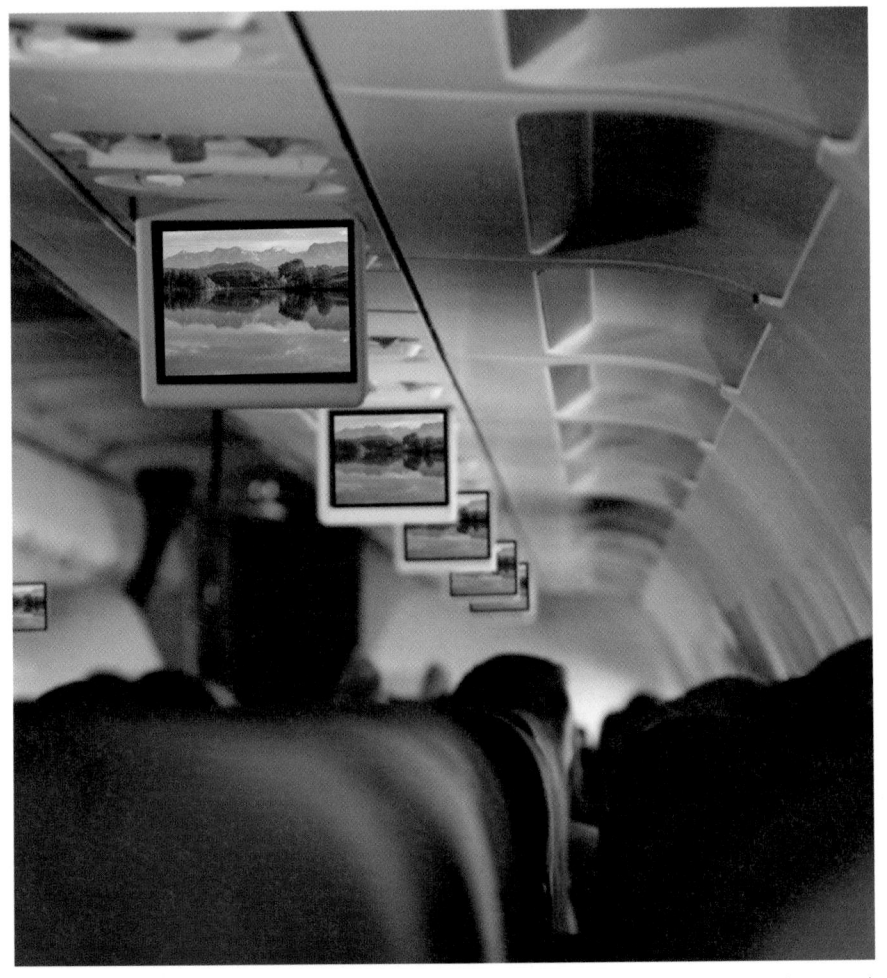

One signal – different pictures (image courtesy of iStockphoto.com)

In the perfect world there would be a way of making sure that all TVs could synchronize their settings for brightness, contrast and color, and the unique color characteristics of each TV could be measured and taken into account when displaying a picture. If this could be achieved we could then send 10 different TVs the same picture and the image would appear nearly identical on all of them, irrespective of make, model or age. In the world of digital photography, Adobe has made the illusive goal of color consistency possible by implementing a concept and workflow called 'color management'. Color management, at first glance, can seem like an incredibly complex science for the keen amateur to get their head around, but if just a few simple steps are observed and implemented then color consistency can be yours.

Don't position your monitor so that it faces a window and lower the room lighting so that your monitor is the brightest thing in your field of vision (image courtesy of iStockphoto.com)

1. Preparing your print workshop

The first step is to optimize the room where your monitor lives. Ideally, the monitor should be brighter than the daylight that lights the room and positioned so that it does not reflect any windows or lights (the biggest problems will be what is behind you and over your shoulders as you sit at the monitor). Professionals often build hoods around their monitors to prevent stray light from falling onto the surface of the monitor but if you carefully position it in the room you should be able to avoid this slightly 'geeky' step. Stray light that falls on your monitor will lower the apparent contrast of the image being displayed and could lead you to add more contrast when it is not required. The color of light in the room (warm or cool) is also a critical factor in your judgement of color on the screen. It is advisable to light the room using daylight but this should not be allowed to reflect off brightly colored surfaces, e.g. brightly painted walls or even the brightly colored top you may be wearing when you are sitting in front of your monitor. If the room is your own personal space, or your partner supports your passion/obsession/addiction for digital imaging, then you could go that bit further and paint your walls a neutral gray. Avoid the possibility of warm sunlight streaming into the room at certain times of the day. The brightness of the daylight in the room can be controlled with blinds or you can introduce artificial daylight by purchasing color-corrected lights, e.g. SoLux halogen globes or daylight fluorescent lights. If the above recommendations are difficult to achieve, lower the level of the room lighting significantly.

Overview of step 1 > Position your computer monitor so that it does not reflect any windows, lights or brightly colored walls in the room (when you sit at the monitor a neutral colored wall, without a window, should be behind you). Use daylight or daylight globes to light the room and make sure the lighting is not as bright as the monitor (the monitor should be the brightest thing in your field of view).

2. Preparing the monitor

Purchase a monitor calibration device (available for as little as US$100 from X-Rite, ColorVision or Pantone) and follow the step-by-step instructions. The calibration process only takes a few minutes once you have read through the instructions and adjusted a few settings on your monitor. It is now widely accepted that photographers should choose a D65 whitepoint (which affects how cool or warm tones appear on your monitor) and a gamma of 2.2 (this controls how bright your midtones are on your monitor). The next time you use your calibrated and profiled monitor, Photoshop Elements will pick up the new profile to ensure you are seeing the real color of the image file rather than a version that has been distorted by the monitor's idiosyncrasies and inappropriate default settings.

MONITOR CALIBRATOR RECOMMENDATIONS

If you are on a budget I recommend the ColorVision Spyder 2 Express or the Pantone Huey. If you have a little more money and are looking for a really professional tool, then the Eye One Display 2 is my personal favorite, although it costs a little more. If you decide on the Spyder 2 Express, I found the only hiccup in an otherwise easy-to-follow guide was the instruction on how to decide whether your LCD monitor has a 'brightness' or 'backlight' control. As the vast majority of LCD monitors use a 'backlight' to control brightness, I think this information is a possible source of confusion. The tiny Pantone Huey is really easy to use, completes the process in just a few minutes, and has an option to measure the brightness of the room and then adjust the brightness of the monitor accordingly. I would recommend that you lower the brightness of the LCD monitor to a setting of between 50 and 75% before calibrating an LCD screen with the Huey. The automatic brightness adjustment of the monitor is only useful if you can't maintain a standard level of illumination in your room. If you think small is cute, then the Huey will do an admirable job and you can put it in your shirt pocket when you're done.

If you are working on a tired and old CRT monitor (one of the ones that look like an old TV) and would like to pursue color consistency, now might be the time to treat yourself to that sleek new LCD monitor you have been promising yourself for ages (the useful life expectancy for a CRT for color-critical work is no more than three years). If you currently use a laptop screen I would recommend that you purchase a separate desktop monitor for your color-critical editing work

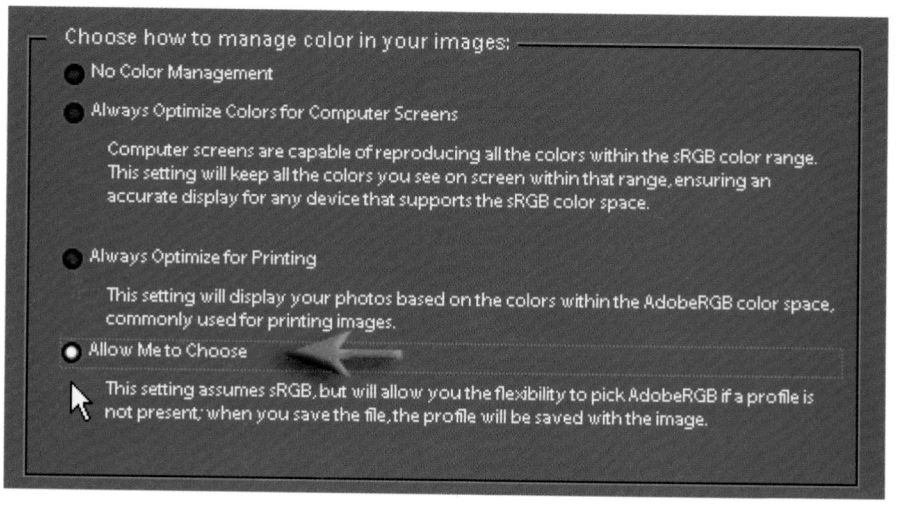

3. Preparing Photoshop Elements' Color Settings

Photoshop Elements can work with the range of colors (called a color gamut) that can be displayed on a monitor but also those that can be printed using inks and dyes. To work with these additional colors, which are out of the range of most monitors, Adobe implemented the concept of using a 'working space' instead of a monitor space for editing digital images. Photoshop Elements has a choice of two working spaces, sRGB and Adobe RGB. When creating images for screen or web viewing use the sRGB working space and when preparing images for print use the Adobe RGB working space. The Adobe RGB color space makes use of a larger color gamut than sRGB – a range of colors that can typically be reproduced by inkjet printers. Go to your Edit menu in Photoshop Elements and open the Color Settings dialog box. Select the Allow Me to Choose option.

PERFORMANCE TIP

When preparing the same images for both print and the web, use the Adobe RGB profile. After optimizing the images for print you can then duplicate them and convert the color profiles of those destined for the web to sRGB (Image > Convert Color Profile > Apply sRGB Profile).

4. Preparing to print to your own inkjet printer

Just as the color characteristics of the monitor have to be measured and profiled in order to achieve accurate color between camera and monitor, a profile also has to be created that describes the color characteristics of the printer. This ensures color accuracy is maintained between the monitor and the final print. When an accurate profile of the printer has been created, Photoshop Elements, rather than the printer, can then be instructed to manage the colors to maintain color consistency. Photoshop Elements can only achieve this remarkable task because it knows (courtesy of the custom profile) how the printer skews color.

Adobe RGB (1998)   Epson R2400

If you hope to achieve optimum print quality at home it is recommended that you use a photo-quality printer (one with six or more inks) that will let Photoshop Elements manage the colors for the best results. A custom profile is only accurate so long as you stick to the same ink and paper. Additional profiles will need to be created for every paper surface you would like to use. Printers are shipped with profiles but these are of the 'one size fits all' variety, affectionately known as 'canned profiles'. For optimum quality, custom printer profiles need to be made for the unique characteristics of every printer (even if they are of the same brand and model number).

PERFORMANCE TIP

In an attempt to make the first time not too memorable (for all the wrong reasons), check that your ink cartridges are not about to run out of ink and that you have a plentiful supply of good-quality paper (same surface and same make). Refilling your ink cartridges with a no-name brand and using cheap paper is not recommended if you want to achieve absolute quality and consistency. I would recommend that you stick with the same brand of inks that came shipped with your printer and use the same manufacturer's paper until you have achieved your first successful workflow.

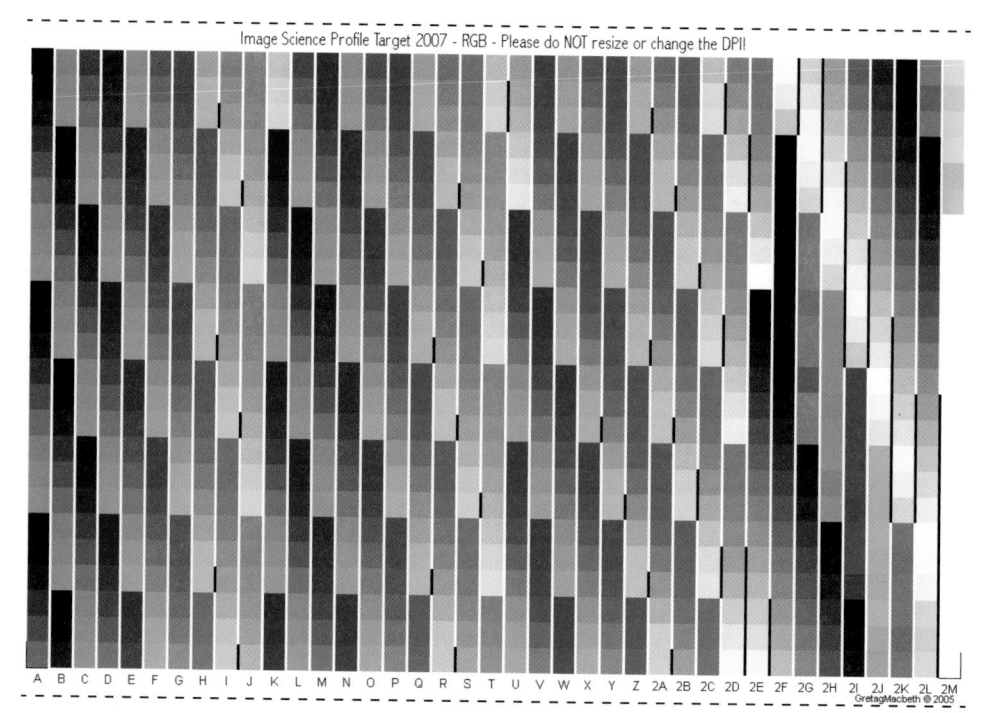

Image Science Profile Target 2007 - RGB - Please do NOT resize or change the DPI!

A B C D E F G H I J K L M N O P Q R S T U V W X Y Z 2A 2B 2C 2D 2E 2F 2G 2H 2I 2J 2K 2L 2M

5. Download a profile target

You can profile your printer, but the equipment is expensive. You can, however, print out a sample pattern and mail it to a company that has the equipment and will make the profile for you. Download a profile target from the website of the company who will create your custom printer profile. The target print can be mailed back to the company and your profile can be emailed back to you once it has been created by analyzing the test print you created.

6. Open the profile target file in Photoshop Elements

Open the target print you have downloaded from your profile service provider and select 'Leave as is' in the Missing Profile dialog box. If the file opens and no dialog box appears then close the file and check that you have changed the Color Settings as outlined in step 3. The color swatches on the target print must remain unchanged by the color management mechanisms for this process to be effective.

7. Print settings in Photoshop Elements

When the target image is open in Photoshop Elements, proceed to File > Print.

1. Select your printer from the Printer menu.
2. Click on Page Setup to choose the size of your printing paper (large enough to print the target image at 100%). **Note > You can also rotate the image or rotate the paper orientation within the Page Setup dialog box.**
3. Make sure that the scale is set to Actual Size (100%).
4. Go to More Options > Color Management (Photoshop Elements 7 users will see the Color Management section on the right-hand side of the main Print dialog) and select No Color Management from the Color Handling options. The Image Space (Source Space in Elements 7) should read Untagged RGB and there will be a reminder to switch off the color management in the Printer Preferences dialog, which we will do in the next step.

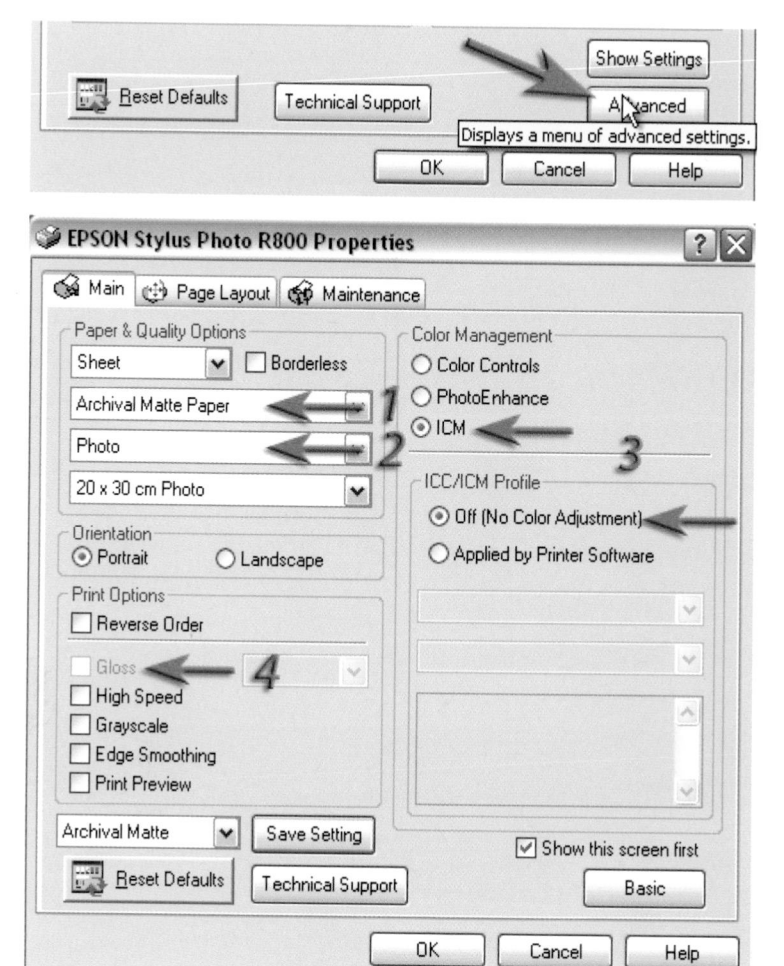

The printer driver of an Epson R800 – the layout and naming of the various options will vary between different makes and models of printers

8. Printer Preferences

Click on Printer Preferences in Photoshop's Printer dialog box (in the Color Management section) and then choose the Advanced options in your printer driver, if available. In the Printer Driver dialog box choose the paper or media type (1), photo print quality (2) and switch off the color management (3). Also switch off any Auto settings and a 'Gloss' option (4) if available and, for owners of Canon printers, make sure the Print Type is set to 'NONE'. The precise wording for switching off the color management in the printer driver will vary depending on the make of the printer and the operating system you are using. When using an Epson or Canon printer you may see that color management is referred to as ICM or ICC. Other manufacturers may refer to letting the software (Photoshop Elements) manage the color. When you print the target print, the colors are effectively printed in their raw state. In this way the lab that creates your profile can measure how the colors vary from one printer to another and they can then create a unique profile that best describes what your printer does with standard 'unmanaged' color.

9. Install your custom profile

Send the target print to the profiling company so that it can be measured using the sophisticated and expensive profiling hardware and software that is best left to the experts. They will email you the profiles after just a few days as an attachment. Right-click the profile and choose Install, and Windows will install it in the correct location. Apple Macintosh users must placew the profiles in the following folder: Macintosh HD > Library > ColorSync > Profiles.

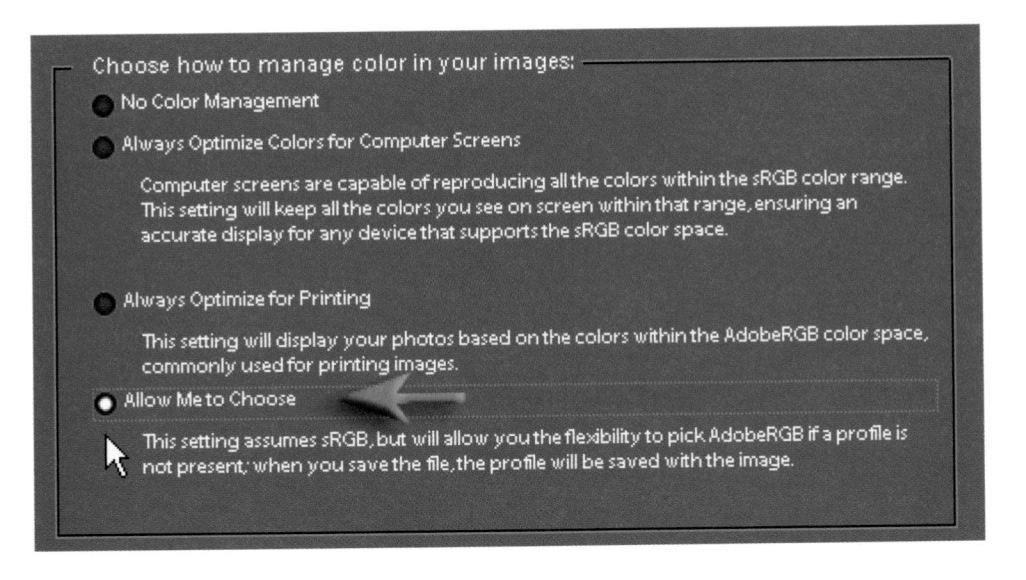

10. Tag your images with the Adobe RGB profile

When you have installed your custom printer profile make sure that your images destined for print are tagged with the Adobe RGB profile. Select the Adobe RGB profile in the camera if possible (digital SLR cameras and many prosumer fixed-lens digicams allow the photographer to choose this setting). Change the Color Settings in Photoshop Elements (Edit > Color Settings) to Always Optimize for Printing. This step will ensure any files being opened from ACR will automatically be tagged with the Adobe RGB profile rather than the sRGB profile.

11. Select Photoshop Elements Manages Colors

It is recommended that the first print you make using your custom profile is a test image – one that has a broad range of colors and tones. A test image with skin tones can be very useful for testing the accuracy of your new print workflow. A small test image is provided on the supporting DVD. When you next open the Print dialog box make sure you change the previous setting used to print the profile target from Printer Manages Colors to Photoshop Elements Manages Colors. Then select your new custom profile from the Printer Profile menu.

12. Making printer presets for quick and easy printing

From the Printer Preferences menu select the same settings that were used to print the profile target (don't forget to ensure the color management is turned OFF). Save a 'preset' or 'setting' for all of the printing options so that you only choose this one setting each time you revisit this dialog box. View your first print using bright daylight and you will discover, if you have followed these directions to the letter, that you have almost certainly found a solution to one of the mysteries of digital color photography – the search for predictable color.

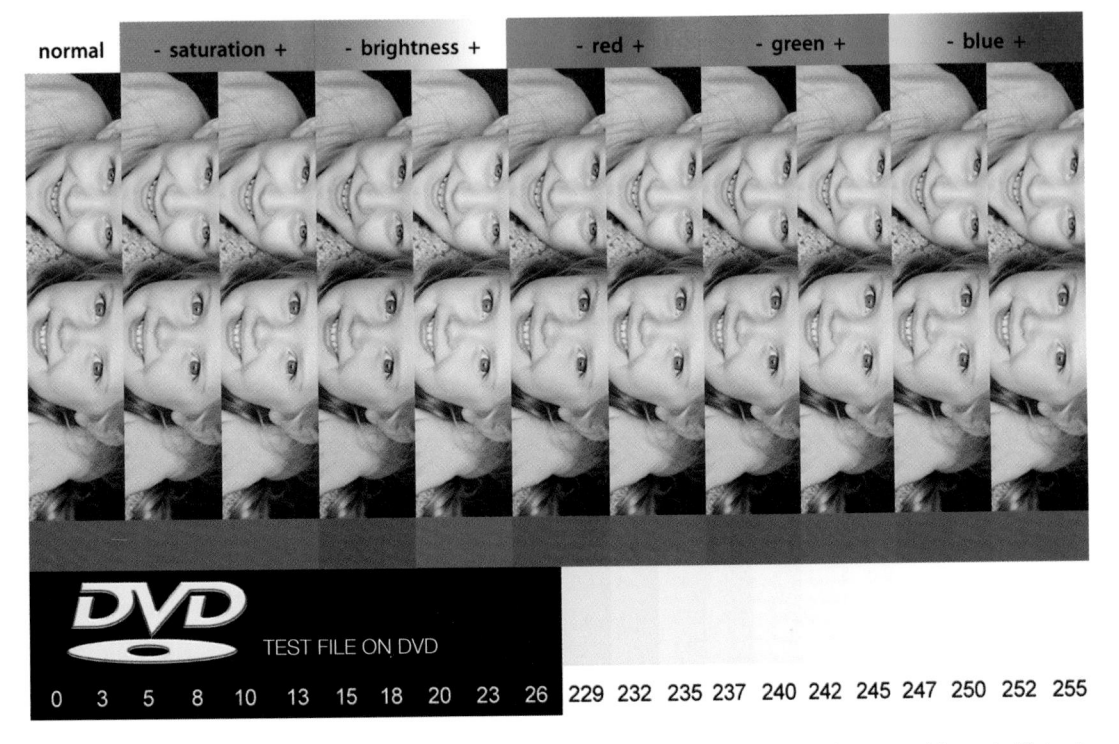

| normal | - saturation + | - brightness + | - red + | - green + | - blue + |

TEST FILE ON DVD

0 3 5 8 10 13 15 18 20 23 26 229 232 235 237 240 242 245 247 250 252 255

Use the test file to help you target the perfect color balance quickly and efficiently

13. Assessing the test print for accuracy

View the print using daylight (not direct sunlight) when it is dry, and look for differences between the print and the screen image in terms of hue (color), saturation and brightness.

1. Check that the color swatches at the top of the image are saturated and printing without tracking marks or banding (there should be a gradual transition of color). If there is a problem with missing colors, tracking lines or saturation, clean the printer heads using the Maintenance setting in the Printer Driver.
2. View the skin tones to assess the appropriate level of saturation.
3. View the gray tones directly beneath the images of the children to determine if there is a color cast present in the image. The five tones on the extreme left are gray in the image file. If these print as gray then no further color correction is required.

PERFORMANCE TIP
Any differences between the monitor and the print will usually now be restricted to the differences in color gamuts between RGB monitors and CMYK printers. The vast majority of colors are shared by both output devices but some of the very saturated primary colors on your monitor (red, green and blue) may appear slightly less saturated in print. Choose a printer with an inkset that uses additional primary inks if you want to achieve the maximum gamut from a printer.

14. Maximizing shadow and highlight detail

Examine the base of the test strip to establish the optimum highlight and shadow levels that can be printed with the media you have chosen to use. If the shadow tones between level 15 and level 20 are visible on screen but are printing as black then you could try either choosing an alternative media type in the printer driver or establishing a Levels adjustment layer to resolve the problem in Photoshop Elements. The bottom left-hand slider in the Levels dialog box should be moved to the right to reduce the level of black ink being printed (raise it to a value of no higher than 10 if you wish to preserve your black point). This should allow dark shadow detail to be visible in the second print.

Note > It is important to apply these Output level adjustments to an adjustment layer only, as these specific adjustments apply only to the output device and media you are currently testing.

PERFORMANCE TIP

Materials

Start by using the printer manufacturer's recommended ink and paper.
Use premium-grade 'photo paper' for maximum quality.

Monitor

Position your monitor so that it is clear of reflections.
Let your monitor warm up for a while before judging image quality.
Calibrate your monitor using a calibration device.

Adobe

Set the Color Settings of the Adobe software to allow you to use the Adobe RGB profile.
Select Photoshop Elements Manages Color.
Use a six-ink (or more) inkjet printer for maximum quality.
Select the Media Type in the Printer Software dialog box.
Select a high dpi setting (1440 dpi or greater) or Photo quality setting.
Use a custom printer profile.

Proofing

Allow print to dry and use daylight to assess the color accuracy of the print.

part 2

enhance

Project 1

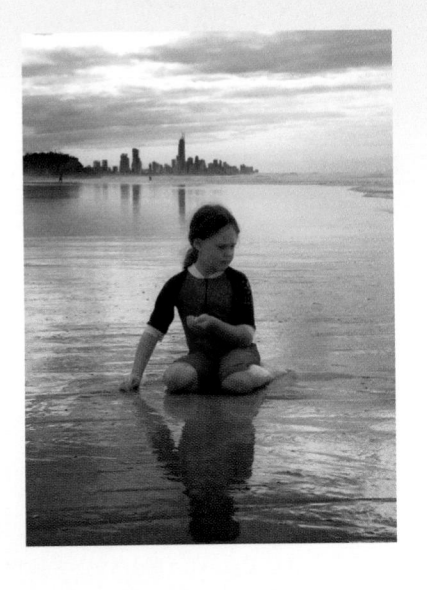

Depth of Field

The Gaussian Blur filter can be used creatively to blur distracting backgrounds. Most digital cameras achieve greater depth of field (more in focus) at the same aperture when compared to their 35 mm film cousins, due to their comparatively small sensor size. This is great in some instances but introduces unwelcome detail and distractions when the attention needs to be firmly fixed on the subject.

There is often a lot to think about during the capture of an image, and the time required to consider the appropriate aperture and shutter speed combination for the desired visual outcome often gets the elbow. Photoshop Elements can, however, come to the rescue and drop a distracting background into a murky sea of out-of-focus oblivion. Problems arise when the resulting image, all too often, looks manipulated rather than realistic. A straight application of the Gaussian Blur filter will have a tendency to 'bleed' strong tonal differences and saturated colors into the background fog, making the background in the image look more like a watercolor painting than a photograph. The Gaussian Blur filter will usually require some additional work if the post-production technique is not to become too obvious.

Decrease the depth of field to emphasize your subject

1. Not all subjects lend themselves to automated extraction processes. Professionals using the full version of Photoshop often make use of 'channels' to start the process of creating a mask when there is not sufficient contrast between the subject and its background. As channels are off-limits for Photoshop Elements users (Photoshop Elements uses them but you are not allowed to see them) we need to use a workaround. We can borrow or hijack a layer mask from an adjustment layer for our purposes in this project.

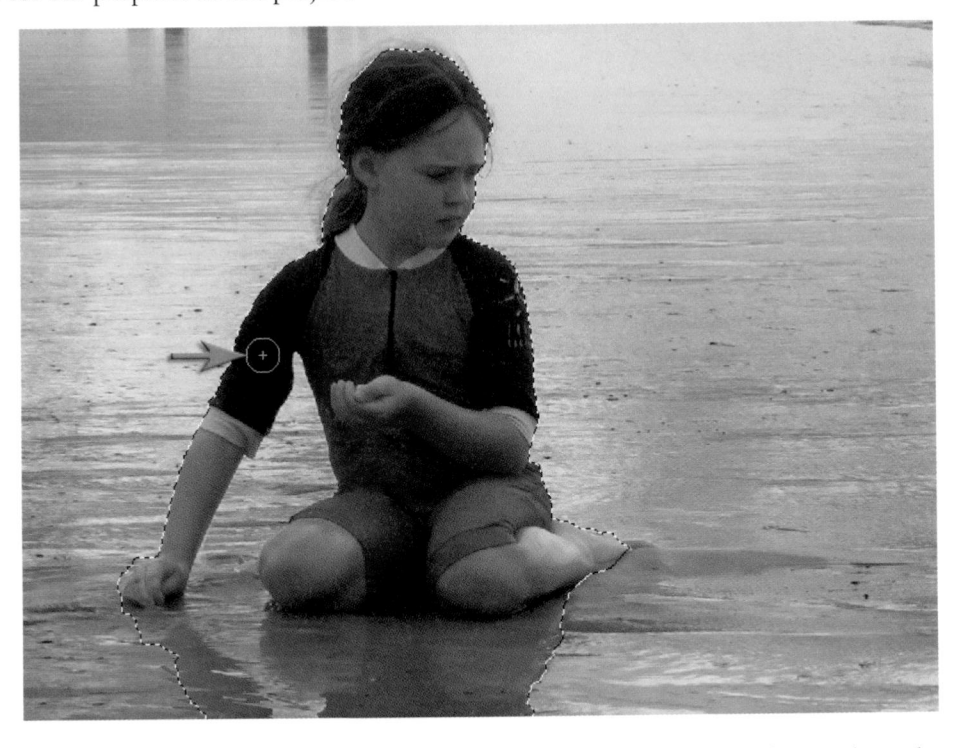

Choose the Quick Selection tool from the Tools panel and drag the tool over the girl and her reflection in the water. The Quick Selection tool will probably include the water underneath the girl's arm as part of the initial selection.

2. Reduce the diameter of the brush size by clicking on the Brush Picker icon in the Options bar. Hold down the Alt/Option key and then paint over any areas of water that need to be excluded from the selection.

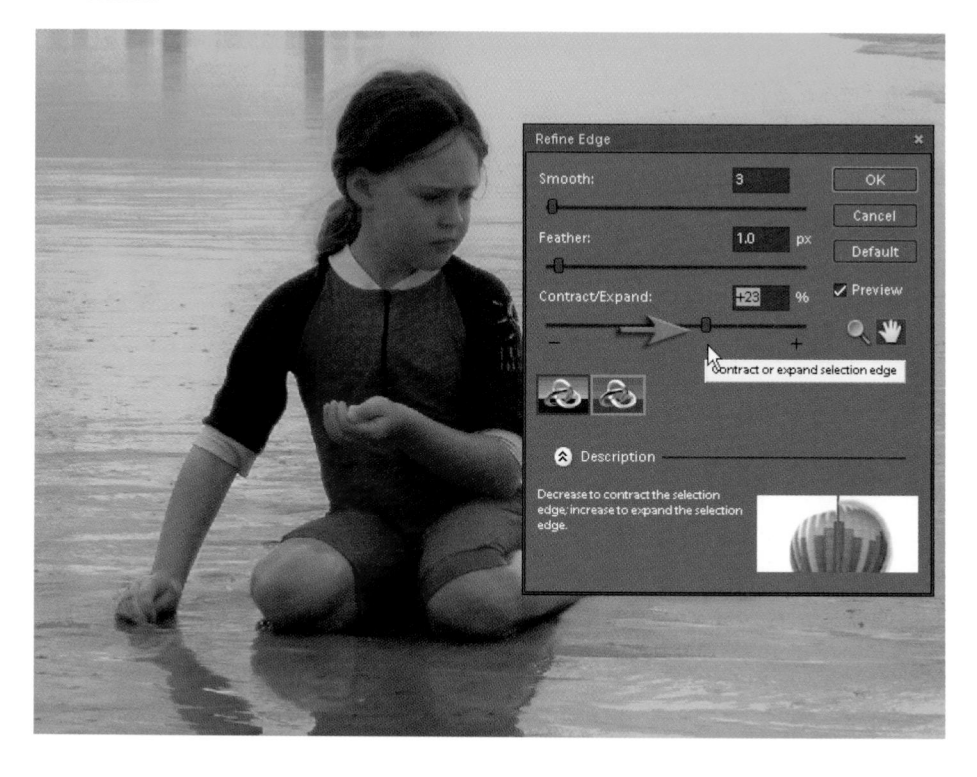

3. Click on the Refine Edge button in the Options bar and choose to view the selection with a mask by selecting the Custom Overlay Color option. Set Smooth to a value of 3 and enter a 1-pixel Feather to soften the edge of the selection. Drag the Contract/Expand slider to the right so that the edge of the mask color sits directly over the edge of the girl. Select OK to apply these adjustments to the selection.

4. From the Select menu choose Inverse. In the Layers panel select Levels from the Create Adjustment Layer drop-down menu. The selection will create a layer mask and this will become the area of sharp focus. Make no adjustment in the Levels dialog box – just select OK (Elements 7 only). Hold down the Alt/Option key and click on the layer mask to view the contents of the mask.

5. Focus is not a brick wall, i.e. it does not start and end suddenly – it gradually fades in and out. Think Gradient tool when you are thinking of fading between masked and unmasked (sharp and unsharp). Choose the Gradient tool in the Tools panel. Choose the Black, White gradient from the drop down menu in the Options bar and then select the Reflected Gradient option and set the mode to Multiply. Drag a gradient from the base of the girl to somewhere around the horizon line in the distance (holding down the Shift key as you drag will constrain the gradient so that it is not crooked). Drag the gradient a second time to darken the mask further. The resulting gradient will extend the focus in front and behind the girl. This will become our plane of focus.

Note > The TIFF file for this project has a saved selection (Selection > Load Selection > DOF). Creating a layer mask with this active selection will automatically create the layer mask in step 5.

7. Drag the background layer to the New Layer icon and then drag it to the top of the layers stack (shortcuts: Ctrl/Command + J to duplicate background layer, then Ctrl/Command + Shift +] to move this duplicate layer to the top of the layers stack). Group this background copy layer with the adjustment layer below (Layer > Create Clipping Mask (Group in Elements 7) or Ctrl/Command + G or by holding down the Alt/Option key and clicking on the dividing line between the two layers).

6. Switch to the Linear option in the Options bar, set the mode to Screen and select the Reverse option. Drag a gradient from the base of the image to the point just below where the girl is in contact with the sand. This will help to reduce focus in the reflection slightly.

8. Go to Filter > Blur > Gaussian Blur and apply a generous amount of blur (20 pixels in this project). How much you drop the focus is pretty much a subjective step. Very shallow depth of field is achieved with larger apertures, a close vantage point and larger format cameras. If you are generous with the pixel radius in the Gaussian Blur filter, the image will appear as though it was created with a large format film camera – something that is impossible to achieve with a digital compact unless you are shooting an insect or flower in macro mode. The power of this effect is to remove distracting background clutter, isolate the subject and keep the focus entirely on the focal point of the image. Unfortunately the effect at this stage has a few shortcomings. The effect of blurring the background has bled some of the darker and more saturated tones into the lighter, more desaturated background. A tell-tale halo is forming that indicates this effect has been achieved in post-production rather than in-camera.

9. The problem is resolved by careful application of the Clone Stamp tool. Select the background copy layer, then pick the Clone Stamp tool. In the Options bar, check the Aligned option and set the mode to Lighten. Hold down the Alt/Option key as you select some pixels further away from the edge, where the bleed has not extended to, and paint these pixels back into the affected border regions. Switch from Lighten to Darken modes if you encounter brighter tones bleeding into a darker background.

Note > This action is part of the Maximum Performance actions from the DVD.

11. The viewer's attention can be further restricted to the central subject by adding a subtle vignette so that the image progressively gets brighter towards the center (we are visually drawn to the light). Click on the Guided option in the Edit drop-down menu (Guided tab in Elements 7) and select the Action Player. Select Vignettes and the 'Oblong-Darken with image' option before clicking the Play Action button. This vignette option protects the bright highlights in the sky from excessive darkening.

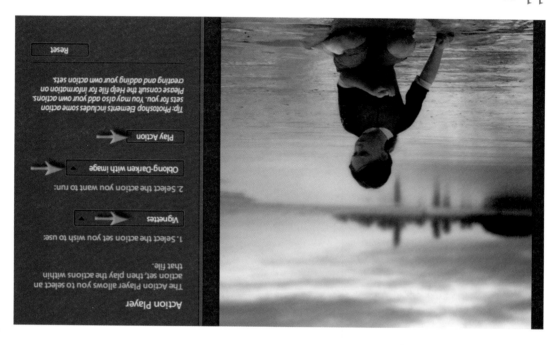

10. Adjustment of the sharpness of the image can be made to the background layer as this is the only portion of the image that remains in focus. There is some noise present in this image so sharpening is best achieved using the Unsharp Mask (Enhance > Unsharp Mask) with the Threshold slider raised to 7 or 8.

FUTURE DEVELOPMENTS SHIFTING FOCUS

If digital cameras are eventually able to record distance information at the time of capture, this could be used in the creation of an automatic depth map (the Lens Blur filter in the full version of Photoshop can already use channels or layer masks to create automated depth of field effects, but the channel must still be created manually using the techniques outlined in this project). Choosing the most appropriate depth of field could be relegated to post-production image editing in a similar way to how the white balance is set in Camera Raw.

IMAGE ON DVD

Project 2

Shafts of Light

Here we explore the science of making good photographs even more memorable. Discover how to add drama to your landscape images using the 'Fingers of God' tool (aka the Gradient tool with customized settings). Creating effective landscape images is not exactly rocket science. Choose a beautiful landscape just after dawn, or just before sunset, and add dramatic natural lighting to create emotive and memorable landscape images.

GRADIENT PRESET ON DVD

Let there be light – create dramatic lighting effects to enhance the drama of your images

Clear blue skies are great for holidays on the beach but the best natural lighting for photography is provided by broken or filtered sunlight through partial cloud cover. The most memorable of all lighting is when shafts of light break through the clouds. Finding partial cloud cover when the sun is low is relatively easy; being present when shafts of light flood your selected vista, however, can be an elusive and rare event. This final ingredient requires patience, persistence and good fortune – or a good helping of post-production editing courtesy of Photoshop Elements.

1. Open the Raw project from the DVD into Adobe Camera Raw (ACR). We will optimize the tonality and color of the Raw file twice, once for the foreground and then again for the sky. The first step is to set a black point for the image as the darker tones are very weak due to the morning mist at the time of capture. Drag the Blacks slider just to the point where the blacks start to clip (the triangle above the left side of the histogram must remain black).

2. Hold down the Alt/Option key and drag the Exposure slider to the right to clip the lighter tones in the distant hills. The threshold view in the image preview will guide you to the point where clipping starts to happen in the foreground. An Exposure adjustment of around +2.00 to +3.00 stops will clip all of the middle distance sunlit hills and also the sky (we are expanding the contrast for the foreground fields only at this stage)

3. Finish optimizing the foreground by lowering the Brightness and Vibrance sliders. The Brightness slider can be moved significantly darker (approximately -50) due to the generous Exposure adjustment applied in the previous step. Click on the Open Image button to open the image in the main Edit space of Photoshop Elements.

4. After the image has opened in the main Edit space go to File > Place and browse to and open the same Raw file. This time optimize the Raw file for the sky. Click on Default to zero the exposure settings. The Exposure can now be dropped half a stop from the default 0.0 setting while the Contrast, Clarity and Vibrance sliders can be pushed to their maximum settings of +100. Select OK to open this version as a layer above the first version, opened in the previous step.

5. This second version opens as a Smart Object above the background layer. The big cross that you can see indicates that we can scale this layer if we want to. As we require perfect registration with the layer below (we don't want to scale this layer) we can right-click on the layer and select Simplify Layer to turn this Smart Object into a regular layer.

Note > Smart Objects can be scaled multiple times without losing any quality.

6. To selectively merge the best of both exposures on the two layers we will mask the foreground of the top layer. Click on the background layer to select it. Click on the Create New Fill or Adjustment Layer icon at the base of the Layers panel and select a Levels adjustment. Select OK if you are using Elements 7. Select the Gradient tool from the Tools panel and the Black, White and Linear options in the Options bar. Drag a short gradient from the dark foreground to the sunlit hills in the middle distance. Now select the top (Shafts-of-Light) layer and from the Layer menu select Create Clipping Mask. Select the Move tool from the Tools panel and then click on the Levels adjustment layer mask. Click and drag the layer mask up or down while holding the Shift key to create the perfect balance of exposure between the two layers.

7. If the foreground fields appear too dark or too light then add a second Levels adjustment layer just above the background layer (click on the background layer before adding a new adjustment layer). Drag the central Gamma slider underneath the histogram to the left or to the right to perfect the foreground brightness.

8. Select the top (Shaft-of-Light) layer and then add an empty new layer above it. Set the mode of this new layer to Overlay. Select the Gradient tool from the Tools panel and choose Black as the foreground color (Press D to select the default colors). Choose the Foreground to Transparent option from the Gradient drop-down menu in the Options bar. Select the Linear option and set the opacity to 50% in the Options bar. Hold down the Shift key and drag a short gradient from the top of the image preview to a position where the clouds are breaking to add drama to the top of the image.

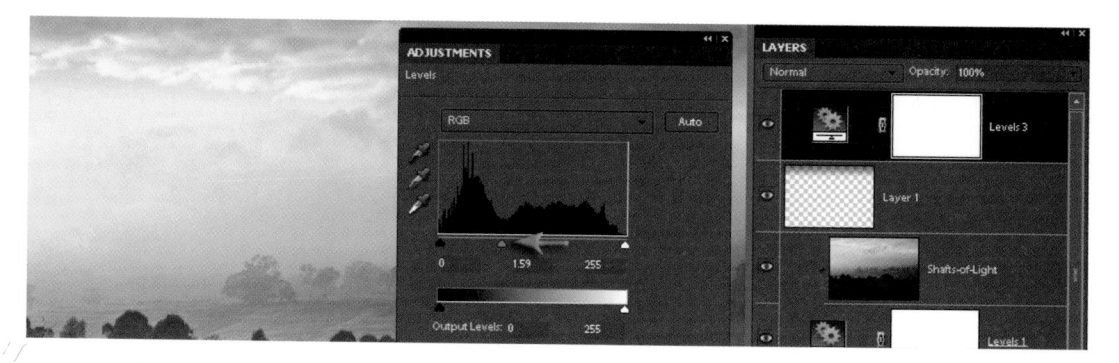

9. Over the next few steps we will instill a sense of drama throughout the image by creating some shafts of light to appear through those breaking clouds. Create a third Levels adjustment layer and increase the brightness of the image significantly by moving the central Gamma slider to the left (by around 1.6 in this project).

10. Choose black as the foreground color and select the Gradient tool in the Tools panel and click on the Edit button in the Options bar to open the Gradient Editor. Click on the Transparent Stripes gradient. Edit the gradient using the following pointers. The aim of editing the gradient is to make the stripes irregular widths with soft edges to emulate the nature of shafts of light. The white stops on the top of the editing ramp indicate full transparency whilst the black stops indicate full opacity of the foreground color. Click and drag the stops into groups of four. A white stop should be on either end of a grouping of four with two black stops next to each other in the middle. Moving the black stops further apart will broaden the stripe. Moving the white stop further away from the central black stops will broaden the area of transition between full opacity and full transparency. To add a stop hold down the Alt/Option key and drag an existing stop a short distance. To remove a stop drag it away from the gradient ramp. To add this modified gradient to the presets, click on the New button and give your shafts of light a suitable name (don't worry that the shafts are colored black for the moment). This gradient can be loaded from the preset that is available on the DVD.

Note > A black stop can be changed to a white stop or vice versa by clicking on it and then adjusting the Opacity slider at the bottom of the Stops section of the Gradient Editor.

11. Make sure the Linear gradient option is selected in the Options bar and set the opacity to 100% and the mode to Normal, and check the Transparency option. The foreground color should still be set to black. Click on the left side of the image window and drag your mouse cursor to the right-hand side of the image window. The length of the line you draw will be the initial width of the shafts, although this can be modified using the Transform command outlined in the following step.

12. From the Image menu select Distort from the Transform submenu. Click on each of the corner handles and drag them to fan the shafts of light. Move the cursor into the Transform bounding box, and click and drag the bounding box to reposition the shafts of light. When you're satisfied with the shape, double-click inside the distorted bounding box to accept the transformation.

Note > You may need to extend the image window so that you can drag the corner handles to the required angle.

13. Go to the Filter menu and select Invert from the Adjustments submenu. This will turn the black stripes to white and return the brightness level of the rest of the image to normal. The next step will aim to fade the top and bottom edges of this striped gradient.

14. Select the Gradient tool and choose the Foreground to Transparent gradient. Drag a short gradient from just below the hard edges a short distance into the shafts to conceal the hard edges. Repeat the process to fade the bottom of the shafts, this time dragging from the bottom of the hard edge a short distance into the gradient. Drop the opacity of the Gradient tool in the Options bar to 50% and drag a gradient from either side to fade the intensity of the outer shafts.

Note > It is possible to increase the intensity of the shafts of light by switching the blend mode of the adjustment layer to Screen. Adjust the opacity of the adjustment layer to fine-tune the effect.

16. To soften the mask further, choose Filter > Blur > Gaussian Blur. Select a pixel radius that will soften the edges of the shafts so that the effect is subtle.

15. The brightness or color of the shafts of light can now be adjusted to suit the landscape. In this project I have selected the blue channel in the Levels dialog and moved the central Gamma slider underneath the histogram to the right slightly to warm the shafts of light.

17. We will now improve the appearance of the breaks in the clouds so the shafts of light look they could be appearing from behind them. Click on the Create a New Layer icon in the Layers panel. Switch the mode of the layer to Color. Click on the foreground color swatch in the Tools panel to open the Color Picker. Choose a bright blue color and select OK. Select the Brush tool and choose a soft-edged brush and drop the opacity to 30% in the Options bar. Paint blue where you can see a break in the clouds and adjust the opacity of the layer to fine-tune the color.

18. Create a Brightness/Contrast adjustment layer and raise the brightness to +50. Fill the Layer mask with black by going to Edit > Fill and choosing black as the contents. Select the Brush tool and choose white as the foreground color. Choose a soft-edged brush and set the opacity to 50% in the Options bar. Paint to brighten the break in the clouds at the top of the shafts of light. Paint multiple times to increase the brightness. Add a vignette to taste and the illusion is complete. Now, the only problem with this technique is that it is almost too effective and therefore tempting to sneak it into too many images in your personal portfolio. When this happens the cat will be well and truly out of the bag!

The techniques used to create this image have been taken from Projects 2, 3 and 4 in this section of the book

IMAGE ON DVD

Project 2: Shafts of Light

Project 3

The original color image and the result of choosing the less-than-satisfactory Remove Color command

Maximum Performance

Black and White

When color film arrived over half a century ago, the pundits who presumed that black and white images would die a quick death were surprisingly mistaken. Color is all very nice but sometimes the rich tonal qualities that we can see in the work of the black-and-white photographic artists are something to be savored. Can you imagine an Ansel Adams masterpiece in color? If you can – read no further.

Black and white – when 'luminance' is more important than color. Original image by Michael Weinrich

16 BIT/CHANNEL IMAGE
ON SUPPORTING DVD

The conversion from color to black and white

The creation of dramatic black and white photographs from your color images is a little more complicated than simply converting your image to Grayscale mode or choosing the Desaturate command. Ask any professional photographer who is skilled in the art of black and white and you will discover that crafting tonally rich images requires a little knowledge about how different color filters affect the resulting tonality of a black and white image.

Convert to Black and White allows you to mix the tonal differences present in the color channels. Simply select a style and then adjust the intensity sliders to create your own custom conversion

As strange as it may seem, screwing on a color filter for capturing images on black and white film has traditionally been an essential ingredient of the recipe for success. The most popular color filter in the black and white photographer's kit bag, which is used for the most dramatic effect, is the red filter. The effect of the red filter is to lighten all things that are red and darken all things that are not red in the original scene. The result is a print with considerable tonal differences compared to an image shot without a filter. Is this a big deal? Well, yes it is – blue skies are darkened and skin blemishes are lightened. That's a winning combination for most landscape and portrait photographers wanting to create black and white masterpieces.

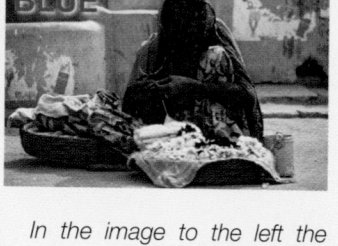

PERFORMANCE TIP

The Maximum Performance actions on the DVD include a series of automated black and white conversions (see the introductory section for installing Maximum Performance actions). The Black&White_Luminosity action creates a single monochrome layer containing the luminosity values of the RGB file (usually a superior black and white conversion when compared with the Remove Color command). The Red, Green and Blue Channel actions allow you to place one of the three color channels as a black and white layer. These actions would also be useful for accessing the best contrast in order to create a mask, as in the 'Depth of Field' project.

In the image to the left the Red channel was used as this offered the best detail in the dark skin tones. The contrast was then increased by duplicating the layer and switching the blend mode to Soft Light. The opacity of this duplicate layer was then dropped to 30%. A vignette was added to complete the project

The Convert to Black and White command (Enhance > Convert to Black and White) allows the user to selectively mix the differences in tonality present in the three color channels, but unfortunately it is not available as an adjustment layer. This means we are unable to make use of the layer mask that typically comes with an adjustment layer. It also means that we would be unable to modify the color conversion at a later date without returning to the original color file. This approach to the conversion (although vastly superior to anything present in previous versions of the software) limits the usefulness of the technique for those users who wish to extract the maximum amount of control and flexibility out of the process of black and white conversion. The famous digital guru, Russell Preston Brown, has come up with a workaround that enables us to retain complete control over black and white conversion using multiple adjustment layers.

1. Drag the Layers panel from the Panel Bin (this will be your command center for this technique). Click on the Adjustment Layer icon in the Layers panel and scroll down the list to select and create a Hue/Saturation adjustment layer. Make no adjustments for the time being but simply select OK (version 7 only) to close the dialog box. Set the blend mode of this adjustment layer to Color.

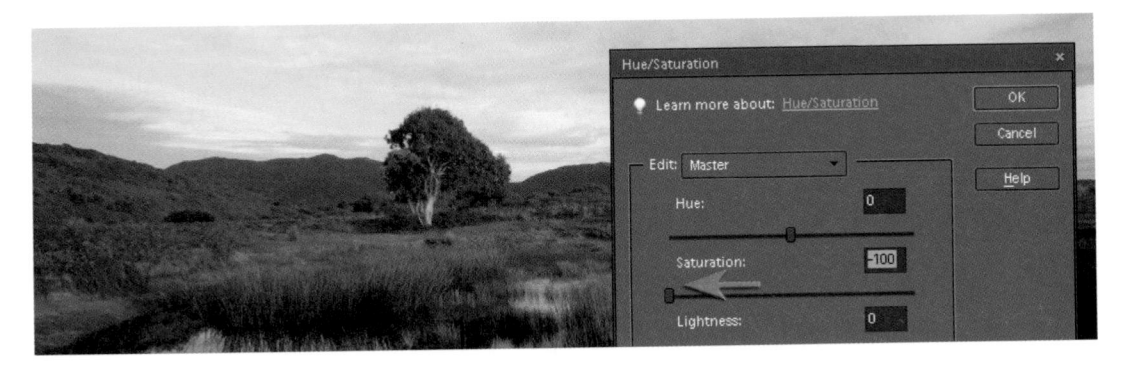

2. Create a second Hue/Saturation adjustment layer. Move the Saturation slider all the way to the left (–100) to desaturate the image. Select OK (version 7 only). The image will now appear as if you had performed a simple Convert to Grayscale or Desaturate (remove color) command.

Note > This second adjustment layer should be sitting on top of the layers stack.

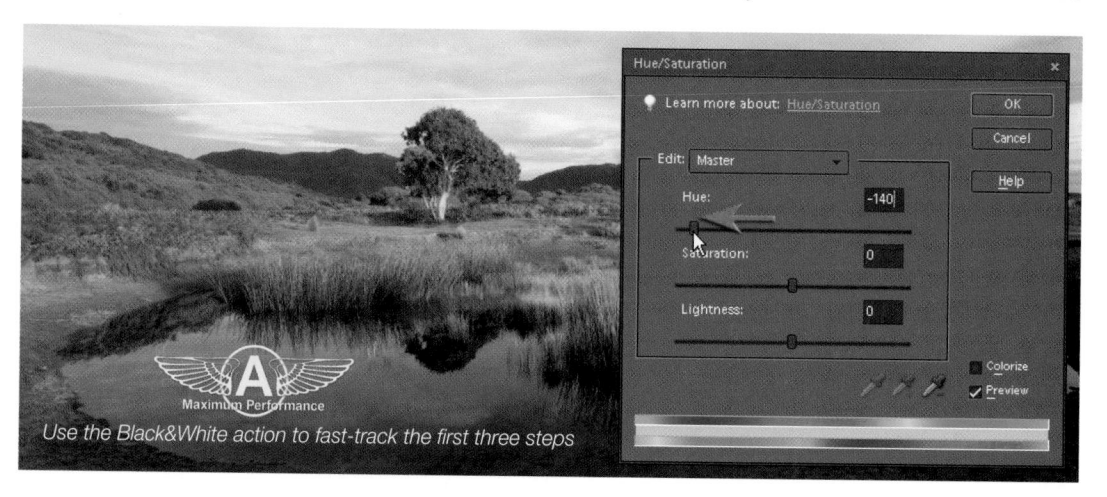

Use the Black&White action to fast-track the first three steps

$3.$ Select the first Hue/Saturation layer that you created (Elements 7 users will need to double-click the layer thumbnail to reopen the Hue/Saturation dialog box). Move the Hue slider in this dialog box to the left. Observe the changes to the tonality of the image as you move the slider. Blues will be darkest when the slider is moved to a position around −150. Select OK (version 7 only). The drama of the image will probably have been improved quite dramatically already but we can take this further with some dodging and burning.

Note > A Maximum Performance action is available to fast-track the first three steps in this project (see the introductory section for installing and using Maximum Performance actions).

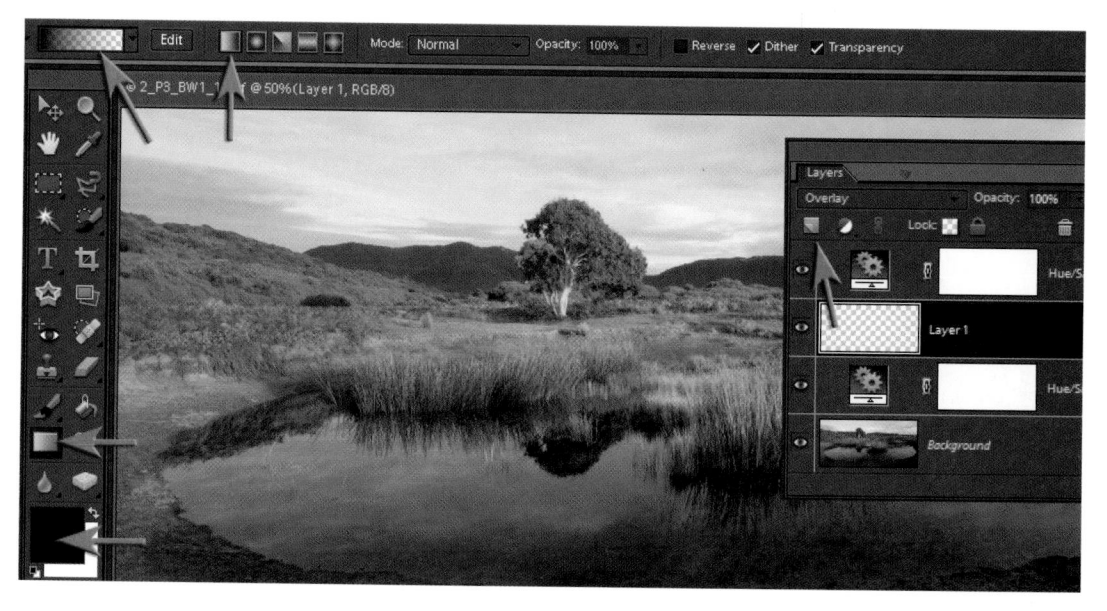

$4.$ Click on the New Layer icon in the Layers panel. Set the blend mode of the layer to Overlay. Set the color swatches in the Tools panel to the default, black and white (click on the small Black and White Swatch icon or press D on the keyboard). Select the Gradient tool and in the Options bar select the Foreground (black) to Transparent and Linear gradient options.

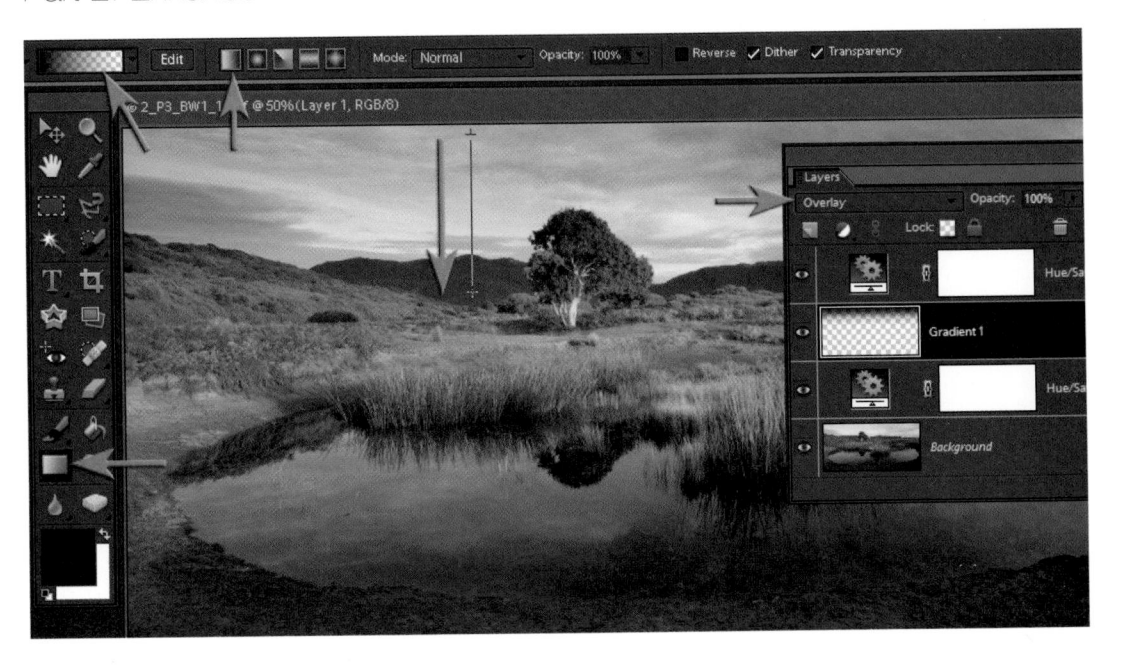

5. Drag a gradient from the top of the image window to the horizon line. This will have the effect of drawing the viewer into the image and will create an increased sense of drama. Lower the opacity of the layer if the effect is too strong and duplicate the layer if you want to increase the drama further. Rename the Gradient layers by double-clicking on the layer names.

6. Press the Alt/Option key and click on the New Layer icon. In the New Layer dialog box set the blend mode to Overlay and select the Fill with Overlay-neutral color (50% gray) option. Select the Brush tool, choose a soft-edged brush from the Options bar and lower the opacity to 10–15%. A layer that is 50% gray in Overlay or Soft Light mode is invisible. This gray layer will be used to dodge and burn your image non-destructively, i.e. by not working on the actual pixels of your image. Paint onto the gray layer with black selected as the foreground color to burn (darken) the image in localized areas or switch to white to dodge (lighten). You can fill or paint using selections to control the dodging and burning process if required. Rename this layer 'Dodge & Burn'.

7. Select the top layer and then create a Levels adjustment layer (one adjustment layer to rule them all) to sit above all of the other layers. Make sure the histogram extends all the way between the black and white sliders. Move the sliders in to meet the histogram if this is not the case.

PERFORMANCE TIP

Try experimenting with the introduction of some of the original color. Duplicate the background layer by dragging it to the New Layer icon. Then drag the background copy to the top of the layers stack. Reduce the opacity of this layer and set the blend mode to Color to let the black and white version introduce the drama once more.

Project 4

Toning

Burning, toning, split-grade printing and printing through your mother's silk stockings are just some of the wonderful, weird and positively wacky techniques used by the traditional masters of the darkroom that are waiting to be exposed (or ripped off) in this tantalizing digital project designed to pump up the mood and ambience of the flat and downright dull. The tonality of the project image destined for the toning table will be given a split personality. Shadows and highlights will be gently blurred to add depth and character at the same time as retaining full detail for emphasis and focus. Selected colors will then be mapped to the new tonality to establish the final mood.

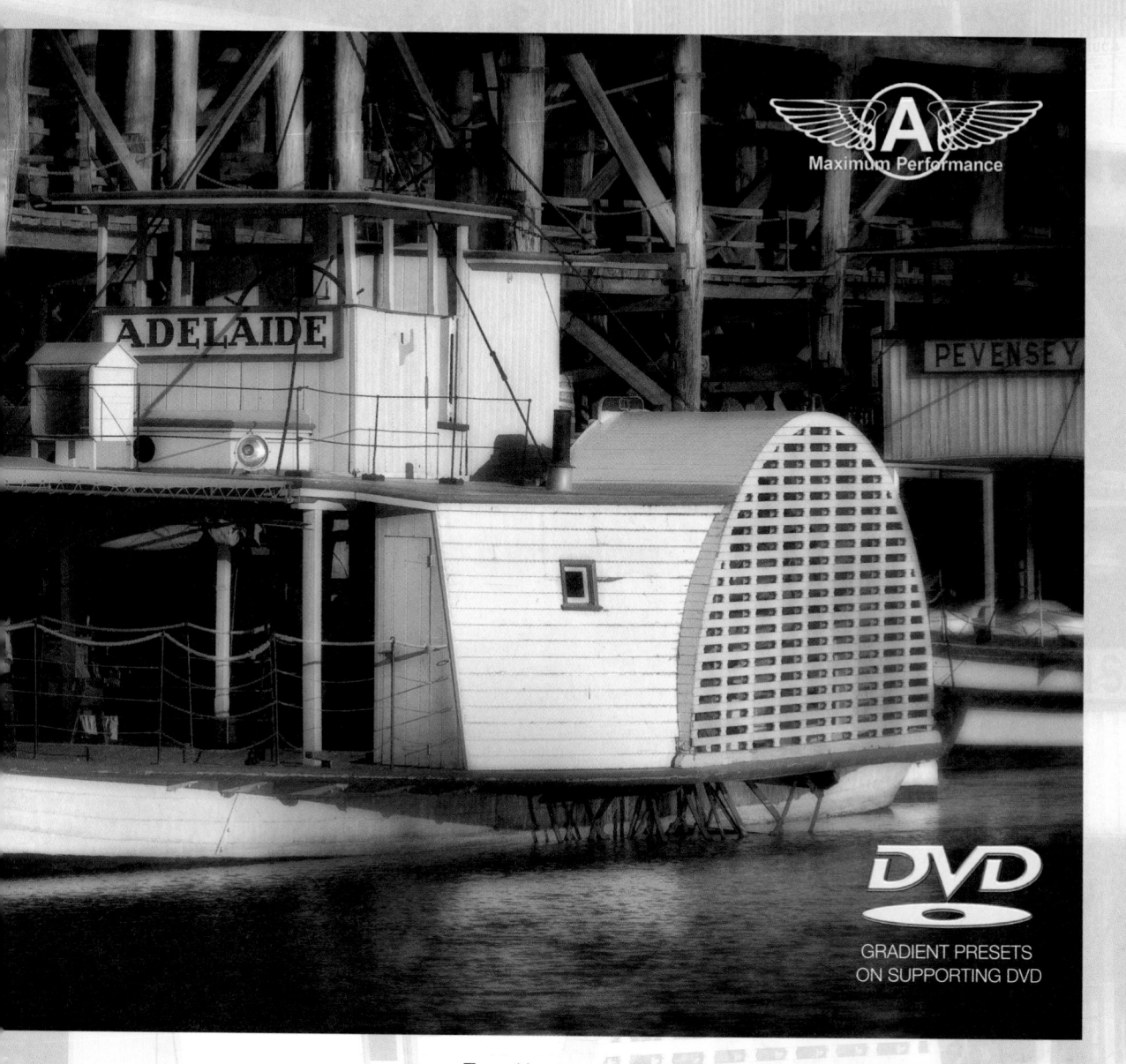

Toned images – exploring the land between black and white and color

It probably comes as no small surprise that 'color' injects images with mood and emotional impact. Photographers, however, frequently work on images that are devoid of color because of the tonal control they are able to achieve in traditional processing and printing techniques. Toning the resulting 'black and white' images keeps the emphasis on the play of light and shade but lets the introduced colors influence the final mood. With the increased sophistication and control that digital image-editing software affords us, we can now explore the 'twilight zone' between color and black and white as never before. The original image has the potential to be more dramatic and carry greater emotional impact through the controlled use of tone and color.

1. This first step will create some soft, smooth tones that we can use to recreate the early morning mood. Duplicate the background layer by dragging it to the Create a New Layer icon in the Layers panel. Go to Filter > Blur > Gaussian Blur and increase the Radius to 15 pixels.

2. Set the mode of the layer to Multiply. The image will appear very dark until we restore the luminance values to the pixels over the next four steps. We can achieve this using a combination of two adjustment layers. Hold down the Alt/Option key while you select a levels adjustment layer from the Create Adjustment Layer menu in the Layers panel. In the New Layer dialog box that opens check the Use Previous Layer to Create Clipping Mask option (the option is called Group With Previous Layer in Elements 7). This will enable us to modify the tonality of the blur layer without affecting the background layer. Elements 7 users will need to click OK to open the Levels dialog while Photoshop Elements 8 users will have access straight away.

3. Move the Shadow Output slider to the right to prevent the deeper shadow tones from becoming too dark: Choose a value of 60 to 100 depending on how dark the shadow values in the image are. We can start with a value of 60 and refine this later, after applying the second adjustment layer. Select OK (version 7 only) to apply the Levels adjustment.

4. Hold down the Alt/Option key while you select a Levels adjustment layer from the Create Adjustment Layer menu in the Layers panel. In the New Layer dialog box that opens set the mode of the new layer to Screen. Select OK to open the second Levels adjustment layer.

Note > We do not need to select the Use Previous Layer to Create Clipping Mask option as we are about to adjust the overall tonality rather than just the background copy layer.

5. The Screen mode applied to this second adjustment layer will lighten all tones. Drag the white Output slider to the left to restrict this adjustment to just the shadow tones and midtones (a value of 128 has been used in this project). This will prevent the highlights from becoming too bright. Move the central Gamma slider to the left to increase overall brightness in the midtones.

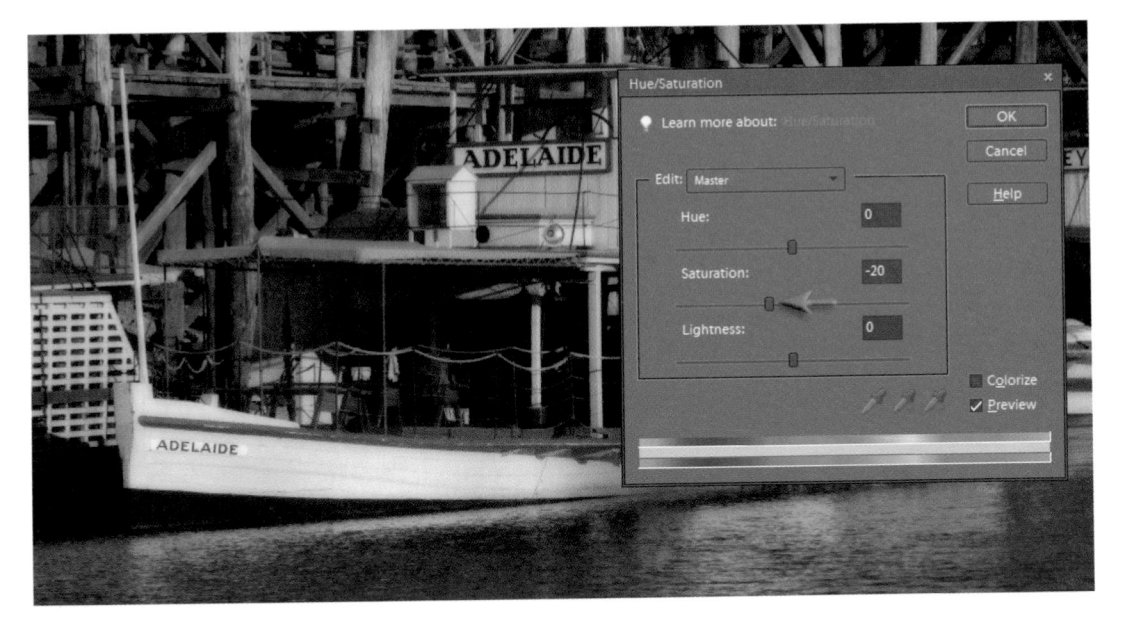

6. The original brightness of the image should now be restored but the saturation values will be slightly higher. Select a Hue/Saturation adjustment layer from the Create Adjustment Layer menu in the Layers panel and lower the saturation to -20.

Note > The Maximum Performance action 'Smooth Tone' can be used to automate the last six steps in this tutorial.

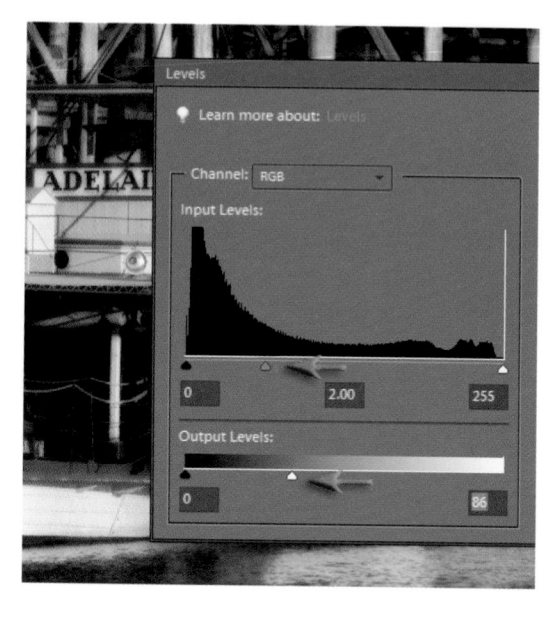

7. At any stage in this project you can modify the impact of the Blur layer on the image by adjusting the sliders in the two Levels adjustment layers. Select the first adjustment layer that is grouped with the background copy layer (Elements 7 users will need to double-click the thumbnail to open the dialog) and then drag the white Input slider to 140 and the central Gamma slider to 0.35 to increase the apparent blur in the image. Raise the black Output slider to 70. Select OK (version 7 only) to apply the changes. Select the second adjustment layer (the one set to the Screen mode) and drag the central Gamma slider to 2.00 and the white Output slider to 86 to adjust the overall tonality.

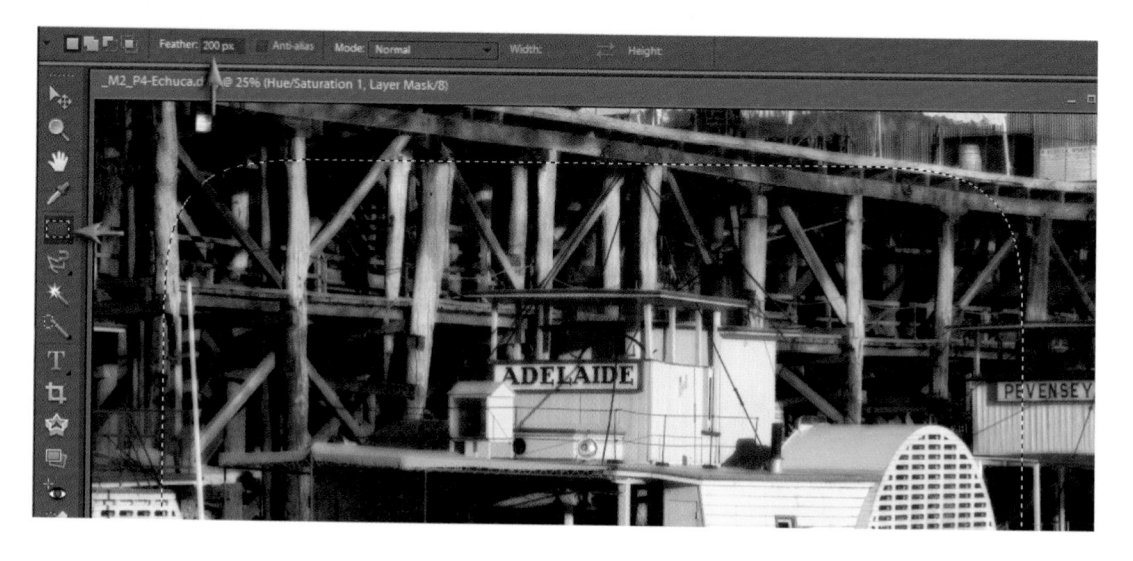

8. We will now add a vignette to this image. Select the Rectangular Marquee tool in the Tools panel. Set the feather radius to 200 pixels in the Options bar. Click and drag from the top left-hand corner of the image to the bottom right-hand corner to make a selection.

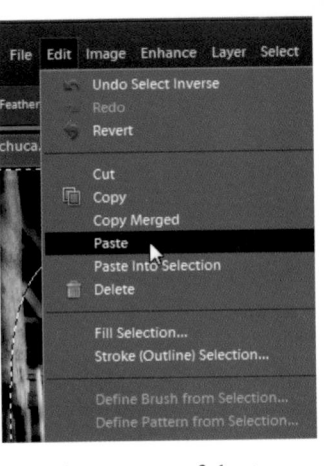

9. From the Select menu choose Inverse so that the edge, rather than the center, of the image is selected. From the Edit menu choose Copy Merged and then from the Edit menu again choose Paste.

Note > The Copy Merged command allows you to copy the visible pixels rather than just the pixels on the active layer.

10. The pixels on this new layer (currently making no difference to the appearance of the image) can be used to darken the image by setting the mode of the layer to Multiply. Lower the opacity of the layer if the vignette is too dark, using the opacity control in the Layers panel.

11. Set the foreground colors in the Tools panel to their default black and white settings. Click on the Create Adjustment Layer icon in the Layers panel and choose Gradient Map from the menu. Click on the gradient in the Gradient Map dialog to open the Gradient Editor dialog.

Note > The gradient must start with black and end with white, otherwise your image will not use the full dynamic range possible.

12. The Gradient Editor dialog allows you to assign colors to shadows, midtones and highlights. Click underneath the gradient to create a new color stop. Slide it to a location that reads approximately 25% at the bottom of the dialog. Click on the color swatch to open the Select Stop Color (Color Picker) dialog.

13. Cool colors such as blues or cyans are often chosen to give character to shadow tones. In the project image the HSB values (hue, saturation and brightness) are adjusted to 208°, 19% and 35% (this brightness value is lighter than the 25% position of the color stop and opens up the dark shadow detail in this image). Select OK in the Select Stop Color dialog to assign this color.

14. Create another stop and move it to a location that reads approximately 75%. This time try choosing a bright warm color to contrast with the blue chosen previously. HSB values of 52°, 14% and 80% have been selected for the project image. Select OK to assign this color to the highlights.

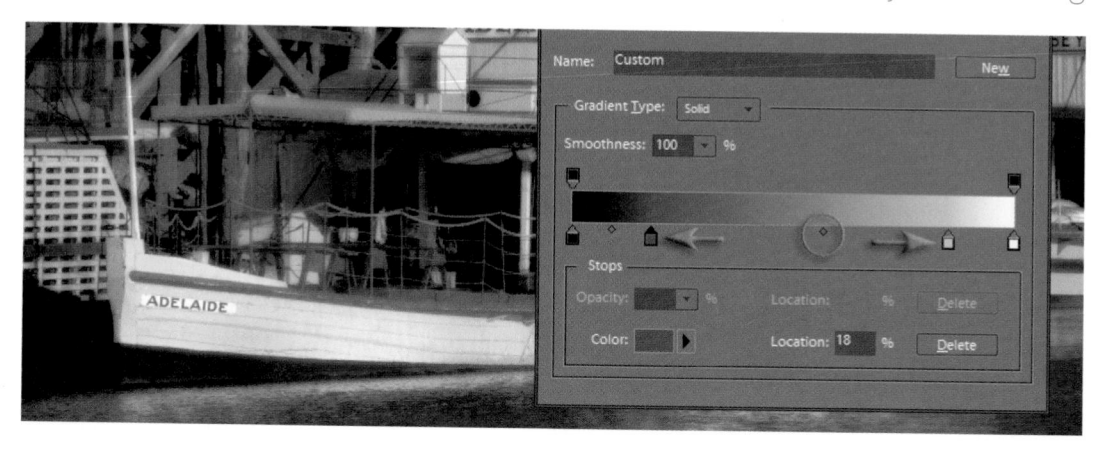

15. The Color stops can be moved to modify the contrast of the image. Pushing the two color stops further apart will reduce the contrast, giving increased detail to the shadows and highlights. When a Color stop is moved, color midpoints are visible that can also be moved along the color ramp to fine-tune the effects of the gradient on your image.

Note > Avoid moving the color stops or Midpoint too close to each other as this can cause tonal banding or posterization in the image.

16. Add another Color Stop in the middle of the gradient for maximum control over the toning process. HSB values of 37°, 18% and 59% have been selected for the project image. Select OK to assign this color to the Midtones. This Color Stop increases the warmth in the midtones and completes the toning process.

17. A custom gradient can be saved as a Gradient preset. Enter a name for your gradient and then click on the New button. The New Gradient will appear in the presets. Gradients can be saved to other locations (such as your desktop or an external drive) so that they can be loaded into imaging projects using a different computer.

18. Select OK in the Gradient Editor dialog to commit the changes. In the Layers panel reduce the opacity of the Gradient Map layer to introduce some of the original colors to the image.

PERFORMANCE TIPS

The gradient map used in this toning project can be downloaded from the supporting DVD and loaded directly from the Gradient Editor dialog or via the Preset Manager (go to Edit > Preset Manager > Gradients > Load). Then browse to the Maximum_Performance.grd preset and select OK. Quick split-tone effects can be accessed via the Maximum Performance split-tone actions available on the DVD.

Try blurring the Vignette layer by going to Filter > Blur > Gaussian Blur. A 10-pixel blur will give the image an interesting soft-focus effect.

TONAL MAPPING IN ADOBE CAMERA RAW

In the 'Toning' project we softened the majority of the tones and remapped the colors. In contrast to this smooth tone technique there are several techniques for expanding midtone contrast to give you the 'crunchy' look or treatment.

Detail can be boosted by pushing some of the sliders in ACR to the max. One of the cutting-edge treatments in commercial photography that has been all the rage recently, is expanding maximum detail and surface texture along with mid-tone contrast. The final effect is one where the image seems to be part photograph, part illustration. Take a look at http://www.davehillphoto.com/ to get an idea of how this treatment is being applied by one popular US photographer. It is also referred to as an HDR effect as this expanded midtone contrast can be created when photographers merge images with different exposures and then map the resulting detail. This effect can, however, be created in ACR and the main editing space of Photoshop Elements.

To expand the mid-tone contrast and edge detail within the image, move the Recovery, Fill Light, Contrast and Clarity sliders all the way to the right (to a value of +100). Lower the Vibrance slider to reduce the excessive saturation in the image that results from raising the contrast slider.

The massive adjustments may upset the brightness of the image. Click on both of the triangles above the histogram to switch the clipping warnings on. Adjust the white point of the image by dragging the Exposure slider to the left or right until thin red lines appear around the edges of the brightest parts of the subject. Adjust the black point of the image by dragging the Blacks slider to the left or right until thin blue lines appear around the edges of the darkest parts of the subject. Drag the Brightness slider to alter the overall brightness of the image and then click the triangles above the histogram to switch the clipping warnings off.

TONAL MAPPING IN THE EDIT SPACE

Midtone contrast can also be applied after first applying the smooth tone technique from the 'Toning' project. Crunchy midtone contrast is even more effective when placed over some tones that have been blurred. Hold down the Ctrl/Command, Alt/Option and Shift modifier keys and then (whilst still holding down the modifier keys) press the letter E. If your new layer, Stamp Visible, is not on top of the layers stack, click and drag it to the top of the Layers panel.

Go to Enhance > Color > Remove Color and set the layer to Soft Light or Overlay mode. Go to Enhance > Lighting > Shadows/Highlights and drag all three sliders to 100% to create a similar effect to the one we achieved in ACR. Select OK and adjust the strength of the effect by lowering the opacity of the layer.

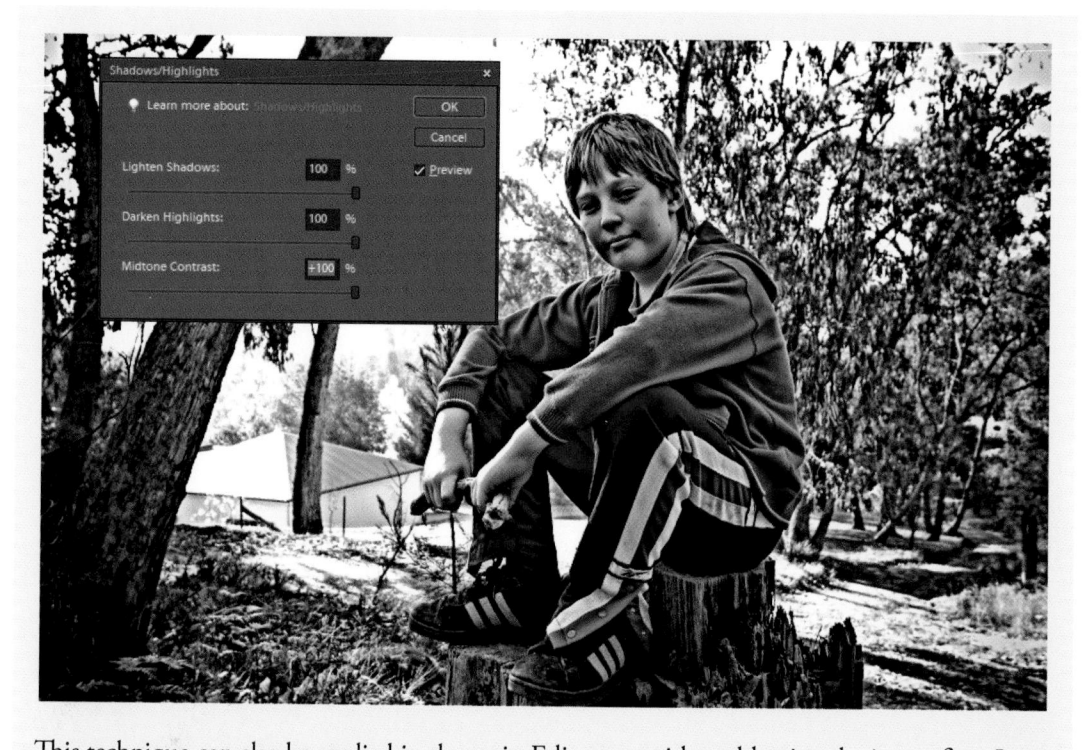

This technique can also be applied in the main Edit space without blurring the image first. Just duplicate the background layer and apply the Shadows/Highlights adjustment outlined on the previous page.

To 'bleed' the underlying colors, duplicate the background layer and apply an 8-pixel Gaussian Blur. Although not as sophisticated as the smooth tone technique outlined in the main tutorial, it does work quite well under the midtone contrast layer that ensures the image appears sharp.

Project 5

Character Portrait

It is often possible to unleash the hidden potential of an image without the hassle of making fiddly selections. This project demonstrates how the tonality of an image can be enriched using duplicated layers, blend modes and a couple of filters to shape and sharpen. Dust off your trophy shelf – I feel an award coming on!

The beauty of these techniques is that we can let Photoshop Elements do all of the hard work and extract an image that has all of the hallmarks of a professionally lit, studio-quality portrait from one that is illuminated with nothing more than ambient light. The secret to success, if you plan to reuse this recipe on one of your own images, is to start with a razor-sharp image illuminated by soft directional light (diffused window light is ideal).

DVD
16 BITS/CHANNEL IMAGE
ON SUPPORTING DVD

Cooking up some character – a recipe for success

Preparing the image

Before we start our culinary masterpiece we should prepare the main ingredient – the image. This should include optimizing the histogram via a manual or auto Levels adjustment (if you have the luxury of accessing a 16 Bit/Channel file via a Raw capture or a 48-bit scan, your histogram will appreciate the Levels adjustment prior to hitting the 8 Bits/Channel option in the Image > Mode submenu). Start the project by removing any distractions in the image so that the viewer's focus will not wander from the *pièce de résistance* – the face containing the character and majesty of our sitter. Keeping it simple is a key to clean and effective design.

$1.$ You can either paint directly on to the background layer or duplicate it if you want to preserve the background layer unadjusted. Remember you have the option to undo any brush stroke that is not absolutely effective. In fact, Photoshop Elements allows you to undo 50 steps by default. Check the preferences and adjust the number to suit your own workflow if required. I think 50 is overly generous and can consume excessive portions of the computer's usable RAM that would serve us better by being made available for the more memory-intensive editing tasks we are about to engage in. There is no need to restart the computer if you decide to lower the number of History States to 20.

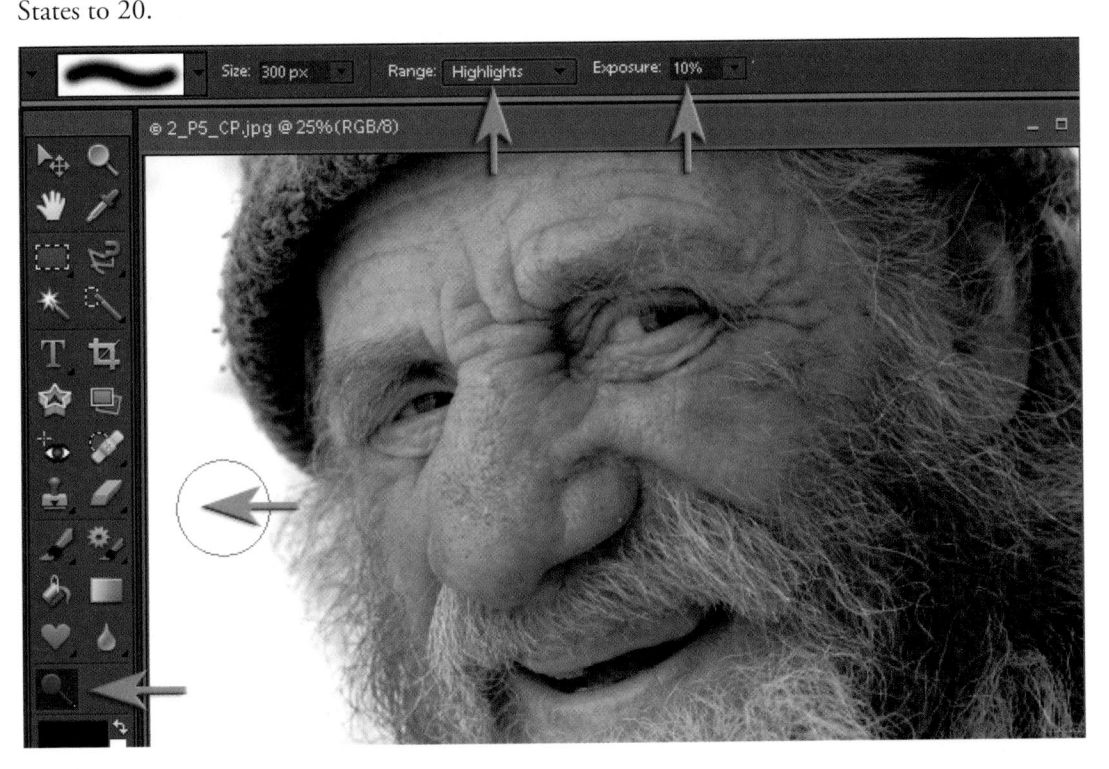

Dodge tool > Use a soft-edged brush and paint with the Dodge tool set to Highlights. Reduce the opacity to around 20–30% to ensure that you lighten the background in the top left-hand corner without unduly affecting the sitter's hat. Lower the opacity to 10% to lighten the rest of the background on this side (around the beard). The following steps will ensure that this backdrop will look like something from a studio (rather than the bus shelter where this image was captured).

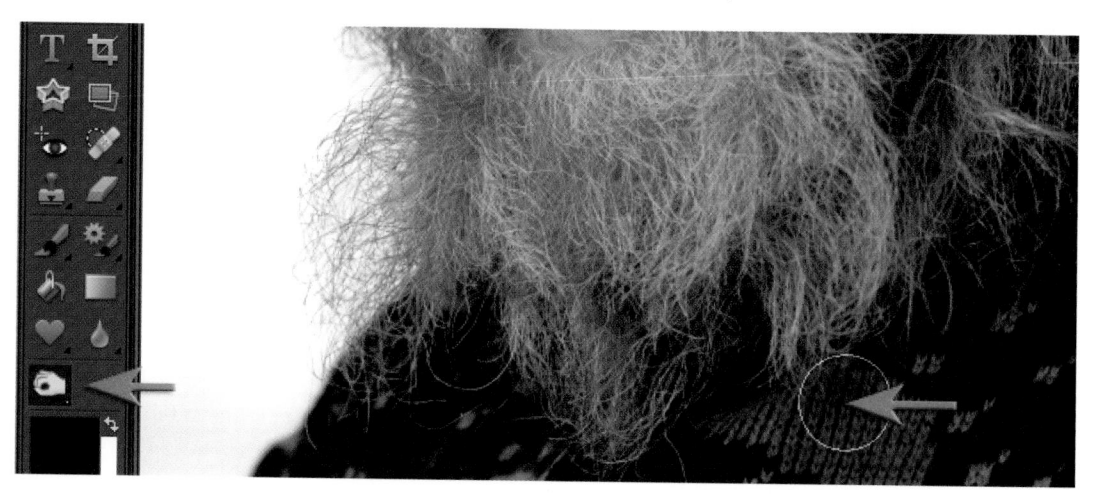

Burn tool > Use a similar soft-edged brush and paint with the Burn tool set to Midtones to reduce the distracting pattern of the clothing. You are not aiming to remove the texture – just subdue it.

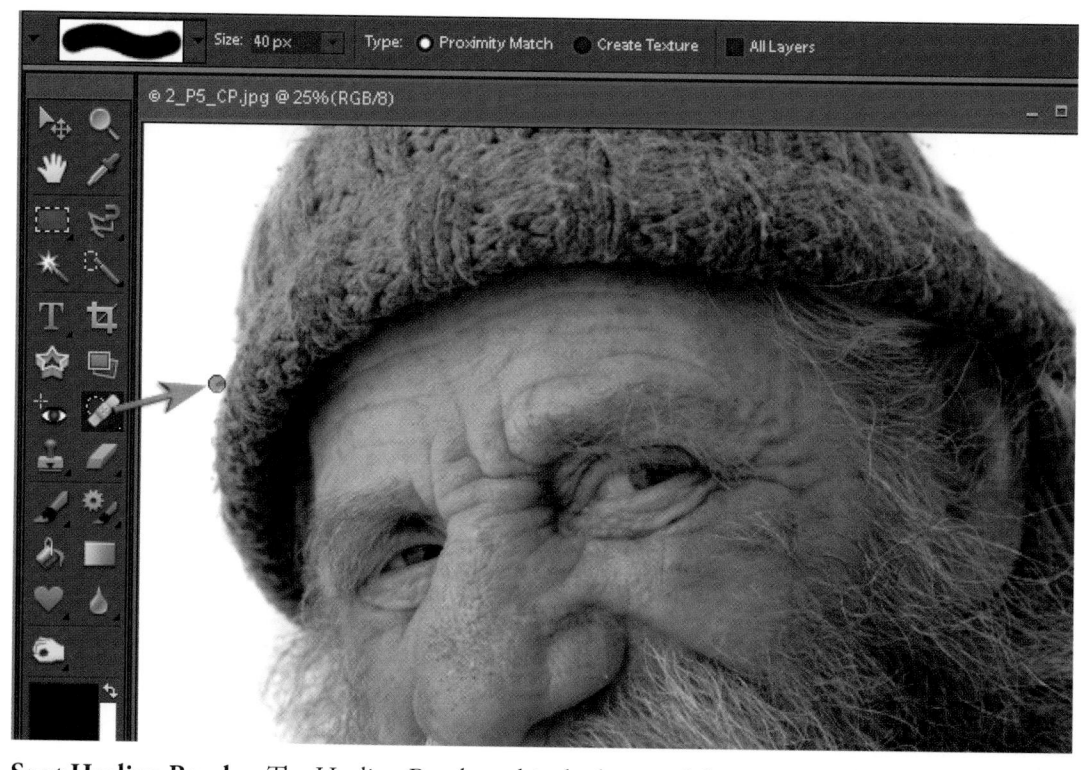

Spot Healing Brush > The Healing Brush tool is the best tool for removing distracting details or dust marks. Use a hard-edged Healing Brush when working in areas of large tonal difference, e.g. removing the dark woollen bobbles that are surrounded by the white background. This will ensure the healing area is not contaminated with the adjacent tones of the nearby hat.

2. To start working on the tonality we need to separate the 'luminance' or brightness values from the color component of the image. Start the process by dragging the background layer to the New Layer icon in the Tools panel to duplicate it (alternatively use the keyboard shortcut Ctrl/ Command + J). From the Enhance menu choose the Remove Color command from the Adjust Color submenu. This will create a desaturated layer sitting above the colored background layer.

3. The fine detail of this portrait is going to be more pronounced if we create some smooth underlying tones. These smooth tones will also help to increase the three-dimensional quality of the portrait. Duplicate the desaturated layer using the keyboard shortcut Ctrl/Command + J and then go to the Filter menu and choose Gaussian Blur from the Blur submenu. Choose a generous Radius value – one where the skin tones are very smooth but the facial features can still be made out. When the Blur Radius is selected choose OK.

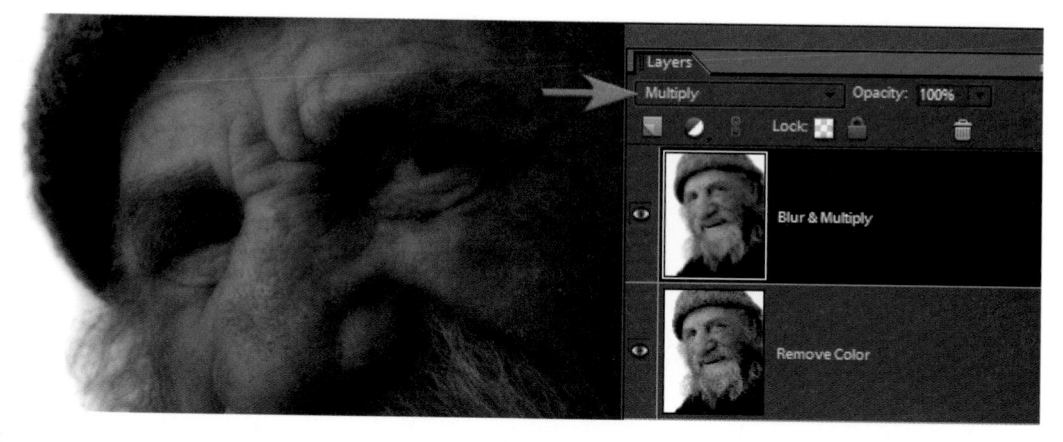

4. Switch the blend mode of the blurred layer to Multiply. The Multiply mode blends the blurred tones back into the sharp detail underneath but renders the image temporarily dark. The shadow information, although very dark, is not lost or clipped by this blending technique. The overall brightness of the image will be restored in the next step so that we can appreciate how effective this technique has been.

Multiply mode > The Multiply blend mode is one of the most useful blend modes for creative editing of digital images. The Multiply blend mode belongs to the Darken family grouping. The brightness values of the pixels on the blend layer and underlying layer are multiplied to create darker tones. Only values that are multiplied with white (level 255) stay the same.

5. To restore the majority of the brightness values to this image simply create a new Levels adjustment layer and switch the blend mode to Screen. The action of first multiplying and then dividing (screening) has, however, incorporated the Blur layer into the pixel stew and the visual outcome is altogether different from the starting image.

Screen mode > The Screen mode belongs to the Lighten family grouping and has the opposite effect to the Multiply blend mode.

PERFORMANCE TIP – BEFORE AND AFTER

When working on a long project it is often necessary, or reassuring, to perform a quick taste test, i.e. gain a quick reminder of how life started out for this image and whether the techniques you are using are creating positive or negative visual outcomes. Rather than clicking on each individual layer's Eye icon, to switch the visibility off (one by one), you can simplify the process by simply holding down the Alt/Option key and clicking only the Eye icon on the background layer. This action switches all of the other layers off in a single click, enabling you to see how life for this image started out. Alt/Option + click a second time to switch all of the layers back on. Looking good? Then let's proceed.

PERFORMANCE TIP – STAMP VISIBLE

One of the really essential techniques for multilayered image editing is the ability to take all of the combined elements from the visible layers and stamp them to a single new layer. It is so important that Adobe have decided to keep the shortcut a secret. The long way to achieve this stamping process involves choosing Select All from the Select menu, Copy Merged from the Edit menu, and then selecting Paste, again from the Edit menu.

Stamp Visible – the mother of all keyboard shortcuts

The shortcut involves several key presses, but will save you considerable time as this technique is used over and over again in this style of editing. It will also impress the socks off image editors who are self-taught and who are most unlikely to have come across this permutation, as it involves holding down nearly all of the left side of the keyboard! Hold down the Ctrl/Command, Alt/Option and Shift modifier keys and then (whilst still holding down the modifier keys) press the letter E. If your new layer is not on top of the layers stack, click and drag it to the top of the Layers panel.

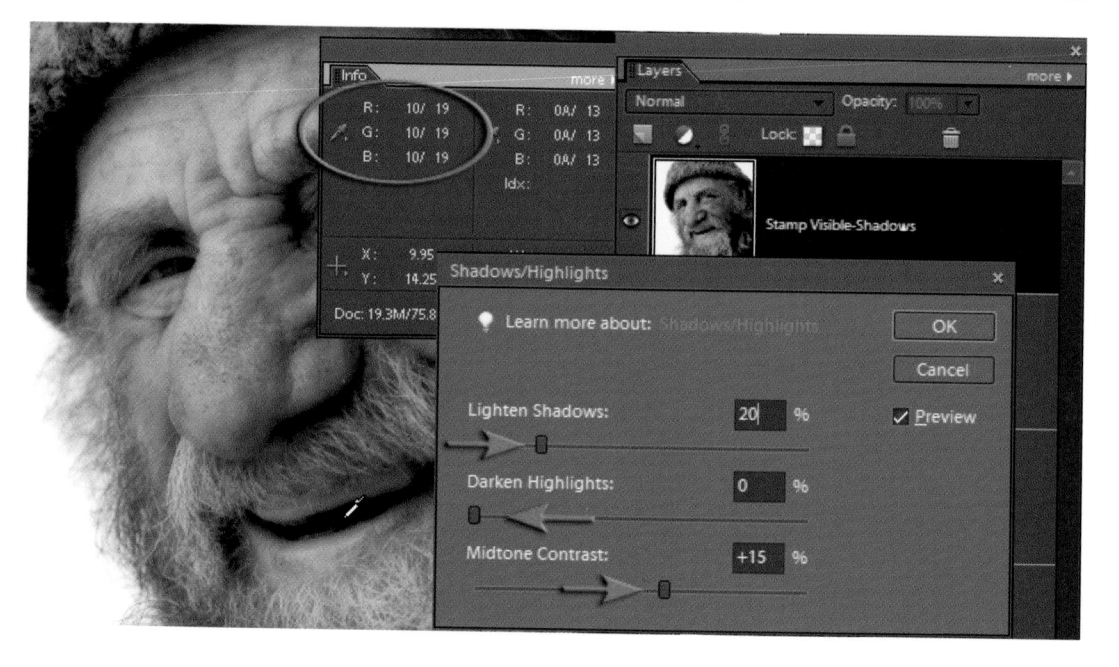

6. Sometimes tones need to be rescued if they are getting too close to 0 or 255. As the shadows are starting to make friends with level 0 and getting a little too close for comfort, we must instigate a rescue attempt. We will need to stamp all of the visible elements to a new layer (see previous performance tip) if we are to utilize our good friend and ally – Shadows/Highlights. Choose Enhance > Adjust Lighting > Shadows/Highlights. Move the Lighten Shadows and Midtone Contrast sliders to values that will raise the darkest shadows above level 15.

The Shadows/Highlights adjustment feature is an excellent tool for targeting shadow or highlight tones that need to be massaged in isolation and brought back into the range of tones that can be comfortably printed using an inkjet printer. Although the Screen blend mode did an excellent job of moving the midtones and highlight tones back to their former glory, the shadows of this image are still struggling to emerge above a level where they are likely to print with detail (between level 10 and level 20 depending on the type of paper, ink and printer being used). The adjustment feature can be accessed via the Enhance > Adjust Lighting menu. Before accessing the adjustment feature it is probably worth having either the Histogram panel and/or the Info panel open so that you can gauge when the shadows have been restored to a value that will print on your trusty inkjet printer. Raising the Midtone Contrast slider can also inject some life and drama into the tonality of the image. You may need to do a balancing act between the two sliders whilst observing the numerical or visual effects on your tonal range if you intend to make use of the Midtone Contrast slider.

PERFORMANCE TIP – SHADOWS/HIGHLIGHTS

The Shadows/ Highlights adjustment feature is the most sophisticated tool for lowering excessive contrast in Adobe Elements. The tool made a very welcome appearance in Elements 3.0 and forms part of the sophisticated armory of adjustment features that can enable users to edit the tonal qualities of an image with control and confidence.

7. The next step involves getting rid of the distracting white background and replacing it with something a little more dramatic. Before creating a gradient make sure that black is the foreground color in the Tools panel (type D on the keyboard to return the color swatches to their default setting). From the Create Adjustment Layer menu in the Layers panel choose Gradient. The creation of a radial gradient or 'vignette' involves fours steps. First choose the Radial and Reverse options in the Gradient Fill dialog box and enter a value of 150% in the Scale field, and then choose an appropriate angle (I have followed the angle of the face). The second step involves clicking on the gradient to open the Gradient Editor. Choose the Foreground to Transparent preset and move the opacity stop on the far right of the gradient ramp to the left to clear the face of any tone, thereby pushing the starting point of the gradient to the edge of the face. For the third step select OK to close the Gradient Editor and then drag inside the image window to move the center of the gradient to the perfect position. Finally (step 4) select OK and adjust the opacity of the layer to balance the background tone with the portrait.

PERFORMANCE TIP – GRADIENT LAYERS

Although Gradient layers represent an important and powerful editing tool, the good people at Adobe have overlooked a very important aspect in this adjustment layer feature, making it one feature short of a full load. Gradients have a nasty habit of 'banding', either in the screen view and/or in the printed image, giving the tonal transition a posterized appearance that is not at all in keeping with the rich tonal qualities of advanced image-editing techniques. The banding can only partly be reduced by selecting the Dither option (not a default option for the gradients). To ensure this banding does not raise its ugly head the user must add noise to any areas of smooth tone after any gradients have been applied. Gradient layers unfortunately do not contain pixels to which noise can be added, so this can become especially problematic and requires an additional Noise layer to resolve the problem.

8. Adding rather than reducing noise may sound strange. One has to remember, however, that the gradient is completely artificial and noiseless – something that cannot be matched even with a low-noise image captured on a digital camera using a low ISO setting. By adding noise we are merely trying to match the noise present in the rest of the image and at the same time eliminate or reduce the problem of banding. You can add noise directly to the Gradient Fill layer but you will have more flexibility and control if the noise is added to a separate layer. To create a Noise layer hold down the Alt/Option key and click on the New Layer icon in the Layers panel. In the New Layer dialog box choose Overlay as the mode and click on the 'Fill with Overlay-neutral color (50% gray)' checkbox.

Select OK and then switch off the visibility of the Gradient layer so that we can see the original white background. Only one selection is used in this project and it is used to isolate the background for the noise treatment. Select the Magic Wand from the Tools panel and then the Sample All Layers option in the Options bar. Deselect the Contiguous box and lower the tolerance to 20 to ensure that the selection is painless – a single click should do the trick. You will need to add a generous amount of feather (100 pixels or more) to this mask to create a gradual transition between noise and no noise (Select > Feather). After feathering the selection, switch the visibility of the Gradient Fill layer back on. Zoom in to 100 or 200% (avoid magnifications that do not give an accurate screen view, e.g. 66%, 133% etc.).

9. With the selection still active select the Add Noise filter from the Filter > Noise submenu. Select the Monochromatic option and choose an amount that will create a noise level that is consistent with the rest of the image file. To check that the noise level is OK zoom in to Actual Pixels (View > Actual Pixels) and then hold down the Spacebar to enable you to drag the image between the gradient (with added noise) and the face (with no added noise). When the texture is consistent select OK.

Note > Adding noise is an essential component of using gradients. Think gradient – think noise.

10. The localized contrast is already vastly improved from the original file, but if you want to see how far you can take this tonal manipulation you may like to try the following technique that can add depth and volume to a seemingly lifeless and flat image. Stamp the visible elements yet again to another new layer (Ctrl/Command + Alt/Option + Shift and then type E) and then switch the blend mode to Overlay. From the Filter menu go to the Other submenu and choose the High Pass filter. When this filter is used as an alternative to the Unsharp Mask filter a small radius of between 1 and 5 is usually selected, depending on the resolution of the image file and the output medium, but in this case the Radius slider can be moved much higher whilst observing the effects on the image file. At the moment the effects may appear a little excessive, but lowering the opacity of the layer and/or switching its blend mode to Soft Light can refine the overall effect.

11. The rich tonality will now serve as an excellent canvas for the fine detail that we are about to sharpen. Sharpening should always be done late in the editing process to avoid exaggerating any image artifacts or non-image data. If you are to have maximum control over the sharpening process and the flexibility to adjust the level of sharpening after making a test print (images tend to look a little softer when compared to their screen counterparts – especially when using LCD displays), you need to apply the Unsharp Mask to a Copy Merged layer. You know the drill by now – stamp visible to a new layer. When this has been done you should set the blend mode to Luminosity. Switching the layer to the Luminosity blend mode will have zero effect on the visual outcome of the image at this stage. The advantage of this mode change is seen when the color is switched back on in the next and final step of the project. If you are used to applying conservative values in the Unsharp Mask filter this is not the time to exercise restraint. Be generous – very generous – with the Amount slider (200 in this project) but keep the Radius slider to the usual amount (no more than 1.5). The Threshold slider, which is usually raised to avoid sharpening minor details, can either be left at 0 so that all of the image information comes under the global sharpening umbrella or raised to around 5 so that the image noise levels are not excessively sharpened. You will need to print a test strip to your favorite paper surface before you can assess whether the amount of sharpening for this image is correct. If the sharpening seems a little excessive simply lower the opacity of the Sharpening layer until you find the perfect setting for your paper.

PERFORMANCE TIP

You might be so impressed with the tonal qualities of your monochrome masterpiece that the thought of switching the color back on gives you the shivers. It is important, however, to the learning curve of this project to discover how the luminance values of an image file can be edited independently of the color before being reunited. Color can be a major distraction when editing tonality. Switching off the visibility of the three monochrome or desaturated layers sitting directly above the background layer will allow the top layer in Luminosity mode to merge with the color of the background layer. The blend modes are one of the most under-utilized of the editing features to be found in Photoshop Elements. Perhaps it is because of their slightly abstract names and their mathematical approach to multilayered pixel editing, but their creative power and usefulness should not be underestimated. With the digitally remastered dish ready to serve up to your printer, you may need to savor both monochrome and color versions over a period of time before your own personal preference helps you make the final decision. Enjoy!

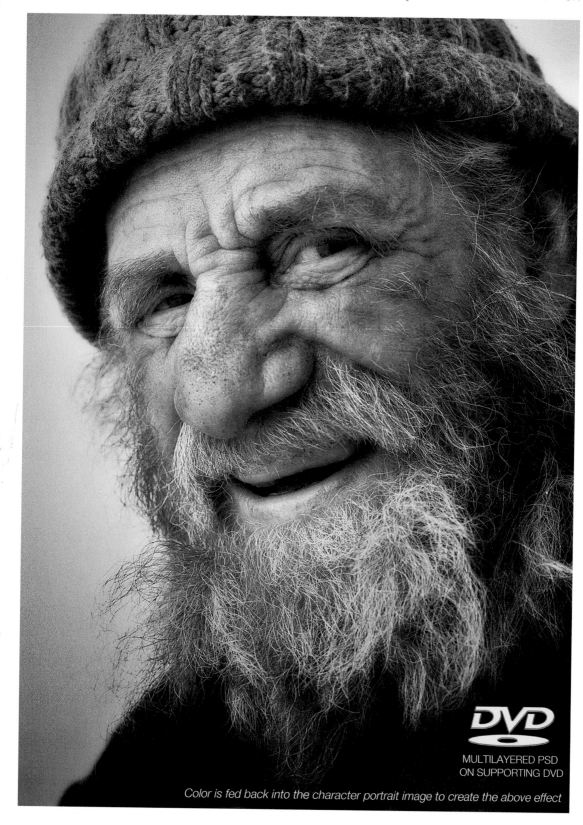

DVD

MULTILAYERED PSD
ON SUPPORTING DVD

Color is fed back into the character portrait image to create the above effect

Project 6

Photograph by Jennifer Stephens

Maximum Performance

Use the Soft Focus action to achieve a lightning-fast makeover (minus the heal and liquify steps)

Glamor Portrait

Cheaper (and more fun) than plastic surgery, we explore how pixel surgery can be used to craft perfect portraits that are bound to flatter the sitter every time.

The glamor portrait offers an excellent opportunity to test the effectiveness of a variety of image-editing skills. The portrait is an unforgiving canvas that will show any heavy-handed or poor technique that may be applied. We will start with a color portrait that has been captured using a soft, diffused light source.

This project will aim to perfect various features and not to make such changes that the character of the sitter is lost to the technique. The techniques used do not excessively smooth or obliterate the skin texture, which would lead to an artificial or plastic appearance. The techniques used smooth imperfections without totally eliminating them.

DVD

16 BITS/CHANNEL IMAGE
ON SUPPORTING DVD

The 15-minute (after practice) makeover – techniques designed to flatter your model

PERFORMANCE TIP

Use window light or diffused flash to obtain a soft, low-contrast light source to flatter the subject. Avoid direct flash unless it is diffused with a white umbrella. Stand back from your sitter and zoom in with your lens rather than coming in close and distorting the features of the face (the closer you stand, the bigger the nose of the sitter appears). A perfect white background is difficult to create if you don't have a studio backdrop and multiple lights but, with a little practise, it is possible to get a near-white background by capturing the sitter in front of a white translucent curtain against a brightly illuminated window and with a single introduced light source.

1. If you can capture using the Raw format then you will have the opportunity of perfecting the histogram and color balance in 16 Bits/Channel mode prior to starting the project. Choose Enhance > Adjust Lighting > Levels, then drag the Shadow and Highlight sliders in to meet the histogram or simply click the Auto button. Drop the bit depth once this has been done to 8-bit mode (Image > Mode > 8 Bits/Channel).

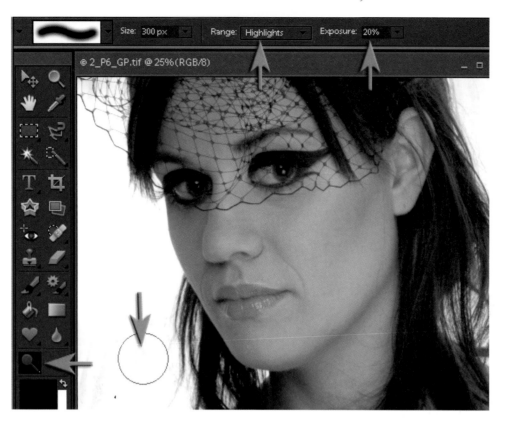

2. Select the Dodge tool in the Tools panel and in the Options bar choose Highlights and an exposure setting of around 20–30%. If you are a little nervous about using this tool on the background layer, duplicate the background layer by dragging it to the New Layer icon in the Layers panel. Stroke the background with a large soft brush until any detail or tone present is rendered white. As the Dodge tool in Highlight mode only lightens the brightest tones on the layer, care only needs to be taken if the skin tones or hair next to the white background are also very bright.

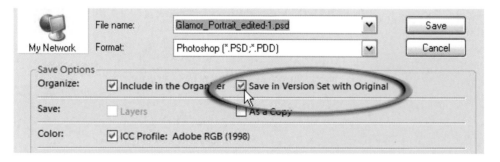

3. As you move through this project it is worth saving consecutive versions. The Organizer in Photoshop Elements (PC version) can keep track of these versions (providing the file is already in the Organizer's catalog) and help name them if you click on the Save in Version Set with Original option when you use the Save As command from the File menu.

4. Select the Healing Brush from the Tools panel to remove or reduce dark lines on the face. A time-saving technique when working with the Healing Brush tool is to either duplicate the background layer or create a new empty layer before starting the healing process. You can simply fade all of your work at the end of the process by dropping the opacity of the Healing layer. If you choose to heal to an empty layer make sure that this is the layer that is selected in the Layers panel and the Sample All Layers option is selected in the Options bar.

PERFORMANCE TIP

Care must be taken when selecting the size and hardness of the brush. If an overly large soft-edged brush is used near the eyes, lips or hair it can draw in color values that can contaminate the skin tones (a selection can be made prior to using the Healing Brush to isolate the healing area from different colors or tones). If the brush is too hard the edges of the healing area will be visible. Sometimes it is better to use a smaller brush and make several passes rather than trying to complete the section with a single pass. The Healing Brush tool, with its protection of surface texture, is a superior alternative to using the Rubber Stamp tool at a reduced opacity.

5. Next we're going to alter the facial features. Select the background layer in the Layers panel. Duplicate the background layer using the keyboard shortcut Ctrl + J (PC) or Command + J (Mac) if you don't want to work directly on the background layer. Choose Filter > Distort > Liquify. The Liquify filter is another tool that works directly on your pixels so you may like to duplicate the background layer if you are feeling nervous about the pixel surgery that follows. The various tools in the Liquify filter dialog box can be used to modify the shape or size of the sitter's features. The Pucker tool and Bloat tool can be used to contract or expand various features, e.g. grow eyes or lips and shrink noses. Perhaps the most useful of the Liquify tools, however, is the Shift Pixels tool. This tool can be used to move pixels to the left when stroking up and to the right when stroking down. It is ideal for trimming off unsightly fat or reshaping features. In this project the brush pressure is dropped to 15% and an appropriate brush size is selected so that the side of the face is not moved along with the nose. If things start to get ugly just remember the keyboard shortcut Ctrl/Command + Z (undo)! If you are happy with your results you could choose Flatten Image from the Layer menu at this stage to keep the total file size small. This is, however, optional if you are the sort of person who never likes throwing anything away!

Note > It is important to exercise great restraint when using the Liquify filter, as the face can quickly become a cartoon caricature of itself when taken too far. The filter also softens detail, becoming obvious when overdone.

173

PERFORMANCE TIP

It is possible to 'freeze' pixels to protect them from the actions of the Liquify filter. There is a freeze brush in the Liquify filter of the full version of Photoshop – but not in Photoshop Elements. To activate the freeze in Elements simply make a feathered selection prior to selecting the Liquify filter. Select the area to be modified, being careful to leave out sections of the face that should be protected from the pixel surgery. With the selection active, open the Liquify dialog box. The areas outside of the selection are now frozen.

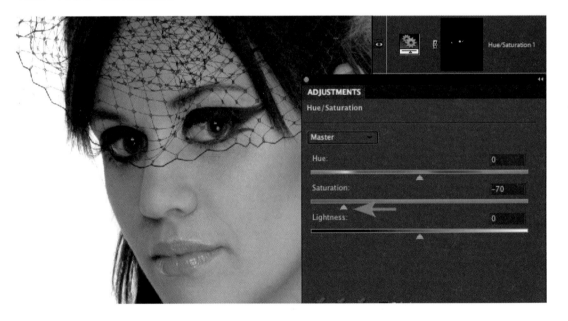

6. Create a Hue/Saturation adjustment layer. Focus your attention on the whites of the eyes and lower the saturation until any discoloring is removed. Disregard the effects to the rest of the face for the time being. Select OK (version 7 only) and then fill the layer mask with black to conceal the adjustment (Alt/Option + Backspace if black is in the foreground color swatch or Ctrl/Command + Backspace if black is in the background color swatch).

Select the Brush tool from the Tools panel. Choose a soft-edged brush just a little smaller than the eye from the Options bar and lower the opacity to 50%. Choose white as the foreground color in the Tools panel. Stroke the whites of the eyes with the brush until they are appropriately drained of color.

7. Create a Levels adjustment layer and move the Gamma slider to the left to brighten the whites of the eyes. As before, select OK (version 7 only) and then fill the layer mask with black to conceal the adjustment once again.

This time brighten the eyes by painting with white at 50% opacity. If you overdo it you can switch colors and paint with black or simply lower the opacity of the adjustment layer.

8. The technique to smooth the tones of the face is quick and very effective. The first step is to merge all of the visible elements of the image into a new layer on top of the layers stack (a process referred to as 'stamp visible'). Hold down all of the modifier keys (the Ctrl/Command, Shift and Alt/Option keys) and then type in the letter E. Make sure the resulting layer is on top of the layers stack and set the blend mode of this layer to Multiply. Go to the Filter menu and choose Gaussian Blur from the Blur submenu. Apply a 20-pixel Gaussian Blur.

Visual warning > It is going to look like someone turned out some of the lights until we carry out the next stage of the process, but if you use your imagination you can probably already see that the skin tones are now smooth and radiant – if just a tad dark.

PERFORMANCE TIP

The precise pixel radius of the Gaussian Blur filter will vary depending on the resolution of your image. The idea is to bleed the tones, but not so much as to lose the features of the face.

9. Create a Levels adjustment layer and set the blend mode to Screen to lighten the image. If the image is still not light enough, drag this adjustment layer to the New Layer icon to duplicate it. The blend mode of this duplicate layer will also be in Screen mode. If this lightens the highlights too much, drag the Output highlight slider towards the center of the histogram to restrict the screening effect to the shadows and midtones only.

10. Create a Hue/Saturation layer above these screened layers and lower the saturation a little. The side effect to smoothing the skin tones using this technique is that saturation increases. Another problem that will need to be resolved is that the deepest shadow tones may be pushed too dark to print. These important shadow tones will need to be rescued in order to produce a professional result.

Fine-tuning the tonality

11. There are a number of different ways we can use to rescue the shadow tones of this image. The first uses the non-destructive Dodge layer technique. Hold down the Alt/Option key whilst you click on the New Layer icon in the Layers panel. Switch the mode to Soft Light and check the 'Fill with Overlay-neutral color (50% gray)' box. Select OK. This 50% gray layer is invisible in Soft Light mode but can be used to lighten or darken the underlying image. Select white as the foreground color and use a soft-edged brush at 50% opacity to paint the darkest areas of the hair lighter. Several passes at a reduced opacity rather than a single pass at 100% opacity will render the dodging a subtle affair.

> PERFORMANCE TIP
> Try switching the blend mode of your Dodge and Burn layer to Overlay mode instead of Soft Light mode for alternative effects when dodging and burning.

12. The Shadows/Highlights adjustment feature from the Enhance > Adjust Lighting submenu can also be used to target and rescue the darker tones of your image. Stamp visible to a new layer before implementing the adjustment. When using a layer mask with the Shadows/Highlights adjustment command it is possible to pump up the level of lightening and midtone contrast without affecting the midtones or highlights in the image.

PERFORMANCE TIP

Shadows/Highlights is a very powerful adjustment feature. Use a layer mask to further limit or restrict the effects of the Shadows/Highlights adjustment. Create a Levels adjustment layer without making any adjustment. Copy the image to the clipboard (Select > All and then Edit > Copy Merged) and paste it into the layer mask of this adjustment layer. In order to paste the image into the layer mask you must first Alt/Option + click the layer mask. When you Alt/Option + click an empty layer mask the image window will appear completely white. From the Edit menu choose Paste. If this action is not taken the copied pixels will be pasted to a new layer. To restrict the adjustment to just the darkest tones of the image you must first invert the image in the layer mask (Ctrl/Command + I) and then perform a Levels adjustment (Ctrl/Command + L) on this layer mask. Move the Shadow slider to the right to restrict the lightening process to just the darkest shadows. Move the Highlight slider to the left to increase the effect of the Shadows adjustment.

13. Smooth skin tones can be unduly sensitive to the application of the Unsharp Mask. It is usual to raise the Threshold slider sufficiently so that areas of smooth tonal gradation are left unaffected. Film grain, image sensor noise and minor skin defects all come in for the sharpening treatment if the threshold is left too low. If the sharpening process is proving problematic using the Unsharp Mask, a selective sharpening technique should be considered. Stamp visible to a new layer, set the blend mode to Overlay and apply the High Pass filter (Filter > Other > High Pass). At this stage the sharpening is global but it can be restricted by using a layer mask borrowed from an adjustment layer or by painting directly into this High Pass layer using 50% gray to eliminate sharpening.

Click on a 50% gray swatch in the Swatches panel or click on the foreground color swatch in the Tools panel and set the HSB values to 0°, 0% and 50%. With 50% gray as your foreground color you can now proceed to paint the smoother areas of skin to ensure they escape the sharpening process.

14. You can add a little lip-gloss (or extra sparkle to the eyes) by duplicating the High Pass layer and filling the rest of the image with 50% gray. Make selections of the lips and/or eyes and then invert the selection. Then choose Fill Selection from the Edit menu and choose 50% gray. Switching the mode of the layer to Hard Light will pump up the effect to maximum.

It might seem like a long road to the final result but this technique can be surprisingly quick when you get into the swing of things. It avoids excessive selections and fiddly work, and a lot of minor blemishes are nuked via the blurred layer set to Multiply mode. Of course the real reward will be the admiration of your photographic skills by the sitter – who will be eternally grateful.

PERFORMANCE TIP

If you can't leave well enough alone, or would just like to explore different approaches to the make-up the model is using, then you can add your own make-up in post-production instead of pre-production. Add a new empty layer set to Darken or Multiply mode. Using a soft paintbrush set to 50% opacity, build up some eye shadow, rouge or lipstick and then lower the opacity of the layer until you create the right effect.

Try clipping/grouping a Hue/Saturation adjustment layer with the make-up layer and move the Hue and Saturation sliders to explore alternative shades quickly and easily. If only getting ready to go out for the evening was this simple!

Ozgurdonmaz (www.iStockphoto.com – image number 4875147)

NEGATIVE CLARITY IN ADOBE CAMERA RAW

Softening the skin tones on a model's face, which previously had to be performed in the main editing space, can now be carried out much faster in Adobe Camera Raw (ACR). In ACR 4.5 and later we have the option to use a Negative Clarity adjustment. This is useful to soften and suppress detail and texture. In the example above, the Clarity slider has been dropped to -50 to illustrate how the adjustment can be used to reduce the excessive detail in the model's skin. Be careful, as excessive amounts of negative clarity will lower the contrast of the image.

Ozgurdonmaz (www.iStockphoto.com – image number 5009631)

SURFACE BLUR FILTER

This filter, unlike the Gaussian Blur filter, has a Threshold slider that, if used correctly, will leave edges crisp and sharp whilst blurring the surfaces inside the edges. This will ensure there are no nasty haloes around the edges of your subject as a result of the blurring process.

Duplicate the background layer before going to Filter > Blur > Surface Blur. It is important to get the balance right between the Radius and the Threshold slider settings for each and every image (there is no one 'perfect recipe' that suits every image). To get a feel for what these two sliders do, set them both to a value between 20 and 25. Now move the Radius slider lower until you detect the surface tone becoming 'mottled' or 'blotchy' and then move it higher again until the surface appears very smooth. Finding the minimum radius that renders the surface smooth is your goal here.

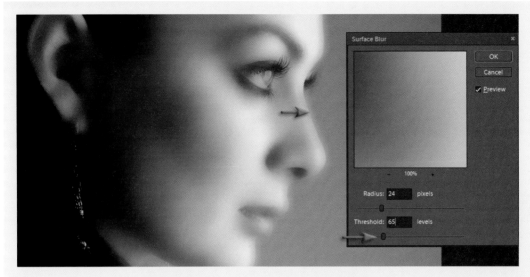

Now drag the Threshold slider higher until you see haloes appear around the edges of your subject. Back the slider off to a point where all of the haloes disappear. If you continue to move the slider lower, after the haloes have disappeared you will start to re-introduce the finer detail that was removed by the Radius slider. Try to make the surface as smooth as possible at this stage as some of the texture and detail can be made visible by lowering the opacity of this layer.

Select OK to apply the Surface Blur filter. Create an adjustment layer below this copy layer and group the background copy layer to the adjustment layer (Layer > Create Clipping Mask, or Group With Previous Layer for users of Elements 7). Fill the adjustment layer mask with black to conceal the surface blur. Select white as the foreground color in the Tools panel and then choose a soft-edged brush and set the opacity to 60–80% in the Options bar. Paint to reveal the blur in the areas of the skin only. You do not need to be too critical about accuracy as areas of fine detail such as the eyelashes and the contours of the face have already been preserved on the Surface Blur layer. You will, however need to avoid painting over areas such as the lips to ensure fine detail is not lost in these areas. Paint a second time to reveal additional softening where needed.

Project 7

Motion Blur

If you have a need for speed and would like to 'move it, move it' this project shows you how to get some ooomph into your stationary wagon. To get some motion magic happening we need to start with nothing more than a half-decent parked car. The example used in this project may look like a professional car shoot but was in fact captured using a fixed-lens digicam in a school car park. With little more than a selection, a couple of blur filters and a little know-how, the static becomes dramatic.

CORVETTE

A 1999 Corvette is polished and taken for a spin in this classic car makeover

The post-production editing or 'car makeover' is simplified when there are not too many reflections in the bodywork or chrome of the car that you captured. Busy reflections will either detract from the final quality or increase the time you spend removing the unwanted detail. In this tutorial you will learn how to smooth out the bodywork, streak the background and spin the wheels, and finally put the icing on the corporate cake by applying the logos to give the image that advertising look.

Stage 1 – Cleaning the paintwork

1. If you are not experienced in using the Healing Brush and Clone Stamp tools I would recommend duplicating the background layer by dragging it to the New Layer icon in the Layers panel. This will give you the option of trashing the layer if all goes horribly wrong. Hold down the Alt/Option key and click on an area of good paintwork and then paint over any scratches, blemishes or damaged areas. Vary both the size and the hardness of the brush to get the best results. If you are working in the middle of a panel the Healing Brush tool usually gives the best results. If you are working close to an edge, you may want to try increasing the hardness of the brush in the Options bar or switching to the Clone Stamp tool. Double-click on the layer name in the Layers panel and name it 'Clean' to differentiate it from the background layer.

2. Make a selection of the car using one of the tools from the Lasso group (the edge contrast is a little too low for the Quick Selection tool). The Magnetic Lasso tool will do a good job of selecting most of the car. Select only the car, excluding its shadow. Click on an edge of the car with the Magnetic Lasso tool and move the tool slowly along the edge to start the process. You will notice that the tool lays down anchor points. When moving the tool over an edge with poor contrast you can help Photoshop along a little by clicking to add an anchor point manually (Photoshop cannot see some edges due to the poor contrast). Alternatively you can fine-tune the sensitivity of the tool by experimenting with the settings in the Options bar. From the Select menu choose Save Selection, give your selection a name such as 'Car' and click OK. Go to Select > Deselect.

3. The next part of the process involves separating the edges of the car from the broader areas of paintwork. This will allow us to smooth out the paintwork whilst retaining the definition and detail of the edges. Duplicate the layer you have just cleaned and healed (if you duplicated the background layer in the first step you will now have three layers in your Layers panel) and apply a 1-pixel Gaussian Blur (Filter > Blur > Gaussian Blur). This prepares the file for the filter used in the next step.

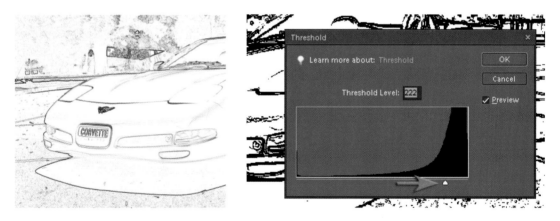

4. Choose the Find Edges filter found in the Stylize submenu (Filter > Stylize > Find Edges) to reduce this layer to the edges only. To increase the contrast and width of the edges, we can apply the Threshold filter from the Adjustments submenu (Filter > Adjustments > Threshold). Drag the slider in the Threshold dialog box to the right until you have well-defined black lines and limited detail visible in the panels. Name the layer you have been working on to save any possible confusion later. I have called mine 'Find Edges'.

5. Select the Brush tool in the Tools panel and white as the foreground color (press the letter D on your keyboard to set the colors to their default settings and then press the letter X to switch the foreground and background colors). Paint to remove any detail in the paintwork that is not required, i.e. anything that is not the edge of a panel or important detail that needs to be pin-sharp. Load the selection (Select > Load Selection) that you saved earlier in step 2. Check the Invert box and then select OK. The background should now be selected.

6. Choose Fill Selection from the Edit menu and select Black for the contents color. Click OK. Your image should now appear as a line drawing of the car with a black background. Choose Deselect from the Select menu.

7. To soften the lines so that detail of the edges fades gradually into the smooth paintwork, we must apply a small amount of Gaussian Blur to this layer. In softening the edges the Gaussian Blur may also reduce the density of the lines, so follow the Gaussian Blur with a Levels adjustment (Enhance > Adjust Lighting > Levels). In the Levels dialog box move the central Gamma slider underneath the histogram to the right until the lines once again appear black. This is now the resource for our mask that we will use to protect the important detail when we smooth out the superfluous detail in the bodywork.

8. To transfer this layer to a mask we need to choose All from the Select menu and then Copy from the Edit menu. Photoshop Elements cannot add a layer mask to a pixel layer so we will need to borrow a mask from an adjustment layer. Create a Levels adjustment layer and then select OK (version 7 only) without making any adjustments. Hold down the Alt/Option key and click on the layer mask of this adjustment layer in the Layers panel. The image window will appear white (you are now viewing the contents of the layer mask, and as yet there is nothing in there). Now choose Paste from the Edit menu and the line drawing of your car should now appear. Alt/Option-click the layer mask a second time and choose Deselect from the Select menu. Although it appears you are still viewing the layer mask you are in fact viewing the layer beneath, which is identical.

9. Click on the Eye icon to hide the visibility of the mask resource layer I have called 'Find Edges' (the one below the adjustment layer) or discard it by dragging it to the Trashcan icon in the Layers panel. Create a duplicate of the layer that you cleaned in step 1 by holding down the Alt/Option key and dragging it to the top of the layers stack. Create a clipping mask (group) for this layer with the adjustment layer supporting your layer mask by going to the Layer menu and choosing the command Create Clipping Mask (Group for Photoshop Elements users).

10. Apply a small amount of Gaussian Blur to this Clean Copy layer – one or two pixels is usually required if you are using a file from a fixed-lens digital compact or prosumer camera. This step will create smooth paintwork by removing superfluous detail and image noise. The important detail such as the crisp edges to the bodywork and panels will not be affected due to the actions of the mask below. If you have used more than 1-pixel Gaussian Blur to smooth the paintwork you may need to add 1% noise to this layer to prevent possible tonal banding or posterization (visual steps of tone instead of a smooth transition of tone).

Stage 2 – Blurring the background

11. Now that the car looks brand new we can add the dramatic element in this project. Load the selection of your car, ensuring the Invert box is checked again (Select > Load Selection). Create another adjustment layer with the selection still active. There is no need to make any adjustment. We are again just using the adjustment layer to access its layer mask. The active selection will create its own layer mask. Again whilst holding down the Alt/Option key, drag a copy of the clean layer to the top of the layers stack. You may want to rename your previous clean copy layer to save any possible confusion or to remember any settings you have used.

12. Before we apply the Motion Blur filter to this copy layer we must prepare the layer so that the car is not streaked into the background, thereby creating a ghost image of itself. Select the Clone Stamp tool from the Tools panel. Choose a large soft-edged brush set to 100% opacity in the Options bar. Clone away the front and the rear of the car by setting a source point in the road. To set the source point hold down the Alt/Option key and click your mouse. Clone away the top of the car by moving the source point to the trees above the windscreen. There is no need to be overly precise with this work, as any imperfections will be hidden when the Motion Blur filter is applied in the next step.

Important > Do not clone away any of the shadow of the car.

13. Go to the Filter menu and choose Motion Blur from the Blur submenu. Drag the Distance slider to the right to increase the apparent speed of the car. Adjust the angle using the little wheel or by entering a figure in the field so that the streaked lines of the blurred background appear to line up with the angle of the car and then select OK. Create a clipping mask for the Motion Blur layer with the adjustment layer beneath by choosing the Create Clipping Mask command from the Layer menu. Although we now have an impressive result the image is not yet perfect.

14. We must now turn our attention to the shadows. The Motion Blur filter may drag lighter tones underneath where the wheels make contact with the ground. This will give the illusion that the car is floating above the road instead of in contact with it. To darken the road immediately next to the tires we can use an adjustment layer. To prevent the adjustment layer from lightening the entire image we simply need to add the adjustment layer to the group. Hold down the Alt/Option key as you click on the Adjustment Layer icon in the Layers panel and select a Levels adjustment layer. When the New Layer dialog box opens check the Use Previous Layer to Create Clipping Mask box and select OK. When the Levels dialog box opens move the central Gamma slider underneath the histogram to the right to darken the road. Pay particular attention to the road directly in front of the rear wheel. Select OK when the tones match. To restrict this darkening process to just a small area around the wheels we must fill the layer mask with black. Go to the Edit menu and choose Fill Layer. Select Black as the contents and click OK. The effects of the adjustment layer will momentarily disappear.

15. Now choose the Brush tool in the Tools panel and select White as the foreground color. Drop the opacity of the brush to 50% and paint where the road requires darkening. Make several strokes with the brush (letting go of the mouse button after each stroke) until the road is darkened sufficiently.

16. The act of adding motion blur to the shadow has made it too long in front of the car so we need to reposition it. Make a selection of the soft leading edge of the shadow using the Lasso tool with a 20-pixel feather selected in the Options bar. Select Copy from the Edit menu and then Paste from the Edit menu. Group this layer with the layer group underneath (Layer > Create Clipping Mask). Select the Move tool and drag the shadow back underneath the car. Ignore the original shadow that may appear to the left, as this will be removed in the next step.

17. To remove any evidence of the original shadow, select the Clone Stamp tool and check the Sample All Layers box in the Options bar. This option will allow you to select the pixels from the layer underneath without first selecting it. Choose a sample point by holding down the Alt/Option key and clicking the mouse. Now the Motion Blur will be convincing and the car will look like it is neither floating nor parked.

Stage 3 – Spinning the wheels

If you examine the pin-sharp wheels of the car you will probably appreciate that there is still more work to do before we can hide the fact that this car is actually static. We must apply a small amount of Motion Blur to the wheels but this needs to be a radial instead of linear Motion Blur.

18. Make a selection with the Circular Marquee tool using a 5-pixel feather. If you need to move the selection before it is complete (letting go of the mouse button will complete the selection) you can press the Spacebar and slide the selection to a better position. Copy the wheel using the Copy Merged command from the Edit menu. The Copy Merged command will copy all of the visible pixels instead of the pixels on the currently selected layer. Choose Paste from the Edit menu to paste a copy of the wheel to a new layer. From the Select menu choose Reselect.

Note > If the ellipse of the selection is slightly crooked when compared to the ellipse of the wheel that you are trying to select, you can rotate the selection by using the Transform command (Image > Transform > Free Transform). You must, however, select an adjustment layer with an empty layer mask to ensure that no pixels are rotated when the elliptical selection is rotated. As none are currently available in this project you would have to create one.

Choose the Transform command (Image > Transform > Free Transform) and drag the side handle of the bounding box until the wheel appears as a circle instead of an ellipse. To get the best result from the Radial Blur filter we must present the wheel on the same plane to the one in which the filter works, i.e. front on.

19. From the Blur group of Filters choose the Radial Blur filter. Check the radio buttons Spin and Best and start with a value of around 20 pixels before clicking OK. If the radial blur is excessive or insufficient choose Undo from the Edit menu and then try the filter using an alternative amount. When you have applied the filter choose the Transform command again and return the wheel to its original elliptical shape. Repeat the process with the rear wheel.

Stage 4 – Adding the graphics

A classic car shot such as this would look great with a little window dressing. Rather than create the graphics from scratch, a couple of extra close-up images were taken of the car model name and its distinctive logo of crossed flags.

20. Open the image 'Logo1' and then click and drag the background layer thumbnail in the Layers panel from this new image file into the window of the car image. Use the Move tool to drag it into position below the car. Set the layer to Luminosity mode in the Layers panel so the background behind the text adopts the same color as the road. You can create a softer edge to the background by using the rectangular Marquee tool and making a feathered selection around the name. I have used a 30-pixel feather in this project.

21. Select the layer beneath the Logo1 layer and then create a Levels adjustment layer (no adjustment required). The active selection will create a mask that we can use to soften the edge of the logo. To make use of this mask select the Logo layer and then choose Create Clipping Mask from the Layer menu. We can disguise the tonal difference of the background by grouping a Levels adjustment layer with the Logo layer (hold down the Alt/Option key and check the option in the New Layer dialog box as in step 14).

22. Move the Gamma slider until the left-side of the logo's background appears the same tone as the road (ignore the fact that the right-side is now lighter than the road) and then select OK (version 7 only).

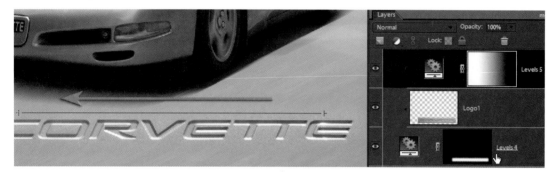

23. Select the Gradient tool in the Tools panel and choose the Black, White gradient and Linear options in the Options bar. Click and drag a straight line from the end to the start of the logo (hold down the Shift key whilst dragging your line to constrain the gradient to a straight line). This will shield the right-side of the gradient from the excessive effects of the adjustment and create a tonal balance or uniformity along the width of the logo.

24. Open and drag in the second logo file. Use the Transform command to rescale the logo and move it into position. In the Effects panel choose the Layer Styles icon and the Bevels subcategory, and apply the Simple Pillow Emboss style by double-clicking its icon in the panel. This will ensure the logo matches the style of the embossed letters. Delete the background surrounding this second logo if you wish to emboss only the flags instead of the entire layer.

Stage 5 – Completing the image

At last we are on the home straight. All we have to do is add a vignette to focus the attention on the car and then, as always, an appropriate amount of sharpening just prior to printing.

25. Create a new layer and make sure it is positioned above all other layers in the Layers panel. Choose the 'Circular Marquee tool' and select a 200-pixel radius in the Options bar. Drag from the top left-hand corner of the image to the bottom right-hand corner. Choose Inverse from the Select menu and sample some of the dark green foliage using the Eyedropper tool. Then choose Fill Selection from the Edit menu and select Foreground Color as the contents. Drop the opacity of the Vignette layer to create the right effect and set the mode of this layer to Multiply.

26. Complete the project by sharpening the image. Select the top layer in the Layers panel and then hold down the Ctrl/Command + Alt/Option + Shift keys and type the letter N followed by the letter E. This keyboard shortcut will copy all of the visible layers and paste them to a new layer. Use a generous amount of sharpening (150 to 200) but keep the radius low (0.8 to 1.5). The threshold can be raised slightly (3 to 6) when using files from a digital compact rather than a digital SLR. Print the image to assess the appropriate amount of sharpening. If the sharpening is excessive, lower the opacity of the Unsharp Mask layer. Perfection on a plate – well, almost. For even more realism don't forget to add that quintessentially important ingredient that I missed in this project – the driver!

iStock_000001143384 (Endless Highway 2 by ra-photos)
iStock_000001300100 (BMW 318i by felixR)

PERFORMANCE TIP

When the movement is towards the camera the illusion of movement can be created by using the Radial Blur filter instead of the Motion Blur filter. To reduce the effects of the blur in the distance the filter can first be applied to a duplicate layer and this duplicate layer can then be grouped with an adjustment layer that contains a radial gradient. The sky was also masked using a linear gradient in Multiply mode.

The car in this illustration came from a separate image and was masked using techniques outlined in Project 1 of the Montage section (Part 3) in this book. The original shadow was preserved using the techniques outlined in Project 6 of the Montage section. The images used in this Performance Tip are courtesy of iStockphoto (www.iStockphoto.com).

Project 8

Low Key

A low-key image is one in which the dark tones dominate the photograph. Small bright highlights punctuate the shadow areas, creating the characteristic mood of a low-key image. The position of the light source for a typical low-key image is behind the subject or behind and off to one side so that deep shadows are created. In the olden (pre-digital) days choosing the appropriate exposure usually centered around how far it could be reduced by the photographer before the highlights appeared dull. In the digital age this approach to exposure at the time of capture should be avoided at all costs, especially when black velvet-like tones are your benchmark for quality.

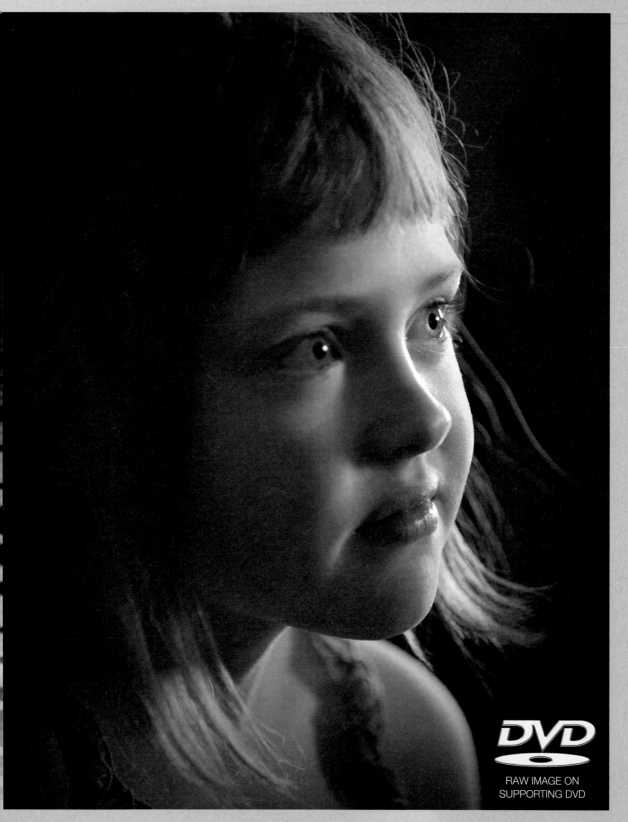

RAW IMAGE ON
SUPPORTING DVD

The classic low-key image – redefining exposure for a digital age

Exposure for low-key images

For those digital photographers interested in the dark side, an old SLR loaded with a fine-grain black and white film is a hard act to follow. The liquid smooth transitions and black velvet-like quality of the dark low-key prints of yesteryear is something that digital capture is hard pressed to match. The sad reality of digital capture is that underexposure in low light produces noise and banding (steps rather than smooth transitions of tone) in abundance. The answer, however, is surprisingly simple for those who have access to a DSLR and have selected the Raw format from the Quality menu settings in their camera. It is to be generous with your exposure to the point of clipping or overexposing your highlights and to only attempt to lower the exposure of the shadows in Adobe Camera Raw (ACR).

1. The first step is the most difficult to master for those who are used to using Auto or Program exposure modes. Although the final outcome may require deep shadow tones, the aim in digital low-key exposure is to first get the shadow tones away from the left-hand wall of the histogram by increasing and NOT decreasing the exposure. It is vitally important, however, not to increase the exposure so far that you lose or clip highlight detail. The original exposure of the image used in this project reveals that the shadow tones (visible as the highest peaks in the histogram) have had a generous exposure in-camera so that noise and banding have been avoided (the tones have moved well to the right in the histogram). The highlights, however, look as though they have become clipped or overexposed. The feedback from the histogram on the camera's LCD would have confirmed the clipping at the time of exposure (the tall peak on the extreme right-hand side of the histogram) and if you had your camera set to warn you of overexposure, the highlights would have been merrily flashing at you to ridicule you of your sad attempts to expose this image. The typical DSLR camera is, however, a pessimist when it comes to clipped highlights and ignorant of what is possible in ACR. Adobe Camera Raw can recover at least one stop of extra highlight information when the Exposure slider is dragged to the left (as long as the photographer has used a DSLR camera that has a broader dynamic range than your typical fixed-lens compact digicam).

Adobe Camera Raw rescues the highlights – sometimes automatically

'Exposing right'

When the Auto checkbox in the Exposure slider is checked, ACR often attempts to rescue overexposed highlights automatically. With a little knowledge and some attention to the histogram during the capture stage, you can master the art of pushing your highlights to the edge. So if your model is not in a hurry (mine is watching a half-hour TV show) you can take an initial exposure on Auto and then check your camera for overexposure. Increase the exposure using the exposure compensation dial on the camera until you see the flashing highlights. When the flashing highlights start to appear you can still add around one extra stop to the exposure before the highlights can no longer be recovered in ACR. The popular term for this peculiar behavior is called 'exposing right'.

PERFORMANCE TIP

If the highlights are merrily flashing and the shadows are still banked up against the left-hand wall of the histogram the solution is to increase the amount of fill light, i.e. reduce the difference in brightness between the main light source and the fill light. If you are using flash as the source of your fill light it would be important to drop the power of the flash by at least two stops and choose the Slow-Sync setting (a camera flash setting that balances both the ambient light exposure and flash exposure) so that the flash light does not overpower the main light source positioned behind your subject.

2. Before we massage the tones to create our low-key image we must first check that our tones are smooth and free from color and luminance noise. Zoom in to 100% magnification for an accurate preview and look for any problems in the smooth dark-toned areas. Setting both the Luminance Smoothing and Color Noise Reduction sliders (found in the Detail tab) to 25 removes the noise in this image. I would also recommend that the Sharpness slider be set to 0 at this point. Selective sharpening in the main editing space may help to keep the tones as smooth as possible rather than committing to global sharpening using the ACR dialog box.

3. Create the low-key look by dropping the Exposure and/or the Brightness sliders in the Adjust tab. You can continue to drop these sliders until the highlights start to move away from the right-hand wall of the histogram. Select the White Balance tool and move your mouse cursor over the deeper shadows – this will give you an idea of the RGB values you are likely to get when this image is opened into the editing space. Once you approach an average of 15 to 20 in all three channels the low-key look should have been achieved.

4. To enhance this image further a vignette has been added. This can be achieved in the ACR dialog box in the full version of Photoshop but in Photoshop Elements the vignette has to be added in the main editing space. In Photoshop Elements the Correct Camera Distortion filter can be used to add the vignette. Uncheck the Show Grid option at the bottom of the dialog box and then drag the Amount slider to the left to darken the corners. Dragging the Midpoint slider to the left will slowly move the darkening effect towards the center of the image.

Note > If you are in 8 Bits/Channel mode and you want to add a vignette using layers, first create a new layer in Multiply mode and fill this layer with white. Hold down the Alt/Option key as you click on the New Layer icon in the Layers panel to access the New Layer dialog box to give you these options.

5. To drop the RGB to black and white I have used a technique that extracts the luminance values from the RGB file. I usually find that this gives a superior result to lowering the saturation or choosing the Remove Color command. Simply click the New Layer icon in the Layers panel and from the Fill Layer dialog box choose 50% gray as the contents color (Edit > Fill Layer > 50% Gray). Create a duplicate of the background layer (or merge the contents if you have placed the vignette on a separate layer) and then move this duplicate background layer to the top of the layers stack. Switch the mode of the background copy layer to Luminosity to create a black and white image from the Luminance values.

6. To complete the project the file should be sharpened for printing. Photoshop Elements has two alternative sharpening filters. Adjust Sharpness (Enhance > Adjust Sharpness) is an excellent alternative to the Unsharp Mask for sharpening images that have little to no noise. To ensure the image does not appear over-sharpened, restrict the Radius to no higher than 1.5. The image preview in this dialog will appear in color as the layer itself has not been dropped to black and white.

Note > If the Adjust Sharpness is making the smoother soft-focus tones appear anything but liquid smooth then consider a localized sharpening technique as described below.

7. Create a Stamp Visible layer (hold down the Ctrl/Command, Shift and Alt/Option keys and press the E key). Apply a generous amount of sharpening using either the Unsharp Mask or Adjust Sharpness (be generous with the Amount slider but restrict the Radius slider to no greater than 1.5).

8. Click on the layer beneath the one you have just sharpened, to make this the active layer. Then click on the Create Adjustment Layer icon in the Layers panel and choose a Levels adjustment layer from the drop-down menu. When the Levels dialog opens make no adjustment – just click OK (version 7 only). Make sure this adjustment layer is below the layer you have sharpened. Click and drag it into position if it needs to move.

9. Fill the adjustment layer mask with black (Edit > Fill Layer > Black).

10. Click on the sharpened layer to make this the active layer. From the Layer menu choose Create Clipping Mask (Group With Previous Layer for users of Photoshop Elements 7).

11. Select the Brush tool from the Tools panel. Select white as the foreground color. Choose a soft brush from the Options bar and drop the opacity of the brush to 50%.

12. Click on the layer mask in the Layers panel to make this active and then move your attention to the main image window. Zoom the image to either 50% or Actual Pixels (100%). Paint in the areas where you would like to increase the sharpness of the image. Painting several times in the same region will slowly build up the sharpness.

PERFORMANCE TIP – A FINAL WORD OF WARNING

To extract the maximum quality from your low-key image you will need to print it on premium quality photo paper or have the image printed at a professional quality print service provider. All the work will be for nothing if the printer or surface quality of the paper cannot handle all of these smooth dark tones. If printed well the print will stand up to close – really close – scrutiny.

Project 9

Channels

You can spend a long time making pointless selections when all Elements needs is to be shown the differences between 'that which must be changed' and the pixels that need to be left alone, based on hue, saturation or brightness. I have learnt to resist the temptation to jump in early with the lasso or tragic wand tool and instead to utilize and exploit the differences that may be lurking beneath the RGB surface of the image. The differences that Photoshop Elements thrives on for selection-free editing can usually be found in the component channels of the RGB image.

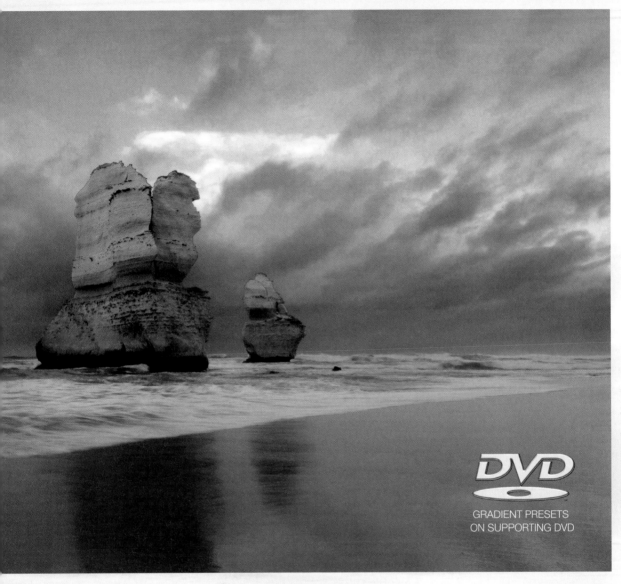

The Apostles – the finished image together with the starting image and the red and blue channels. The red channel is employed to enhance the sky while using the blue channel to mask the effects.

The red channel in this seascape image is information-rich in the sky, whilst the blue channel has excellent contrast that could be utilized for the creation of a mask to control localized adjustments. Users of the full version of Photoshop have this information available in the Channels panel. The Photoshop Elements user must find another way, as the Channels panel is out of bounds. Although Photoshop Elements uses the three primary color channels to create the RGB image, Adobe feels that the Photoshop Elements user does not need to see the component information. Just because you can't see the channels doesn't mean you can't use them.

Part 1 – Extracting the red channel

1. To start the ball rolling duplicate the background layer by dragging it to the New Layer icon in the Layers panel and then add a Solid Color adjustment layer from the Create Adjustment Layers menu in the Layers panel. Select red in the Color Picker (255 Red, 0 Green, 0 Blue).

2. Set the blending mode for the layer to Multiply and then choose Merge Down from the Layer menu. It will probably come as no surprise, but your image has just turned bright red.

3. Duplicate the red layer (background copy) by dragging it to the New Layer icon and from the Enhance menu choose Adjust Hue/Saturation from the Adjust Color submenu (Enhance > Adjust Color > Adjust Hue/Saturation, or use the keyboard shortcut Ctrl/Command + U. Move the Hue slider to +120. Your 'Background copy 2' layer is now bright green.

4. Change the blend mode of this green layer (Background copy 2) to Screen (this will turn the main image yellow as the filtering process begins to take place) and then drag the green Background copy 2 layer to the New Layer icon to copy it. Use the Hue/Saturation adjustment again to change the hue to blue by dragging the Hue slider to +120. The image in your main image window should now appear black and white – these are not just any shades of gray but the gray values that are only present in the red channel of your image. It is a bit too early for the round of applause as we are currently using three layers to achieve this effect.

5. Select all three colored layers by holding down the Ctrl/Command key and clicking on each in turn so that all three are highlighted. From the Layer menu choose Merge Layers. This red layer (dropped to grayscale values) is a useful way to create dramatic black and white images, due to the fact that red filtration of a full color scene makes blue skies darker without darkening any clouds that may be present in the sky. We will, however, take this a few steps further if you are able to stay along for the ride.

Part 2 – Using the red channel layer to darken the sky

6. I have named the background copy layer as 'Red Channel' (really a layer) by clicking on its name in the Layers panel (just so things don't get too confusing). Duplicate the Red Channel layer by dragging it to the New Layer icon and change the blend mode to Multiply. This step is designed to darken the sky and create a lot more drama. Choose Merge Down from the Layer menu to create a single darkened Red Channel layer. Now click on the background layer in the Layers panel to select it and then from the Create Adjustment Layer icon in the Layers panel choose Levels. Don't make any adjustments; just click OK (version 7 only) in the Levels dialog box. We will use the adjustment layer mask on this adjustment layer to mask or hide everything in the Red Channel layer except the sky, which we will leave visible in order to darken it.

7. Click on the Red Channel layer to make it active and then from the Layer menu choose Create Clipping Mask (Group With Previous Layer). Change the blend mode of the Red Channel layer to Luminosity. The Luminosity blend mode will allow all of the color from the background layer to become visible but retain the brightness or 'luminance' values of the Red Channel layer. The mask beneath can hide any of the luminance values that are not required. Adjust the opacity of the Red Channel layer if the drama needs to be lowered a little. You could now just paint in the mask to hide the unwanted luminance values but the idea behind this tutorial is to let Photoshop do all of the work – we are just providing the brains. My brain cells tell me that a mask for those rocks probably already exists in the blue channel of this RGB file. We will typically find that the sky is very light in the blue channel and everything that has no blue component will be dark, i.e. the rocks and foreground beach.

Part 3 – Channel masking

8. Switch off the visibility of the top two layers by clicking on the eye icon next to each layer thumbnail. Using the same technique as in Part 1 of this tutorial create a Blue Channel layer. Instead of selecting red as the Solid Color in step 1, choose 255 blue (the other two channels should be set to 0 in the Color Picker). The rest of the procedure is identical (hallelujah!), using the same +120 Hue value in the Hue/Saturation dialog box each time and the same sequence of blend modes (first apply the Multiply mode to the blue solid color adjustment layer, then apply the Screen mode to the subsequent color layers and Merge Layers).

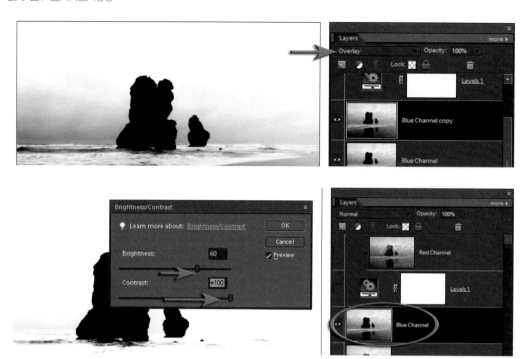

9. After merging the three color layers to create a Blue Channel layer you should see that the rocks in the sea are very dark against the bright sky (the basis of a really effective mask) – the contrast, however, is not quite high enough to act as a layer mask just yet. The aim is to render all of the sky white and the rocks black. To increase the contrast duplicate the Blue Channel layer and then set the duplicate layer to Overlay mode. Then choose Merge Down from the Layer menu. Apply the Brightness/Contrast adjustment feature (Enhance > Adjust Lighting > Brightness/Contrast) to render the sky mostly white and the rocks mostly black.

10. Apply a Levels adjustment to this layer (Enhance > Adjust Lighting > Levels) and drag the white slider underneath the histogram to the left until no traces of gray sky are left. Drag the black slider underneath the histogram to the right until the rocks are solid black. Click OK to apply the changes and create your mask – the only problem now is that it needs to be in the layer mask above and not in its own layer. Switch on the visibility of the Red Channel layer.

11. To transfer this high-contrast Blue Channel layer to the layer mask above select All from the Select menu and then choose Copy from the Edit menu. Hold down the Alt/Option key and click on the adjustment layer mask thumbnail on the Levels 1 layer. The main image window should momentarily appear white, as you are now viewing the empty contents of this layer mask. Choose Paste from the Edit menu to paste the contents of the clipboard into this layer mask. Hold down the Alt/Option key again and click on the layer mask thumbnail one more time to switch off the layer mask view. Go to Select > Deselect. Nothing will appear to have changed until you switch off the visibility of the Blue Channel layer by clicking on the eye icon next to the layer thumbnail. Don't expect perfection just yet as the water and the reflections on the beach will appear slightly weird at this point in time.

12. Apart from some strange tones in the water and on the beach you will probably also notice a halo, or white line, appearing around the rocks where the sky has not been darkened. To remove this halo, first apply a 1- or 2-pixel Gaussian Blur filter to the layer mask to soften the edge (Filter > Blur > Gaussian Blur). This step serves to soften the edge whilst the next step will attempt to realign it.

13. Make a selection with the Lasso tool around any edges that have a thin white halo around them. Apply a Levels adjustment to the mask. Moving both the central Gamma slider underneath the histogram in the Levels dialog box and the white Highlight slider to the left should remove the halo. Go to Select > Deselect when you are done.

14. To finish off this edit we must hide the foreground pixels in the red channel, in order to return normal viewing to both the water and the reflections on the beach. Select the Gradient tool in the Tools panel and choose the Black, White gradient in the Options bar and set the Opacity to 100%. Make sure the Linear gradient option is also selected and change the blend mode to Multiply. Move your mouse cursor into the main image window (this is the only painting tool used in the entire edit), click just around the base of the central rock and drag a short stroke to a point around halfway up the rock. Let go of the mouse clicker to apply the gradient to the layer mask. As the blend mode of the Gradient tool is set to Multiply, this gradient will be added to the existing mask rather than replace it.

$15.$ The last step of this edit is to replace some of the saturation in the sky that was upset when we changed the Red Channel layer to Luminosity mode. It is a really painless process to pick up the selection from the layer mask we have just crafted. Hold down the Ctrl/Command key and click on the layer mask thumbnail. This will load the mask as a selection. With the active selection simply select a Hue/Saturation adjustment layer from the Create Adjustment Layer menu in the Layers panel and increase the intensity of the color to taste.

Not convinced?

You may be thinking that this is a very long process to simply darken the sky of this image. I have, however, learnt all the keyboard shortcuts for every step of this process (including all of the blend modes and merge commands) and I reckon most people would only be halfway around the first rock with their Lasso tool before I had completed the entire editing procedure (all 15 steps). This image edit would normally only take you three or four minutes when you know where you are going. If this is not fast enough be sure to check out the action that comes with this book. Remember – just one click and you have all three channels as layers installed in the Layers panel. A little more brains and a little less playing with your tools now will pay dividends in the amount of time you save later.

part

3

tage

montage

Project 1

Creative Montage

Masks can be used to control which pixels are concealed or revealed on any image layer except the background. If the mask layer that has been used to conceal pixels is then discarded the original pixels reappear. This approach to montage work is termed 'non-destructive'. In the full version of Photoshop the mask can be applied to any layer. In Photoshop Elements layer masks are only available on adjustment layers, but these can be used to mask the pixels on the layer, or layers, above.

Forget cutting and pasting – learn the craft of professional montage using advanced masking techniques

1. Select the Quick Selection tool in the tools panel and then deselect the Auto Enhance option in the Options bar. With subjects that are easy to select, the Auto Enhance option can save you time as the edge quality will be refined as you select. The edge contrast of this subject is low in places and no one tool can easily select the entire subject in this image. When this is the case it is better to turn the Auto Enhance feature off and refine the edge later. After selecting the gold man you will notice the selection may not be perfect. You will almost certainly have to remove the areas from under the arms and between the legs from the selection. To do this hold down the Alt/Option key and click and drag over these areas. You may need to reduce the size of the brush when painting over these regions. Do not spend too long trying to perfect difficult regions of the selection using the Quick Selection tool as we will use additional techniques to complete the process.

2. With the selection active go to the Layers panel and add a Levels adjustment layer from the Create Adjustment Layer menu. Select OK (version 7) without making any adjustments. The selection will have been converted into a layer mask. We can use this layer mask to perfect the selection. Hold down the Alt/Option and Shift keys and click on the adjustment layer mask to view the mask and the image at the same time. The mask is currently indicating the area that is not selected. The mask can be converted back into a selection when we have finished editing it with painting tools or selection tools. Select the Polygonal Lasso tool from the Tools panel and set the Feather value to 0 pixels in the Options bar. Click around any area where the mask color needs to be extended to meet the edge of the gold man. Check that you have black as the foreground color in the Tools panel and then use the keyboard shortcut Alt/Option + Backspace to fill the selected area with the mask color.

3. To create the perfect selection it will be necessary to remove any mask color that appears over the subject. To do this make a selection and fill with the background color (Ctrl/Command + Backspace/Delete). When the edge is difficult to see because the mask color extends over the edge of the subject go to Filter > Adjustments > Invert (Ctrl/Command + I). Now you will be able to see the edge clearly and can then make your selection and fill with the foreground color.

4. If you have a steady hand you can also choose to paint directly into the mask using the Brush tool. Choose a brush setting of 100% hardness in the Options bar and then paint with black to add to the mask or with white to remove the mask color. Zoom in to the image (Ctrl/Command + Spacebar) to ensure the mask is accurate and use the Spacebar to access the Hand tool that will enable you to drag around the image while you are zoomed in. Alternatively use the Navigator panel to navigate around the edge of your subject. Before leaving the mask view make sure that the background is covered in the mask color rather than the gold man (Ctrl/Command + I will invert the mask if required). Alt/Option + Shift click the layer mask to return to the normal view.

5. The edges of the mask will need to be refined before it can be used for a high-quality montage. Select Refine Edge from the Select menu and from the View menu choose Selection to hide the selection edge. Double-click the Custom Overlay Color option in the panel to open the Options dialog and set the Color to dark gray and the Opacity to 100%. Select OK to apply the color change. Set the Smooth slider to 10 and the Feather slider to 1.0 and slide the Contract/Expand slider to the left to conceal the white edge that surrounds your subject.

Note > If the subject is gray instead of the background you need to cancel the process and invert the mask before choosing the Refine Edge command.

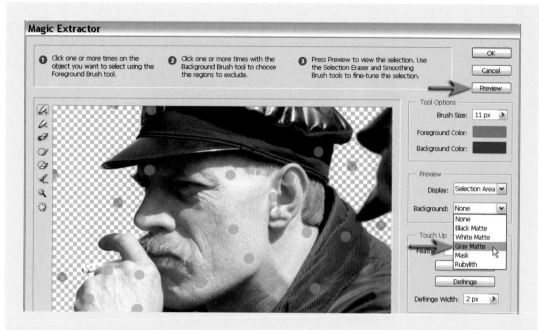

PERFORMANCE TIP

The fact of life is that some extractions can be as painful as pulling teeth! With this in mind Adobe offers you even more magic – the Magic Extractor (Image > Magic Extractor). This is yet another alternative for getting rid of problematic backgrounds. This tool takes a little more time than the Quick Selection tool and is destructive in nature (it deletes the pixels you select with the Background Brush tool) so I would advise duplicating this layer before proceeding. You make little marks or squiggles to advise Photoshop which regions of the image you would like to keep and which regions you would like to delete. Click on the Preview button to see how Photoshop does the hard maths to extract your subject from the background. From the Preview menu choose a matte color to view your extracted subject (choose a different tone from the original background or one that is similar to the new background).

In the Touch Up section of the dialog box select a Feather value (usually 1 or 2 pixels) and then choose a Defringe Width to remove any of the remaining background. Not a bad job – if you don't mind losing the background pixels.

6. Open the new background image and place the two image files alongside each other. Select both layers in the gold man file (hold down the Ctrl or Command key and click on each layer) and then drag the layers into the new background file to create a file containing all three layers.

7. Drag the adjustment layer in the Layers panel so that it is under the layer of the gold man. Select the layer containing the gold man and then choose Create Clipping Mask (Group With Previous Layer in version 7) from the Layer menu. Alternatively you can take your mouse cursor to the dividing line between the two layers, hold down the Alt/Option key until you see the clipping mask icon appear and then click to group them. The original background behind the gold man will now be hidden from view and you will be able to see the new background on the background layer.

8. Select the top two layers (Ctrl/Command+click each layer) and then select the Link Layers option in the Layers panel. This will ensure that the size and position of the mask will match the subject above. Go to Image > Transform > Free Transform (Ctrl/Command + T). Use the keyboard shortcut Ctrl/Command + 0 to fit the Transform bounding box on the screen. Drag a corner handle to resize the image so that it sits nicely against the new background (you will not require all of the legs to replicate the framing in this project). Press the Commit icon or Enter key to apply the transformation.

9. Zoom in and take a close look at the edges. You may notice a white halo along some of the edges (the old background). This can be removed by making a selection of the problem area (use a 5-pixel feather if your selection crosses the edge of your subject) and then applying a Levels adjustment (Enhance > Adjust Lighting > Levels or Ctrl/Command + L) to move the edge of the mask. Move the central Gamma slider to the right to remove any of the old lighter background that may still be visible on the layer above.

10. Click on the background layer in the Layers panel and then choose a Hue/Saturation adjustment layer from the Create Adjustment Layer menu. Select Reds from the Edit menu in the Hue/Saturation dialog and move the Hue slider to the right until the red stripes in the image turn yellow. Adjust the saturation to taste and then select OK to apply the changes (version 7 only).

11. Select the top layer in the Layers panel (the one with the gold man). Hold down the Alt/Option key and select another Hue/Saturation adjustment layer. Holding down the Alt/Option key as you select the adjustment layer will open the New Layer dialog. Choose the Create Clipping Mask (Group With Previous Layer in version 7) option in this dialog and select OK. Clipping the Hue/Saturation adjustment layer to the layer below will ensure the adjustments do not flow down and affect the colors on the background layer.

12. Adjust the saturation of the gold man to match the saturation of the yellows on the background layer. Notice how the adjustments are only affecting the layer below. Select OK to apply the changes (version 7 only). The ability to match the color and tonality of a number of different layers in a composite image is an essential skill for montage work.

13. The basic task of replacing the background is complete. We will now paste a copy of the background layer into the lenses of the dark glasses. Duplicate the background layer (Ctrl/ Command + J) and then drag this copy layer to the top of the layers stack. Switch off the visibility of this copy layer by clicking on the Visibility icon. Select the Quick Selection tool in the Tools panel and click the All Layers option in the Options bar and the Auto Enhance option. Click on each lens in turn to select them.

14. Create a Levels adjustment layer below the background copy layer. Select OK (version 7 only) without making any adjustments. The selection will create a layer mask we can use. Select the background copy layer, switch on the visibility and then group the background copy layer with the adjustment layer. Select Free Transform from the Edit menu and then scale and rotate the layer so that the red stripes appear in the lenses of the sunglasses. You have the option to lower the opacity of the layer in the Layers panel if required.

15. Hold down the Alt/Option key and click and drag the Hue/Saturation 1 adjustment layer to the top of the layers stack. This action will copy the adjustment layer and change the red stripes to yellow but it will also affect the color of the golden Viking. To limit the changes to the reflections in the glasses, group this with the layer below (the transformed background copy layer). Note how you can have more than two layers in a clipping group.

16. Select the Levels 1 adjustment layer in the Layers panel. Go to the Effects panel (Windows > Effects) and click on the Layer Styles icon (two overlapping window frames). Choose Drop Shadows from the drop-down menu. Double-click on the style High to apply the style to the adjustment layer. You will see a drop shadow appear behind the gold man and a blue '*fx*' icon appear on the layer (next to the Link icon). Double-click the '*fx*' icon to open the Style Settings dialog. Move your mouse cursor into the image window and drag the shadow to the right-hand side of the image (the left-hand side of the gold man) to match the direction of the light source in this image. Adjust the Opacity and Size sliders to create the perfect shadow and select OK to apply the changes.

Note > This project has introduced a completely non-destructive approach to montage. Any aspect of the composite image can be re-edited as no pixels were permanently changed or deleted on any layer during the process. The techniques outlined in this project work around the fact that layer masks are only supported on adjustment layers in Photoshop Elements (unlike the full version of Photoshop which supports masks on all layers). We are effectively hijacking an adjustment layers mask to serve this purpose. Although there is a Mask option when using the Selection Brush tool, you are prevented from using the Lasso tools in Elements when working in this mask mode – hence the work we carried out directly on the adjustment layer mask with the mask visible. Same result as the full version of Photoshop – slightly different workflow required to get there.

Project 2

Replacing a Sky

For people who seem to find themselves in the right place at the wrong time!
Have you ever traveled long and far to get to a scenic vista only to find that the
lighting is useless and the sky is a little short of inspiring? Do you make camp and
wait for the weather to change or reluctantly and humiliatingly buy the postcard?
Before you hit the Delete button or assign these 'almost rans' to a never-to-be-
opened-again folder to collect digital dust, consider the post-production alternatives.
Photoshop Elements lets you revisit these uninspired digital vistas to inject the mood
that you were looking for when you first whipped the camera out from its case.

Drama in Venice – change the sky to change the weather

I think every photographer can relate to the intrepid explorers of the Australian Outback who, after scaling the highest peak in the area with great expectations, decided to call it Mount Disappointment! One can only conclude that they were expecting to see something that was simply not there. This something extra could be made real so that all of your landscapes live up to your high expectations – with just a little digital help.

 Check out the supporting DVD to access an extensive stock library of royalty-free skies

1. Select the Quick Selection tool from the Tools panel and deselect the Auto Enhance option in the Options bar. Drag the tool across the sky to make an intital selection of it. Zoom in to 100% (or Actual Pixels) and choose the Selection Brush tool from the Tools panel and the mask option in the Options bar. Paint to add the tops of the buildings that were not included in the mask because of the overzealous behavior of the Quick Selection tool. Exclude the scaffolding and the TV aerials from the mask. Choose the Selection option in the Options bar when this work is finished.

2. From the Layers panel choose Levels adjustment from the Create Adjustment Layer menu. Select the sky image used in this project and from the Select menu choose All. From the Edit menu choose Copy. Return to the Venice image and from the Edit menu choose Paste. From the Layer menu choose Create Clipping Mask (Group With Previous Layer in version 7) or hold down the Alt/ Option key and click on the dividing line between the Sky layer and the adjustment layer below to group the two layers. Don't be alarmed at how bad it looks at the moment; we have several more steps to go before things start to look OK. For the moment we must be content that the sky was captured at a similar time of day to the Venice image and that the direction of that light is also similar.

3. Select Layer 1 and then go to Image > Transform > Free Transform (Ctrl/Command + T). Click and drag inside the Transform bounding box to raise the sky into position. Click and drag on the top-center handle to further enhance the location and shape of the sky to fit the host image. Press the Enter key to commit the transformation.

4. Click on the layer mask to make it active and then go to Select > Refine Edge. Choose a setting of 3 for the Smooth slider and a 1-pixel feather and then move the Contract/Expand slider to the right until the light halo from around the majority of the buildings has disappeared. It is not possible to remove the halo around the buildings on the extreme left-hand side of the image without removing too much edge detail from the rest of the skyline. The halos around these buildings can be fully corrected using the Levels adjustment technique as outlined in Project 1 of this section.

5. Select Layer 1, hold down the Alt/Option key and select a Levels adjustment from the Create Adjustment Layer menu. Select the Create Clipping Mask option (Group With Previous Layer in version 7) in the New Layer dialog. Move the central Gamma slider underneath the histogram to the left to render both the highlights and midtones of the sky very bright so that they match the tones of the distant buildings. Skies that have been captured in less humid conditions will always require this adjustment if they are to look at home in a location where there is reduced contrast together with lighter tones in the distant subject matter. Select OK to apply the changes (version 7 only).

6. Select the Gradient tool from the Tools panel. In the Options bar choose the Black, White and Linear gradient options and an Opacity setting of 100%. Click and drag the gradient from the top of the image to a position just above the horizon line. Hold down the Shift key to constrain the gradient. This will give the sky depth and ensure it retains its drama above the buildings in the foreground.

7. Create a second Levels adjustment and group this to the layer below. The purpose of this second adjustment layer is to increase the intensity of the light on the left-hand side of the image. This will help establish the realism of the effect of the light source that is bathing the buildings on the right-hand side of the image in a warm afternoon glow. Increase the warmth by moving the Gamma slider to the left in the red channel and to the right in the blue channel. Raise the overall brightness in the RGB channel. Observe the effect above the foreground buildings on the left-hand side of the image.

8. Select the Gradient tool from the Tools panel. Select the Black, White and Radial options. Select the Reverse checkbox in the Options bar. Drag a short gradient from behind the buildings on the left-hand side of the image to the top-center. This gradient will enhance the effect of the setting sun.

9. Select the Rectangular Marquee tool in the Tools panel and set the feather to 200 pixels in the Options bar. Click and drag a selection from the upper right-hand corner of the image to the lower left-hand corner. Go to Select > Inverse or use the keyboard shortcut Shift + Ctrl/Command + I. From the Edit menu choose Copy Merged and then Paste.

10. Using the information from the file itself to create a vignette prevents the highlights at the edges of the image from excessive darkening. Set the mode of this new layer to Multiply and adjust the opacity of the layer to make the vignette a little more subtle. The project is now complete and the scene carries all of the mood of an old Venetian painting, courtesy of a dramatic sky.

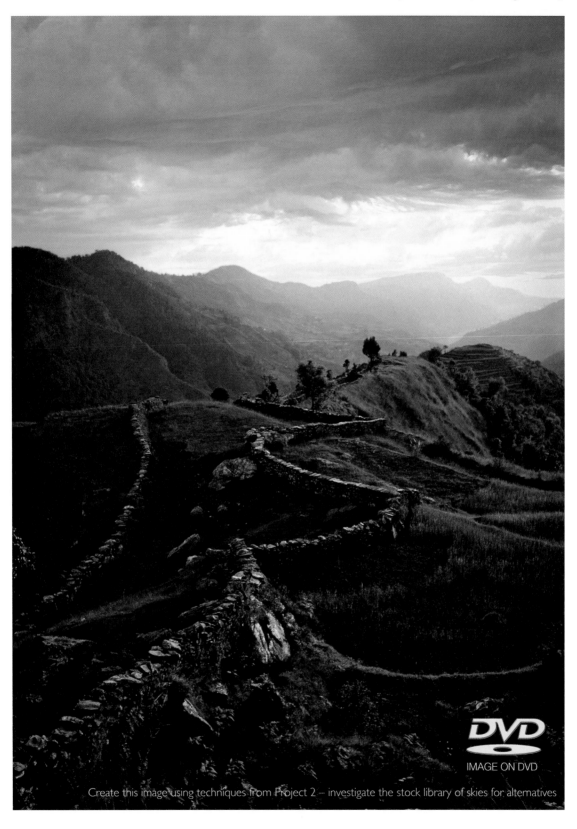

IMAGE ON DVD

Create this image using techniques from Project 2 – investigate the stock library of skies for alternatives

Project 3

Photograph by Abhijit Chattaraj

Layer Blending

The blending technique enables the texture or pattern from one image to be merged with the form in another image. Blending two images on the computer is similar to creating a double exposure in the camera or sandwiching negatives in a traditional darkroom. Photoshop Elements, however, allows a greater degree of control over the final outcome. This is achieved by controlling the specific blend mode, position and opacity of each layer. The use of adjustment layer masks can help to shield any area of the image that needs to be protected from the blend mode.

DVD

RAW IMAGE ON
SUPPORTING DVD

Body art – Blend a texture or pattern with your subject to create a dramatic or surreal effect

1. Click and drag the layer thumbnail of the raindrops image into the body image window. Hold down the Shift key as you let go of the drops thumbnail to center the image in the new window. Use the Move tool to reposition the texture if required. Use the Free Transform command (Image > Transform > Free Transform) if required to resize the texture image so that it covers the figure in the image. Set the blend mode of the drops layer (Layer 1) to Soft Light or Overlay. Experiment with adjusting the opacity of the layer using the Opacity slider in the Layers panel.

2. Turn off the visibility of the water layer (Layer 1). Select the Quick Selection tool in the Tools panel. Deselect the Auto Enhance option in the Options bar. Make an initial selection by dragging the tool over an area of the background. Click and drag over the islands of black background between the subject's fingers to add these areas to the selection (reduce the size of the brush if necessary). Hold down the Alt/Option key and drag over any areas that need to be removed from the selection, e.g. the head.

3. Select the Selection Brush tool in the Tools panel and select the Mask option in the Options bar. Paint over any gaps in the mask (using a brush at 100% Opacity) to perfect the resulting selection. Zoom in and move around the edge of the body to ensure all of the body is fully masked. Switch back to selection mode in the Options bar when this step is complete.

4. From the Create Adjustment Layer menu in the Layers panel select a Levels adjustment layer. The active selection will be converted into a layer mask. Users of version 7 will need to select OK in the Levels dialog without making any adjustments. Switch on the visibility of the raindrops layer and group it with the adjustment layer below (hold down the Alt/Option key and click on the dividing line between the two layers).

5. Click on the layer mask thumbnail in the Layers panel and then from the Select menu choose the Refine Edge command. Double-click the Custom Overlay Color option to access the Overlay options. To get an accurate view of how appropriate the edge of the mask is for our final result we will create a white matte in the Refine Edge dialog to help us choose the optimum settings. Click on the color swatch in the Custom Overlay Color dialog and set the color to white. Set the Opacity to 100% and select OK to close and apply the Custom Overlay Color options.

6. Adjust the Smooth slider to 3 and the Feather slider to 1.0 pixel to help refine the edge and then drag the Contract/Expand slider to the right to hide any of the dark edges from the old black background. Select OK when you have achieved a good clean edge.

7. We need to unlock the background layer to perfect this composite image. Double-click the background layer in the Layers panel to open the New Layer dialog and select OK to accept the 'Layer 0' name. This action will allow us to add a mask to this layer and a new layer below (not possible when the layer is a background layer).

8. Hold down the Ctrl/Command key and click on the Create a New Layer icon in the Layers panel to create an empty new layer below Layer 0. Go to Edit > Fill Layer and choose black as the contents color. Select OK to create a black layer (Layer 2).

9. Hold down the Alt/Option key and click and drag the Levels 1 adjustment layer to copy it. Drag it to a position between Layer 2 (the new black layer) and Layer 0 before releasing the mouse button. Hold down the Alt/Option key again and click on the dividing line between the copy adjustment layer and Layer 0 to create a clipping mask or group. This new mask and the new black layer will ensure a perfect edge when we lighten the background in the final stages of the project.

10. Hold down the Ctrl/Command key and click on the layer mask thumbnail to load the mask as a selection. Click on the raindrops layer (Layer 1) to make this the active layer and then select a Levels adjustment layer from the Create Adjustment Layer menu in the Layers panel.

11. Go to Select > Inverse to invert the layer mask. In the Levels dialog drag the black Output Levels slider to the right to lighten the background to a dark gray tone. From the Channel menu select the blue channel and once again drag the black Output Levels slider to the right to introduce a blue color to the gray background. The precise shade of blue can be controlled by adjusting the black Output levels slider in either the red or green channel. Select OK to apply these changes (version 7 only).

12. Now that the background has been lightened it may be necessary to expand the edge of this layer mask (Select > Refine Edge). The Smooth and Feather sliders can both be set to 0 so the edge does not get softened and smoothed a second time. Adjust the Expand/Contract slider to perfect the edge once again and then select OK.

13. Select the Gradient tool in the Tools panel. Select the Foreground to Transparent and Radial Gradient options with black selected as the foreground color. Set the opacity to 100% and select the Reverse, Dither and Transparency options. Set the mode to Multiply. Click and drag from a position in the center of the man's body out past the top right-hand edge of the image window to create a backlight effect.

14. Select Layer 0 in the Layers panel and use the keyboard shortcut Ctrl/Command + J to duplicate the layer. Group this copy layer with the layer below and from the Enhance menu choose Adjust Sharpness. Select a generous Amount of sharpening with a low Radius setting (300 and 0.8) and click OK. The opacity of this duplicate layer can be lowered to adjust the levels of sharpening for your required output device.

Original image by Abhijit Chattaraj

This image was created using the techniques from this project together with the techniques from Project 5

Project 4

JAGUAR

Displacement

Create a showpiece montage by elevating an old Jag into a classic motor with a little spit and polish and some delectable digital deeds. Wickedly good stuff! The car's paintwork was enhanced before starting the project by increasing the overall saturation of the image and the scratches were removed using the Healing Brush. The tires were made to look like new by using the Burn tool set to 20%. If only it was this easy in real life!

Liquid pixels – a displacement, masking and layer style 'combo'

Stage 1 – Creating a backdrop using the Displacement filter

The layer blend modes are an effective way of merging or blending a pattern or graphic with a three-dimensional form. By using the blend modes the flag in this project can be modified to respect the color and tonality of the undulating silk beneath it. The highlights and shadows that give the silk its shape can, however, be further utilized to wrap or bend the flag so that it obeys the material's shape and sense of volume. This can be achieved by using the Displace filter in conjunction with a 'displacement map'. The 'map' defines the contours to which the flag must conform. The final effect can be likened to 'shrink-wrapping' the flag to the 3-D form of the undulating silk.

How it works > The brightness level of each pixel in the map directs the filter to shift the corresponding pixel of the selected layer in a horizontal or vertical plane. The principle on which this technique works is that of 'mountains and valleys'. Dark pixels in the map shift the graphic pixels down into the shaded valleys of the 3-D form while the light pixels of the map raise the graphic pixels onto the illuminated peaks of the 3-D form.

1. A silk dressing gown was photographed using the available light. For this image to act as an effective displacement map the contrast must, however, be expanded. An effective way of expanding contrast in Photoshop Elements is to duplicate the layer and set the top layer to Overlay blend mode. Note the changes to the histogram by viewing it in the Histogram panel.

Note > Duplicate the silk image resource file to ensure the original file is retained as a master and not lost by this manipulation. Either copy the image file before you start the project or go to File > Duplicate before you proceed to step 2.

2. Go to the Image menu and from the Mode submenu select Grayscale. Choose the option Flatten when the Warning dialog box appears and OK when the the Discard Color Information warning appears.

Note > The displacement map must be in Grayscale otherwise the color channels will upset the appropriate displacement effect.

3. To further improve the effectiveness of the displacement map we must blur the image slightly. This effect of blurring the map will smooth out the lines of the flag as it wraps around the contours of the silk. Too much blur and the undulations will be lost; too little and the lines of the flag will appear jagged as they are upset by any minor differences in tone. Go to Filter > Blur > Gaussian Blur and start by selecting a Radius of around 10 pixels. Increase or decrease this radius when working with images of a different resolution.

4. Save the image (displacement map) as a Photoshop (PSD) file. Close the blurred Grayscale file as the map is now complete. You will need to choose this file when the Displacement filter asks for the location of your map, so make a note of where it has been saved to on your computer.

5. Open or select the original RGB silk file. Also open the flag image. With the flag image as the active window, choose All from the Select menu and then choose Copy from the File menu. Now make the silk image the active window and choose Paste from the File menu. Alternatively you can just drag the thumbnail of the flag image in the Layers panel into the window of the silk image if you can see both image windows on your desktop.

Set the blend mode of the flag layer to Multiply. If you are intending to displace a graphic or a texture it is worth ensuring that you have some elbow room (when we displace the flag it will come away from, and reveal, the edges of the background layer if they are the same size). Use the Free Transform command to enlarge the flag layer so that it is a little larger than the background layer.

6. Go to Filter > Distort > Displace. Enter the amount of displacement in the Horizontal and Vertical fields of the Displace dialog box. The size of the displacement is dependent on the resolution of the image you are working on. Choose amounts of 40 for both fields for the Flag.jpg used in this project. Increasing the amount to greater than 60 for either the Horizontal or Vertical Scale will increase the amount of distortion in this project image, but will also start to break off islands of color from the design of the flag, indicating that the limit of the effect has been exceeded. Select OK in the Displace dialog box and in the Choose a Displacement Map dialog box browse to the displacement map you saved. Select Open and your flag should now miraculously conform to the contours of the silk. If you are not entirely happy with the results go to the Edit menu and choose Undo. Repeat the process choosing smaller or greater amounts in the Displace dialog box.

7. Add an adjustment layer and drag the Highlight slider to the start of the histogram to extend the dynamic range and make the highlights and midtones appear brighter. Your dramatic and colorful background is now complete.

Stage 2 – Creating a montage using masks

The following montage techniques are used for professional results. The techniques covered allow precise control over the alignment and quality of the edge (soft/hard) to ensure that no haloes from the old background are visible (even when using crude selection tools such as the Magic Wand).

Note > Download the completed flag file from the supporting DVD if you would like to start the project at this point.

DISTORTED FLAG ON DVD

8. Open the image of the Jaguar car and add this as a layer above the adjustment layer and flag in the master project file (see step 5 for a guide on combining two images). I have made the background behind the car white in order to make it easier for you to remove it from view in this project.

Select the Magic Wand tool in the Tools panel. Select the Add To Selection icon in the Options bar and set the tolerance in the Options bar to 20. Click on the white background surrounding the car and then click on the rear window behind the back seat to add these sections to the selection. You do not need to delete the white background in order to conceal it (deleting pixels is considered destructive editing and can restrict the control over the edge quality later).

Note > The TIFF image on the supporting DVD has a saved selection of the car.

9. Go to the Select menu and choose Inverse. Then proceed to select an adjustment layer from the Layers panel. It does not matter which adjustment layer you choose as we will only be borrowing its layer mask and not using it to make any adjustments to the layers beneath. Just select OK without making any adjustments. Click on the car layer above the adjustment layer and choose Create Clipping Mask from the Layer menu (Group With Previous Layer in version 7).

Note > The background will now have been removed but the edge still needs to be refined to improve its appearance.

10. The resulting mask is likely to have a 1-pixel white line visible around the edge of the old background. To remove this thin white line choose the Brush tool and paint with black directly into the layer mask of the adjustment layer to remove any white around the outer edges of the mask (the brush size can be large so long as you don't paint over the car. Alternatively a quicker option (if you know your shortcuts) is to select the Levels 2 layer mask and then to make a rectangular selection around the car using the Marquee tool (M), invert the selection (Ctrl/Command + Shift + I) and fill this selection with black (Alt/Option + Backspace/Delete if black is in the foreground swatch).

11. The edge of the mask needs to be softened and moved to conceal the remnants of the old white background. From the Select menu choose Refine Edge. Use a Smooth value of 3 and a Feather value of 1.0 pixel to smooth and soften the edge of the outline of the car. Slide the Contract/Expand slider to the left to hide any white edges from around the car. Select OK to apply the changes to the mask.

12. Now we're going to create a shadow. Select the adjustment layer below the mask layer and then click on the New Layer icon in the Layers panel. Select the Selection Brush tool in the Tools panel and then paint a selection that extends just in front of the tires and underneath the car. Extend some way over the edge of the car as this will be needed later (blurring the shadow will reduce its opacity at the edges). From the Edit menu choose the Fill command, select Black as the color and click OK.

13. Apply a Gaussian Blur filter to this layer and then refine the shadow by setting the blend mode to Multiply and lowering the opacity to around 70%.

Note > A second shadow layer could be added to create some smaller shadows just underneath the wheels and further underneath the car. This refinement will help create the illusion that the car is in contact with the flag.

14. The image just needs a few finishing touches to complete the project. Add the leaping Jaguar and make a selection of the white background surrounding the Jaguar using the Magic Wand tool. Click on the layer below and then add an adjustment layer. Select OK without making any adjustments (version 7 only). Create a Clipping Mask (Layer > Create Clipping Mask) and then use the Refine Edge command (Select > Refine Edge) to perfect the new addition.

15. As the Jaguar does not need to appear to be in contact with the flag we can simply add a drop shadow to this layer rather than create a shadow by hand. Go to the Effects panel and click on a Drop Shadow style. This can be modified or perfected by going to the Layers menu and choosing Style Settings. The angle and distance of the shadow from the object can be controlled from this dialog box or the user can simply click inside the image window and drag the shadow to a different position to obtain the best effect.

16. Complete the image by adding the image of the badge in the lower left-hand corner. Add a drop shadow to this layer and the project is complete.

Car photograph courtesy of www.iStockphoto.com

iStock_000000213548 (Dodge Viper GTS ACR – 2000 by Stan Rohrer)

PERFORMANCE TIP

An American flag is available on the DVD. The steps to creating a USA classic car and flag are pretty much the same as for the British car. A non-destructive Dodge and Burn layer was, however, grouped with the car layer to darken the tires and edge of the windshield. Select the color of the car using the Eyedropper tool and paint in Darken mode at 20% in a new layer grouped with the car layer to darken the paint further.

Project 5

Preserving Shadows

The truck used in this project was photographed in the hills of southern Queensland, Australia, while the river dock hails from more than a thousand miles south on the banks of the Yarra river in Melbourne, Victoria. Unlikely bedfellows, but with a little craft the two can lie together comfortably within the same frame – but only if the shadow retains all of its subtlety and is delicately transplanted to its new home on the wooden dock.

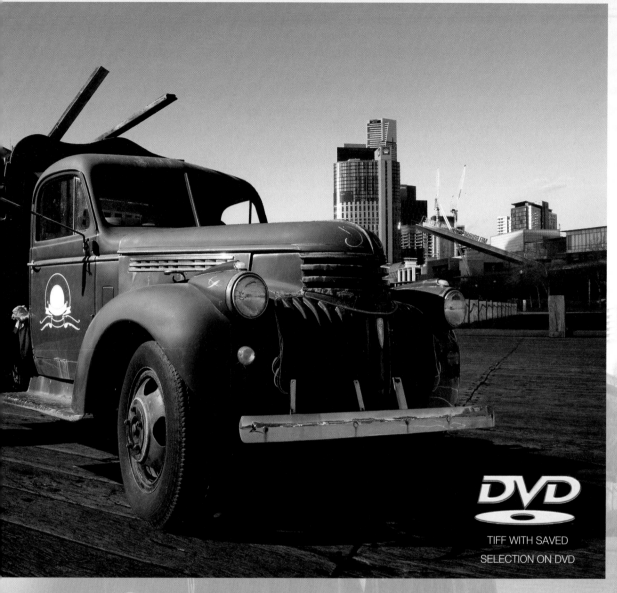

DVD

TIFF WITH SAVED
SELECTION ON DVD

The 'shadow catcher' technique – designed to preserve the natural shadows of a subject

1. Open the Truck TIFF image from the supporting DVD and go to Select > Load Selection. From the Selection menu choose Truck and click OK to load this selection.

Note > This selection has already been refined (see Project 1 in this module) so no further action needs to be taken to optimize the edge quality at this point in time. Raw and JPEG files are also available on the DVD but these do not contain saved selections that can fast-track this project.

2. In the Layers panel choose a Levels adjustment layer from the Create Adjustment Layer menu. Make no adjustment in the Levels dialog and select OK (version 7 only). Go to Filter > Adjustments > Invert to invert the mask so that the truck is masked rather than the background.

Note > We could have inverted the selection prior to creating the Levels adjustment layer but this leads to problems around the edges of the mask when we move and scale the truck later in the project. All subsequent layer masks in this project will be created the same way to avoid problems later on, i.e. creating a mask that then has to be inverted.

3. Hold down the Alt/Option key and click and drag the white input Levels slider to the left. The Alt/Option key will give you a threshold view and as you drag the slider to the left you will see increasing areas of tone being clipped to white. Continue to drag the slider to the left until the shadow appears as an island of black tone surrounded by white clipped tone. Select OK to apply this levels adjustment (version 7 only). Set the mode of the Levels adjustment layer to Luminosity to preserve the original Hue and Saturation values of the shadow tones.

4. Hold down the Ctrl/Command key and click on the adjustment layer mask from the Levels 1 layer to load it as a selection. Invert the selection using the keyboard shortcut Ctrl/Command+Shift+I. From the Create Adjustment Layer menu in the Layers panel choose a Solid Color adjustment layer. Select White as the foreground color and then select OK to create a Color Fill layer.

Note > Make sure the white you pick from the Pick a Solid Color dialog is 255 in all three channels. A quick way of doing this is to select the Only Web Colors option and then click in the top left-hand corner to select white.

5. Invert the layer mask of the Color Fill adjustment layer using the keyboard shortcut Ctrl/ Command + I. Lower the opacity of the Color Fill (Solid Color) layer. Select the Brush tool from the Tools panel and choose a hard-edged brush set to 100% Opacity in the Options bar. Paint over the shadow in black to mask this area on the Color Fill adjustment layer mask (no accuracy is required). When the masking is complete set the opacity of the Color Fill layer back to 100%.

6. Open the river dock image from the supporting DVD and drag the background layer thumbnail into the image window of the truck. Hold down the Shift key as you release the mouse button to center the image. Go to Image > Transform > Free Transform and resize the image to fit the canvas size of the truck image (use the keyboard shortcut Ctrl/Command + 0 to see the bounding box).

7. Hold down the Ctrl/Command key and click on the Levels 1 adjustment layer mask to load it as a selection. Inverse the selection (Ctrl/Command + Shift + I) and then click on the Color Fill adjustment layer to make it the active layer. From the Create Adjustment Layer menu in the Layers panel choose another Levels adjustment layer. Make no adjustment in the dialog and select OK (version 7 only). Invert the layer mask using the keyboard shortcut (Ctrl/Command + I). Hold down the Alt/Option key and click on the dividing line between the Levels 2 adjustment layer and the river dock layer to group them. Set the mode of the river dock layer to Multiply. You should now see the truck and its shadow against its new background.

8. To resolve the lighting direction problem (the shadows are being cast in different directions in the two images) we must flip either the truck or the background. Double-click the background layer and select OK in the New Layer dialog to unlock the background layer. To select multiple layers hold down the Shift key and select the truck layer (Layer 0) and all of the adjustment layers. Go to Image > Transform > Free Transform. In the Options bar deselect the Constrain Proportions checkbox and then enter a minus before the 100% width to flip the image and all of the supporting adjustment layers. Rotate the image anti-clockwise slightly and drag the truck into the best position. Click Commit Current Operation to complete the process.

9. Go to View > Actual Pixels and examine the edge of the truck. Now that the background has changed it may be necessary to expand the edge of this layer mask. Select the Levels 2 adjustment layer and go to Select > Refine Edge. From the View menu choose Selection to hide the selection edges. The Smooth slider can be set to 0 and the Feather sliders may need only a 0.5 pixel adjustment (the edge has already been feathered and smoothed). Adjust the Expand/Contract slider to remove any white halo from around the edge and then select OK.

10. If you are left with a thin dark line on the inside edge of the truck select the Levels 1 adjustment layer mask and then go to Select > Refine Edge once again. Set the Smooth and Feather sliders to 0 and move the Contract/Expand slider to the right to reduce any dark line that may be visible. Select OK to apply the changes.

Note > If any black edges are present in any of the layer masks this will lead to white edges or transparency around the edges of the canvas. Paint with white around the edge of any mask creating a problem.

11. To adjust the density of the shadow click the Levels 1 adjustment layer thumbnail to open the dialog (version 7 users need to double-click). Drag the central Gamma slider beneath the histogram to the left or right to lighten or darken the shadows under the truck.

12. The color temperature (white balance) of the two images is slightly different. To correct this difference add a Photo Filter adjustment layer above the truck layer. From the Photo Filter dialog choose a Warming Filter (85) and adjust the opacity until the white balance between the two images appears consistent.

THE BEST TECHNIQUE FOR SUBTLE SHADOWS

The technique to preserve shadows provides to those photographers burdened with a meticulous eye a useful way of retaining and transplanting subtle and complex shadows. Observe the subtle shadow cast by the leaf above that would be virtually impossible to re-create using any other technique. The primary circumstances that prevent this technique from being used are when the shadow falls over a surface with a different texture to the one in the new location, or the surface over which the shadow falls is particularly uneven or moves from a horizontal to a vertical plane over the length of the shadow.

PSD ON DVD

PERFORMANCE TIP

If it is not possible to preserve the original shadow, try to capture a second image from the direction of the light source. This second image will allow you to create a more accurate shadow than simply using the outline of the subject as seen from the camera angle instead of the direction of the light source.

This process would include the following steps:

• Make a mask of your subject and place it on a layer above a background.
• Import the second image captured from the direction of the light source and position it between the subject layer and the background layer.
• Make a selection of the subject in this second image (your shadow resource).
• Create a new empty layer that sits below the actual subject and above the background layer, and then fill this selection with black.
• Hide or delete the layer that the selection was made from.
• Place your new shadow layer in Multiply mode.
• Lower the opacity of your shadow layer and apply the Gaussian Blur filter.
• Use the Free Transform command to distort and move the shadow into position.

Project 6

6

High Dynamic Range

Contrary to popular opinion, what you see is not always what you get. You may be able to see the detail in those dark shadows and bright highlights when the sun is shining – but can your image sensor? Contrast in a scene is often a photographer's worst enemy. It is a sneak thief that steals away the detail in the highlights or shadows (sometimes both). Wedding photographers will deal with the problem of contrast by using fill flash to lower the subject contrast; commercial photographers diffuse their own light source or use additional fill lighting and check for missing detail using the histogram. Landscape photographers, however, have drawn the short straw when it comes to solving the contrast problem. For the landscape photographer there is no 'quick fix'. A reflector that can fill the shadows of the Grand Canyon has yet to be made and diffusing the sun's light is only going to happen if the clouds are prepared to play ball.

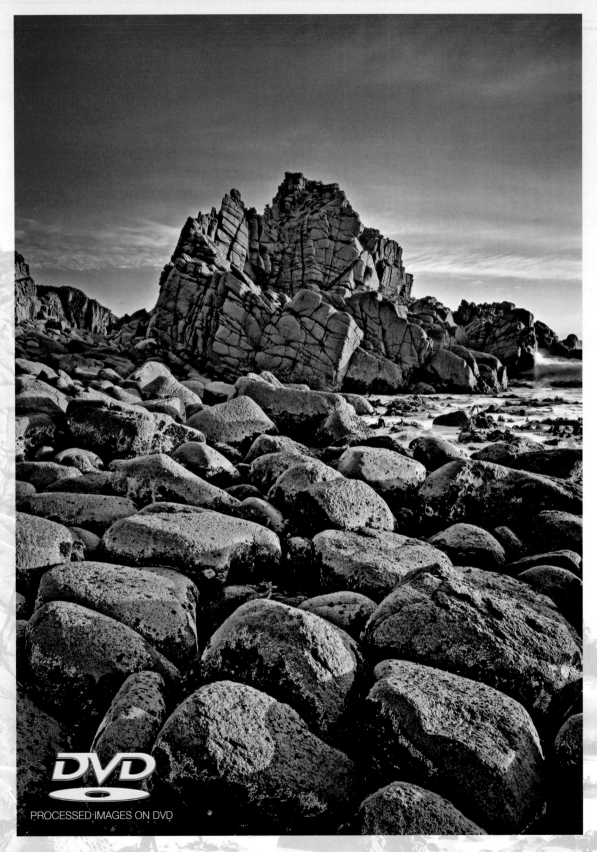

DVD

PROCESSED IMAGES ON DVD

Contrast no problem – discover the secrets to limitless dynamic range

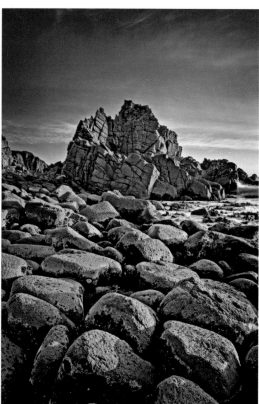

1. If we can't fit all the goodies into one exposure, then we'll just have to take two or more. The idea is to montage, or blend, the best of both worlds (the light and dark sides of the camera's not-quite all-seeing eye). To make the post-production easier we need to take a little care in the pre-production; i.e. mount the camera securely on a sturdy tripod. Take two exposures – one overexposing from the auto reading and the other underexposing from the auto reading. One or two stops either side of the meter-indicated exposure should cover most high-contrast situations.

PERFORMANCE TIP

Setting your camera to Auto Bracket exposure mode and using a remote release means that you don't have to touch the camera between the two exposures, thereby ensuring the first and second exposures can be exactly aligned with the minimum of fuss. The camera will bracket using the shutter speed rather than the aperture to avoid capturing images that have a different depth of field of focus. The only other movement to be aware of is something beyond your control. If there is a gale blowing (or even a moderate gust) you are not going to get the leaves on the trees to align perfectly in post-production. This also goes for fast-moving clouds and anything else that is likely to be zooming around in the fraction of a second between the first and second exposures.

2. Open both the HDR TIFF images from the supporting DVD. These files have been optimized from the Raw files (also available on the DVD) to enhance the shadow and highlight detail. Many HDR workflows use more than two exposures but the two captured for this project provide good shadow and highlight detail without the need for additional files (the advantage of shooting Raw). Go to File > New > Photomerge Exposure (new for Photoshop Elements 8). In the Photomerge Exposure dialog go to the Automatic tab and then select the Smart Blending option. For this project drag both the Highlights and the Shadows slider to 100 to achieve maximum detail from both exposures. Select Done at the base of the Photomerge Exposure dialog to merge the exposures.

Note > An alternative to Photomerge Exposure for Elements 7 users is EnfuseGUI which is currently available as a free download (show your appreciation with a donation) or the budget Bracketeer for Mac users which uses the Enfuse engine. Enfuse is every bit as good as Photomerge Exposure.

3. In the Layers panel choose Flatten Image from the fly-out menu (we no longer have any need for the original exposure on the background layer). Right-click on the new background layer after the file has been flattened and choose Duplicate Layer.

4. Go to Enhance > Adjust Color > Remove Color. This will ensure the color saturation does not increase when we take the next action. In the Layers panel set the mode of the copy layer to Soft Light. This is one of the contrast blend modes so the visual outcome will be to raise the contrast of the image.

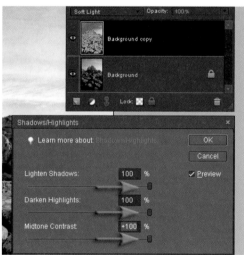

5. Go to Enhance > Adjust Lighting > Shadows/Highlights. In the Shadows/Highlights dialog raise all three sliders to 100%. These very aggressive adjustments will give your image a HDR post-produced appearance that is often referred to as 'tonal mapping'.

Note > If bright halos appear around the edges of your subject you may like to back off the Darken Highlights slider slightly.

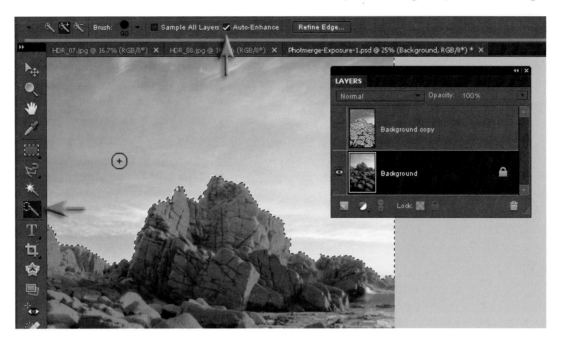

6. Switch off the visibility of the background copy layer and click on the background layer to select it. Select the Quick Selection tool in the Tools panel and check the Auto Enhance option in the Options bar (this will help to refine the edge of the selection). Click and drag the Quick Selection tool over the sky to select it.

7. From the Edit menu choose Copy and again from the Edit menu choose Paste. The sky will be copied to a new layer. In the Layers panel set the mode of this layer to Multiply. This action will darken the sky. A small halo will appear above the dark rocks. We will reduce this halo in the following couple of steps.

8. Hold down the Ctrl key (PC) or Command key (Mac) and click on the sky layer to load the pixels as a selection once again (alternatively you can go to Select > Reselect). Then go to Select > Modify > Border. This will allow you to turn the edges of the current selection into a new selection. Enter in a value of 200 pixels in the Width field (the maximum possible) and then select OK. If you are working with lower-resolution images you may need to reduce this amount. If you need to increase the width of the border selection go to Select > Modify > Expand. We are trying to cover the width of the halo with this selection so be generous with the width rather than conservative.

9. Go to Select > Feather and choose a Feather Radius that is about 25% of the amount you used for the border selection. In this project we have used a value of 50 pixels. Select OK. The feathering process will ensure that when we darken this region of the image it will occur gradually.

10. From the Edit menu choose Copy and then again from the Edit menu choose Paste. This will place a border of sky pixels on a new layer. Set the mode of this border layer to Multiply to darken the sky and remove the halo in this region.

11. Lower the opacity of this layer until the darkening process is subtle (no dark band should be visible). Go to Layer > Create Clipping Mask so that the darkening process does not spill over into the rocks. Select the Eraser tool from the Tools panel and the Brush option in the Options bar and then a large soft-edged brush. Remove any unwanted darkening from the sides and the top of the image and the process of halo reduction is complete.

12. Switch on the visibility of the background copy layer (the Soft Light layer with the Shadows/Highlights adjustment applied). The halo will appear so we need to mask this aspect of this Tonal Mapping layer. Ctrl/Command + click the Layer 1 sky layer to load this as a selection. Go to Select > Inverse to flip the selection so that it is the foreground rocks that are selected.

13. Select Layer 2 in the Layers panel (the border sky layer in Multiply mode). Then add a Levels adjustment layer (go to the Create New Fill or Adjustment Layer icon at the base of the Layers panel and choose Levels from the drop-down menu). The selection will be turned into an adjustment layer mask. Select the background copy layer above the Levels adjustment layer and then from the Layer menu choose Create Clipping Mask. We will now see the sky below and the halo will again be under control.

14. We will now add a vignette to the image. Stamp the visible layers into a new layer (use the keyboard shortcut Ctrl + Alt + Shift + E on a PC or Command + Option + Shift + E on a Mac). Choose the Rectangular Marquee tool and choose a 250 pixel feather in the Options bar. Select the central portion of the image. Then hit the Delete or Backspace key to remove the selected area.

15. Set the mode of this Stamp Visible layer to Multiply to create the vignette effect. Lower the opacity until you achieve a more subtle vignette effect. The foreground rocks will not be a little too dark so we can add another adjustment layer to take care of this. Go to Select > Deselect to remove the selection.

16. Go to the Create New Fill or Adjustment Layer icon at the base of the Layers panel and choose a Brightness/Contrast adjustment layer. Drag the brightness slider to the right to brighten the foreground rocks. Disregard the effects to the sky at this stage.

17. Select the Gradient tool in the tools panel and the Black, White and Linear Gradient options in the Options bar. Drag a gradient from just above the rocks to a position just below the horizon line. Hold down the Shift key to constrain the gradient to a perfect vertical. This gradient will mask the adjustment so that the sky is restored to its former brightness.

18. For even more HDR tonal mapping effect, stamp the visible elements to a new layer once again (see step 14). Go to Enhance > Adjust Color > Remove Color, set the mode of this layer to Soft Light and then go to Filter > Other > High Pass. Raise the radius to a high figure (between 40 and 70 pixels) to increase the localized contrast in the image. Select OK to apply the adjustment and drop the opacity of the layer if the effect is too much.

19. Stamp visible one more time and then sharpen to taste. My preference with these HDR images is to use the Unsharp Mask from the Enhance menu with the Threshold slider raised to 3.

PERFORMANCE TIP

In the full version of Photoshop the user has access to the Advanced Blending options. In this dialog box it is possible to reduce the opacity of the shadow tones on the top layer to reveal the shadow tones beneath. The effect can be faded in gradually, creating a blend of the optimum highlights from the top layer and the optimum shadow tones of the background layer. The Advanced Blending options are only available to users of the full version of Photoshop, but the same results can be achieved using a layer style preset loaded into the Presets folder in Elements. The layer styles provided on the supporting DVD give the Elements user the option of partial transparency based on tonality.

Photoshop Elements users can access the Transparency layer style by first loading the styles and metadata available on the supporting DVD into the Layer Styles folders (<C:\Documents and Settings\All_Users\ApplicationData\Adobe\Photoshop_Elements\7.0 or 8.0\Photo_Creations\layer styles). The styles and metadata were created in the full version of Photoshop but can be read by Photoshop Elements. The software may have to be restarted after loading the styles and metadata into the folder before Photoshop Elements will load the new content.

Note > Vista users will find the Adobe folder in the C:\Program Data folder.

Select the top layer in the Layers panel and then click on each of the four presets in turn (now located in the Effects panel) and choose the one that renders the best tonality.

To improve the midtone contrast proceed to stamp the visible elements of both the dark and light layers into a single layer (hold down the Ctrl/Command + Shift + Alt/Option keys and then type the letter E). Set the blend mode of this Stamp Visible layer to Soft Light and adjust the opacity of the layer if required.

RAW IMAGES ON DVD

Project 7

Photomerge

Photomerge is capable of aligning and blending images without any signs of banding in smooth areas of transition. The new and improved Photomerge first made its appearance in Photoshop CS3 but the maths got even better when it appeared in Photoshop Elements 6 and the stitching is now so clever it will really have you amazed at the quality that can be achieved.

Spot the joins – upgrade to 36 megapixels with seamless stitching

The quality will be even better if you capture vertical images with a 50% overlap using manual exposure, manual focus and Manual White Balance setting (or process the images identically in Camera Raw). The results are now usually seamless – an excellent way of widening your horizons or turning your humble compact camera into a 36 megapixel blockbuster.

The Photomerge feature in version 5 of Photoshop Elements and the full version of Photoshop CS2 left a lot to be desired. All of the flaws and weaknesses of this feature were removed with the release of Photoshop Elements 6.

Now, the only limitation you may come run up against is Photoshop Elements' ability to align and blend strong geometric lines that come close to the camera lens. If the camera is hand-held to capture the component images (i.e. you have not used a specialized tripod head designed for professional panoramic stitching work) then the problem of aligning both foreground and distant subject matter is a big problem for any software (Photoshop Elements handles it better than the rest). The camera should ideally be rotated around the nodal point of the lens to avoid something called parallax error. You will probably not encounter any problems with the new Photomerge feature unless you are working with strong lines in the immediate foreground. Notice how the curved lines in the image above are slightly crooked due to the fact that these images were shot with an 18 mm focal length and the circled lines are very close to the lens. Still pretty good – but not perfect.

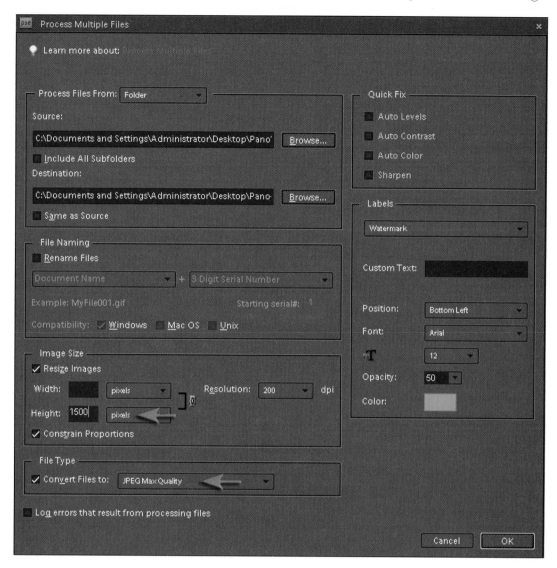

1. The images for this project are available as Camera Raw files but it is strongly recommended when using an older computer or a computer with less than one gigabyte of RAM to downsample the images before attempting this project. To efficiently downsample multiple images go to File > Process Multiple Files. Select the Source folder of the raw images (hit the Browse button) and then select the destination folder where you would like your processed files to be saved. Check Resize Images and select a height of 1500 pixels. Check Convert Files To and choose the JPEG Max Quality option. Select OK to process the images.

Note > If you wish to make a monster panorama (12-megapixel images are used in this project) select all of the Camera Raw files and open them in Adobe Camera Raw (ACR). Choose the Select All option in the top left-hand corner of the dialog box and select OK. Choose Image Settings for these images in ACR and then click Open Images.

2. Select all of the images from the destination folder you created in the Process Multiple Files dialog box. Open the processed images in Photoshop Elements. From the File > New menu choose Photomerge Panorama.

3. In the Photomerge dialog box click on the Add Open Files button and select the Auto radio button in the Layout options. Select OK and let Photoshop Elements do all of the work – and what a lot of work it has to do, aligning and blending all of these images.

Note > Photomerge can also handle multiple exposures and juggle which is the best exposure to use for any given location in the panorama.

4. Prior to Elements 6 many more steps of manual techniques were required to circumnavigate the shortcomings of Photomerge – but as you can see from the results in this project we just about have perfection handed to us on a plate. Fantabulous! (I know that's not in the dictionary but neither is Photomerge – yet.) If you have used the full-resolution images you probably had to go and make a cup of coffee while Photoshop Elements put this one together (all 60 megapixels of it) and will now be considering downsampling your file – but wait, we have a couple of small glitches in this result.

PERFORMANCE TIP

The Auto layout setting gets it right pretty much all of the time. Occasionally you may need to select either the Perspective or Cylindrical options for very wide panoramas. Interactive Layout can be selected when Photoshop Elements is having trouble deciding where one or two of the component images should be placed. This can occur when there is little detail in the image to align, e.g. a panorama of a beach scene where the only obvious line in the image is the horizon. When this occurs you will need to drag the problem file into the best location in the Interactive Layout dialog box.

PERFORMANCE TIP

If you downsample before you flatten your file you will probably encounter hairline cracks after reducing the image size. The solution to this problem is to either flatten the file or stamp the visible content to a new layer (Ctrl/Command + Shift + Alt/Option and then type the letter E) before you reduce the size of the image.

If you hold down the Alt/Option key and click on each layer mask in turn you will notice that Elements uses hard-edged layer masks to hide or reveal the piece of the jigsaw puzzle that makes up the final panorama. The panorama has seamless joins because Photoshop has adjusted or 'blended' the color and tonality of the pixels on each layer. Any pixels concealed by the layer masks have not been subjected to these color and tonal adjustments. This, in effect, means that the user cannot override which bit of each layer is visible as the hidden pixels have not been color-matched.

5. Stamp the visible elements to new a new layer (Ctrl + Shift + Alt and then type the letter E on a PC or Command + Shift + Option and then type the letter E on a Mac). Crop away that which is surplus to requirements before flattening the file, be sure to select the No Restriction option in the Options bar and leave the Width and Height fields blank. This is a big image (especially if you used the full-resolution files) so don't be surprised if things are a little slower in computer land right now.

6. There is a small area of transparency at the top of the frame that will need cloning (I did not want to crop too tight at the top of the frame). Select the Clone Stamp tool from the Tools panel and then clone in some new sky from immediately below the transparent area. I have created an empty new layer to clone into and have checked the Sample All Layers option in the Options bar. Only when I am happy with the patch job will I select Merge Down from the Layers fly-out menu.

7. When stitching just two or three images Photomerge Panorama gets it right pretty much all of the time. When stitching much wider panoramas where there is a good deal of foreground detail you may find a couple of alignment errors. These images were captured using a wide-angle lens and the foreground rocks are just in front of the tripod. If I had used a specialized panorama tripod head the effects of parallax error would not be a problem. Photomerge in this instance, however, has met its match. The foreground rocks all match perfectly but that horizon line has a small break and is undulating. We can fix this. Select the Rectangular Marquee tool and make a selection that just touches the horizon line at the lowest point. Make sure the feather option in the Options bar is set to 0. From the Select menu choose Inverse.

Note > The stitching errors may change depending on the resolution (pixel dimensions) of the files you choose for Photomerge to align and blend.

8. Go to Filter > Distort > Liquify. Choose either the Warp tool or the Shift Pixels tool to nudge the horizon line down towards the red frozen area (created from the selection you made in the last step). Increase the size of the brush to 400-500 pixels and decrease the Brush Pressure to a lowly 5 pixels. If using the Warp tool just click and drag to push the pixels into alignment. If using the Shift Pixels tool click and drag to the left in short strokes. When the horizon line is sitting on top of the red rectangle click OK to apply the changes to the image

9. Pushing the pixels down onto the selection in Liquify will create an unnaturally hard edge to the horizon. This can be fixed by selecting the Blur tool in the Tools panel and a Strength setting of 50% in the Options bar. Zoom in so you can see the effects of your painting and then paint along the edge to soften it.

10. If you find that there are still a few areas of the horizon line that could be nudged straighter you could either repeat the Liquify step or make a selection just below the horizon line again and Inverse the selection (Select > Inverse). Then use the Smudge tool with a very low Strength setting to push the pixels towards the selection edge. Remember that only selected pixels can be moved.

11. If you find a physical break in the horizon line or on the rocks either side of the horizon line you can create a patch to hide the awkward break. Use the rectangular Marquee tool with a feather radius of 10 pixels and make a small selection just next to the break. Choose Copy and then Paste from the Edit menu to put the patch onto its own layer. Then go to Image > Transform > Free Transform. You can now slide and rotate the patch into position. Hold down the Ctrl key (PC) or Command key (Mac) to distort the shape of the patch so that you can achieve a seamless fix.

12. If the Patch does not match the color of the tones then you can create an empty new layer and set the mode of this layer to Color. Select the Brush tool in the Tools panel, hold down the Alt or Option key and click on a more appropriate color to load this into the Foreground Color Swatch in the Tools panel. Then paint over the area that needs adjusting to further perfect the patched area.

13. You can finish this project by stamping the visible layers to a new layer (Ctrl + Shift + Alt + E for a PC or Command + Shift + Option + E for a Mac), setting the mode to Soft Light in the Layers panel and removing the color (Enhance > Adjust Color > Remove Color). Then go to Filter > Other > High Pass. Use a generous setting (60 to 70 pixels) to enhance the midtone contrast and then select OK. Lower the opacity of the layer if you want a more subtle effect.

14. To sharpen this project start by stamping the visible layers again and set the mode of the layer to Luminosity in the Layers panel. Go to Enhance > Unsharp Mask and use an appropriate amount of sharpening to enhance the details within the image (I have used settings of 150 for the amount, 1.0 for the Radius and 3 for the Threshold).

PERSPECTIVE OR CYLINDRICAL

When I selected Auto in the Layout section of the Photomerge Panorama dialog, Photoshop elected to use the Cylindrical option. This option is usually preferable and is usually selected by Auto when you are stitching wide panoramas. When stitching two or three images together you may find that Photoshop decides to use the Perspective option or you can choose this option to override the Cylindrical option if it is chosen by Auto. The Perspective option creates a bow-tie effect when stitching three images and is useful for creating a realistic perspective with straight horizon lines. When this option is used for more than three images, however, the distortion required to create the effect tends to be extreme for the images on the edge of the panorama and cannot therefore be considered as a usable option.

PHOTOMERGE GROUP SHOT

Photomerge also has a Group Shot option. This allows you to merge the best aspects of several images into the same image – especially useful when someone in a group has blinked or looked away. In this group shot (if you can call one boy and his dog a group) it has been decided to combine two images (captured hand-held) so both the boy and his dog are looking at the camera. In the Group Shot dialog box you just scribble over the part of the 'source' image that you would like to merge with the 'final' image. Although Photomerge will align and blend the component images with the same skill as the Panorama option, the user will be presented with an additional flattened file when Group Shot has finished weaving its magic.

For those users who are amazed at the results that can be achieved using Photomerge, but who mourn the loss of layers when using Group Shot, the Panorama option can still be used – even for group images. This is, however, only recommended for those photographers who use Manual White Balance rather than Auto White Balance in-camera. When the Panorama option has finished aligning the images it will have no idea of the 'best bits' it should include in the final result. In the image above it has decided that neither the boy nor the dog need to be looking at the camera. Note how the layer masks – yes, layer masks – are concealing the best bits of each image. Fear not, for we can modify these layer masks so we do get the bits that we want.

Clear both of the layer masks by clicking on each one in turn and then filling them with white. If white is the foreground color hold down the Alt/Option key while pressing the Backspace key. Then choose the Brush tool and paint with black into the mask to shield any of the pixels you do not want to see on this layer. This may seem like a novel approach to montage as we are now enjoying layer masks without having to hijack one on an adjustment layer. You will need to crop the image to finish your project. If you can see the value of this technique then you will quickly realize that taking multiple shots the next time you are presented with a group (or even just one man and his best friend) ensures the decisive moment is history (sorry Henri).

PHOTOMERGE SCENE CLEANER

The newest Photomerge feature (introduced with Photoshop Elements 7) is the Scene Cleaner. The Scene Cleaner is designed to rid your scenic shots of tourists. You no longer have to wait for the scene to be empty before capturing your shot. Just take multiple shots (no tripod required) as the people move around and you can then clean the scene using the new Photomerge Scene Cleaner. The process is remarkably simple; just drag one of your images into the Final window and then click on any of the other images in the Project Bin to set it as the source image. Then paint over any tourist in the Final window or any part of the source file on the left that does not have a tourist (no accuracy is required in the painting action) and the scene in the Final window on the right is cleaned automatically. Move your mouse off the image and the strokes will disappear. The auto-align component of the Photomerge dialog means that the patch is seamless.

PHOTOMERGE FACES

The strangest of the automated features in the Photomerge bag of tricks called Photomerge Faces. The results are often delightfully random, even though you are supposed to define the bits you want merged. You must first use the Alignment tool to indicate where the eyes and mouth are in each image and then click the Align Photos button. In the top part of the example above, the boy's eyes have been merged seamlessly into the girl's face, while in the lower examples Photomerge has happily lifted the nose and lower portion of the ears in the source image in order to achieve a seamless stitch. Great fun (if slightly disturbing) – absolutely no commercial value – but will keep the kids amused for hours!

Project 8

Photograph by Daniel Stainsby

Maximum Performance

Use the Mask Hair Against White action
to fast-track this technique

Hair Transplant

One of the most challenging montage or masking jobs in the profession of post-production editing is the hair lift. When the model has long flowing hair and the subject needs to change location many post-production artists call in sick. Get it wrong and, just like a bad wig, it shows. Extract filters, Magic Erasers and Tragic Extractors don't even get us close. The first secret step must be completed before you even press the shutter on the camera. Your number one essential step for success is to first shoot your model against a white backdrop, sufficiently illuminated so that it is captured as white rather than gray. This important aspect of the initial image capture ensures that the resulting hair transplant is seamless and undetectable. The post-production is the easy bit – simply apply the correct sequence of editing steps and the magic is all yours. This is not brain surgery but follow these simple steps and you will join the elite ranks of image-editing gurus around the world. Celebrity status is just a few clicks away.

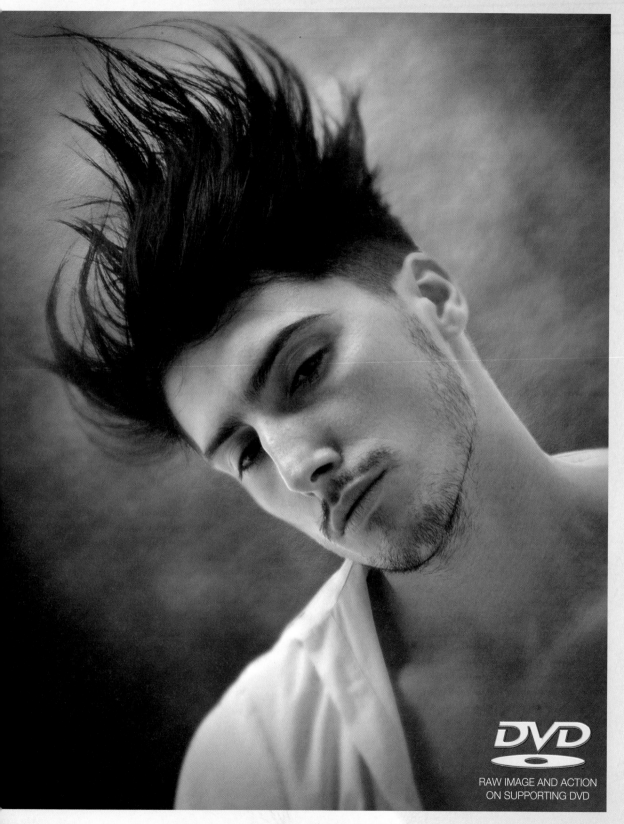

DVD

RAW IMAGE AND ACTION
ON SUPPORTING DVD

Hair extraction – not as painful as pulling teeth

Stage 1: Masking hair – tips for tremendous transplants

1. The initial steps of this tutorial are concerned with creating a mask that can be used in the final montage. Start by dragging the background layer to the New Layer icon to duplicate it. Choose Remove Color from the Adjust Color submenu found in the Enhance menu (Enhance > Adjust Color > Remove Color). Drag this desaturated/monochrome layer to the New Layer icon in the Layers panel to duplicate it. Set the blend mode of this new layer (now on top of the layers stack) to Overlay mode.

2. From the Layer menu choose Merge Down to create a single high-contrast monochrome layer. Select Black as the foreground color and the Brush tool from the Tools panel. Choose a large hard-edged brush and 100% opacity from the Options bar and set the mode to Overlay (also in the Options bar). Painting in Overlay mode will preserve the white background and darken the rest of the pixels. Accuracy while painting in Overlay mode is not a concern when the background is white or is significantly lighter than the subject. Avoid going anywhere near the tips of the hair at this stage.

3. Even the bright tones of the white shirt can be rendered black by repeatedly clicking the mouse while using a large brush in Overlay mode. Again it is important to avoid going anywhere near the tips of the hair.

4. Darken the body of the hair near the scalp but avoid the locks of hair that have white background showing through. Painting these individual strands of hair will thicken the hair and may lead to haloes appearing later in the montage process.

PERFORMANCE TIP

Switch the blend mode of the brush in the Options bar to Normal when painting away from the edge of the subject. This will ensure a speedy conclusion to the mask-making process. The mask is now ready to use in the montage.

Note > If any of the background has been darkened in the process of creating a black and white mask, switch the foreground color to white and choose Overlay in the Options bar. Paint to render any areas of gray background white. It is again important to avoid painting near the edges containing delicate hair detail.

5. With the Remove Color layer selected add a Levels adjustment layer. Without making any adjustment simply select OK (version 7 only). This Levels adjustment layer has a layer mask that we can use to house the mask that we created in the previous step.

6. The next step relocates the mask you have just created into the layer mask of the adjustment layer. From the Select menu choose All and from the Edit menu choose Copy Merged. Hold down the Alt/Option key and click on the layer mask thumbnail in the Layers panel. The image window will momentarily appear white as you view the empty contents of the layer mask. From the Edit menu choose Paste to transfer the contents of the clipboard to this layer mask. Click on the layer below to select it and then click on the Visibility icon of this layer to switch it off. This mask layer serves no purpose now that it has been successfully transferred to the adjustment layer mask. Go to Select > Deselect to lose the active selection.

7. The new background is placed on its own layer above the figure and mask layers. Open the background image and drag the thumbnail of this new file into the image window of your project file from the layer thumbnail in the Layers panel. Group this new background layer with the adjustment layer beneath (Layer > Create Clipping Mask). Alternatively you can hold down the Alt/Option key and click on the dividing line between the two layers to create the Clipping Mask.

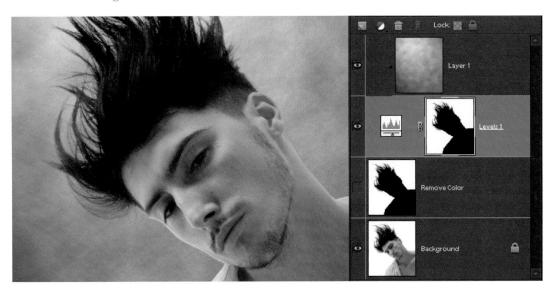

8. Grouping the new background with the adjustment layer will mask the background in the region of the figure but the quality will not yet be acceptable. Setting the blend mode of the adjustment layer to Multiply will bring back all of the fine detail in the hair. The background will not be darkened by applying the Multiply blend mode as white is a neutral color. The subtle details in the fine strands of hair will, however, be preserved in all their glory.

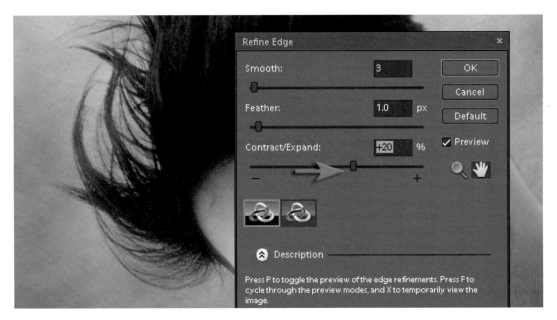

9. The accuracy and quality of the edge of the mask will usually require some attention in order for the subject to achieve a seamless quality with the new background. Go to the Select menu and choose Refine Edge. Choose the default values for the Smooth and Feather sliders (3 and 1.0) and then move the Contract/Expand slider to the right to hide any white edges from around the body and shirt.

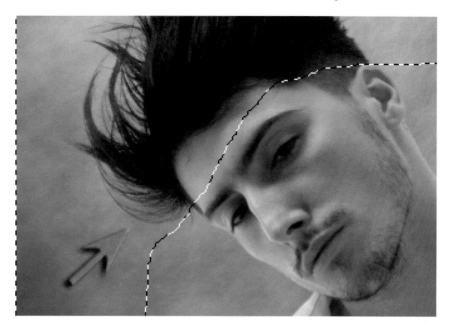

10. In most instances the hair is already looking pretty fabulous but to modify and perfect it even further you will need to make a selection of just the hair with the Lasso tool. Select the Levels 1 layer mask and then choose Enhance > Adjust Lighting > Levels and move the central Gamma slider to the left to increase the density of the hair and eliminate any white haloes that may be present. Moving the white slider to the left a little may help the process of achieving a perfect blend between subject and background. Select OK (version 7 only) and choose Deselect from the Select menu.

PERFORMANCE TIP

Make a selection of any portion of the edge that requires a localized adjustment using the Lasso tool with a small amount of feather entered in the Options bar. Use a Levels adjustment (Enhance > Adjust Lighting > Levels) to optimize this portion of the edge.

PERFORMANCE TIP

Any localized refinement of the mask can also be achieved manually by painting with a small soft-edged brush directly into the layer mask. Paint with white at a reduced opacity (10–20%) to remove any fine haloes present in localized areas. Several brush strokes will slowly erase the halo from the image.

11. The true test of an accurate mask for a subject who was photographed against a white background is when you place the subject against a very dark background. Grouping a Levels adjustment layer with the new background layer can darken the background image used in this project. Hold down the Alt/Option key when you select a Levels adjustment layer from the Layers panel. Click on the Create Clipping Mask box in the New Layer dialog box (Group With Previous Layer in version 7) and then select OK to open the Levels dialog. Move the Gamma slider to the right in order to preview your subject against a darker background in the image window.

Stage 2: Split-tone styling and depth of field tweaking

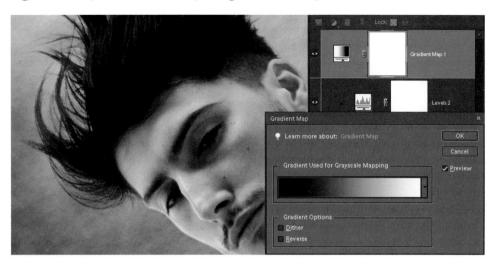

12. Now that the hair transplant is complete the styling can commence. Select the top layer in the Layers panel and then click on the Create Adjustment Layer icon and choose Gradient Map. I have applied one of the split-tone presets that are available on the supporting DVD. See the 'Toning' project in Part 2. A split tone that has a cool shadow tone and a warm highlight tone has been used to achieve the split-tone effect for this project. The opacity of the Gradient Map layer is then lowered.

13. A shallow depth of field can be achieved by first merging the contents of all of the layers to a new layer. With the top layer in the Layers panel selected choose All from the Select menu and then choose Copy Merged from the Edit menu. Click on the New Layer icon in the Layers panel and then choose Paste from the Edit menu. The keyboard shortcut for the last sequence of commands is to hold down the Ctrl, Shift and Alt keys (PC) or Command, Shift and Option keys (Mac) and then press the letter E on the keyboard. Apply a 4-pixel Gaussian Blur to this layer (Filter > Blur > Gaussian Blur).

14. Click on the layer beneath the merged layer (the one you have just blurred) and then create a Levels adjustment layer. Select OK without making any adjustments (version 7 only). Create a clipping mask for the layer above with this adjustment layer and then click on the adjustment layer mask to select it. Select the Gradient tool from the Tools panel and choose Reflected Gradient and the Black, White option from the Options bar. Click in the central part of the model's face and drag outwards to a position just beyond the ear. The sharp focus should now be restored to the central portion of the face only.

15. Create a vignette for this image. Select Layer 2 and then hold down the Alt/Option key and click on the Create a New Layer icon. In the New Layer dialog box set the mode to Multiply and choose the 'Fill with Multiply-neutral color (white)' option. A selection is then made using the Elliptical Marquee tool, feathered by 100 pixels (Select > Feather) and then in the Fill Layer dialog box, in the Contents section, choose Use Black (Edit > Fill Selection). The vignette is then subdued by lowering the opacity of the layer. Go to Select > Deselect to remove the selection.

Note > A small amount of noise must be added if you are creating a vignette in a very smooth-toned background in order to prevent any tonal banding (Filter > Noise > Add Noise).

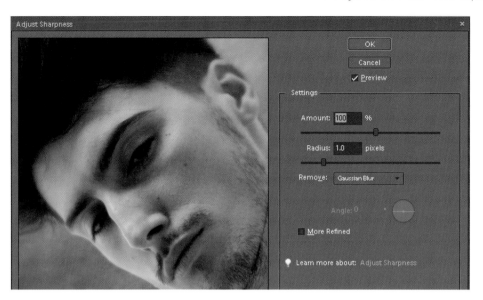

16. Create a merged copy of all of the layers (hold down the Ctrl + Shift + Alt keys (PC) or Command + Shift + Alt keys (Mac) and type the letter E as in step 13) and apply Adjust Sharpening (Enhance > Adjust Sharpening) to complete the project.

To change the scenery (background) simply trash the sharpened and blurred layers and cut and paste a new image into the layer that was clipped with your adjustment layer mask. One face, lots of hair – a million locations. Now you don't have to put a hat on to go traveling.

MAXIMUM PERFORMANCE

When masking hair that was shot against a black background, setting the Levels adjustment layer (the one holding the mask) to the Screen Blend mode is the secret to success. Note the difference between Normal mode and Screen Blend mode in the illustrations above.

You will need to invert the layer mask when using a model shot against a black background (Filter > Adjustments > Invert). Paint in Overlay mode as in steps 2 to 4 of the 'Hair Transplant' project. Apply a Levels adjustment to the layer mask and fine-tune the brightness of the hair against the background by moving the Gamma slider.

Maximum Performance

Use the Mask Hair Against Black action to fast-track this technique

image courtesy of www.iStockphoto.com

iStock_00000803940 (Blond Goddess by Iconogenic)

Jargon Buster

A

ACR: Adobe Camera Raw. Raw processing utility supplied with Photoshop Elements.

Adjustment layers: Non-destructive (always editable) image adjustment placed on a layer.

Aliasing: The display of a digital image where a diagonal or curved line appears jagged due to the square pixels.

Anti-aliasing: The process of smoothing the appearance of lines in a digital image.

Artifacts: Pixels that are significantly incorrect in their brightness or color values.

B

Bit: Short for binary digit, the basic unit of the binary language.

Bit depth: Number of bits (memory) assigned to recording color or tonal information.

Blend mode: The formula used for defining the mixing of a layer with those beneath it.

Brightness: The value assigned to a pixel in the HSB model to define the relative lightness of a pixel.

Byte: Eight bits. Standard unit of data storage containing a value between 0 and 255.

C

CCD: Charge-coupled device. A solid-state sensor used in digital image capture.

Channel: A division of color or luminance data.

Clipboard: Place for the temporary storage of something that has been cut or copied.

Clipping group: Two or more layers that have been linked. The base layer acts as a mask, limiting the effect or visibility of those layers grouped with it.

Cloning tool: A tool used for replicating pixels.

Color fringing: Bands of color on the edges of lines within an image.

Color gamut: The range of colors provided by a hardware device, or a set of pigments.

Color management: A system to ensure uniformity of color between the subject, monitor display and final print.

Color Picker: Dialog box used for the selection of colors.

Compression: A method for reducing the file size of a digital image.

Constrain proportions: Retains the proportional dimensions of an image when changing the image size.

Continuous tone: The illusion of smooth gradations between highlights and shadows.

Contrast: The difference in brightness between the darkest and lightest areas of the image or subject.

Crash: The sudden operational failure of a computer.

Crop: Reduce image size to enhance composition or limit information.

Curves: A control, in the full version of Adobe Photoshop only, for adjusting tonality and color.

D

Default: A 'normal' or 'start' setting as chosen by the manufacturer or user.

Depth of field: The zone of sharpness variable by aperture, focal length or subject distance.

DNG: Digital Negative (Adobe's Raw file format).

Dpi: Dots per inch. A measurement of resolution.

E

Editable text: Text that has not been rendered into pixels.

Exposure: Combined effect of intensity and duration of light on a light-sensitive material or image sensor.

Exposure compensation: To increase or decrease the exposure from a meter-indicated exposure to obtain an appropriate exposure.

F

Feather: The action of softening the edge of a digital selection.

File format: The code used to store digital data, e.g. TIFF or JPEG.

File size: The memory required to store digital data in a file.

Format: The orientation or shape of an image or the erasure of a memory device.

Freeze: Software that fails to interact with new information.

G

Galleries: A managed collection of images displayed in a conveniently accessible form.

Gaussian Blur: A filter used for defocusing a digital image.

Gigabyte: A unit of measurement for digital files, 1024 megabytes.

Grayscale: An 8-bit image used to describe monochrome (black and white) images.

H

High Dynamic Range (HDR): A subject brightness range that exceeds the ability of the capture medium (film or sensor) to record both the highlight and shadow information simultaneously.

Highlight: Area of subject receiving highest exposure value.

Histogram: A graphical representation of a digital image indicating the pixels allocated to each level.

Hue: The name of a color, e.g. red or green.

I

Image size: The pixel dimensions, output dimensions and resolution used to define a digital image.

Interpolation: Increasing the pixel dimensions of an image by inserting new pixels between existing ones within an image.

ISO: International Standards Organization. A numerical system for rating the speed or relative light sensitivity of a film or sensor.

J

JPEG (.jpg): Joint Photographic Experts Group. Popular but lossy (i.e. destructive) image compression file format.

K

Kilobyte: 1024 bytes.

L

Lasso tool: Selection tool used in digital editing.

Latitude: Ability of the film or device to record the brightness range of the subject.

Layer mask: A mask attached to an adjustment layer that is used to define the visibility of the adjustment. It can also be used to limit the visibility of pixels on the layer above.

Layers: A feature in digital editing software that allows a composite digital image in which each element is on a separate layer or level.

Levels: Shades of lightness or brightness assigned to pixels.

Luminance adjustment: The ability to adjust the brightness of a color without affecting either the hue or saturation.

M

Magic Wand tool: Selection tool used in digital editing.

Marching ants: A moving broken line indicating a digital selection of pixels.

Marquee tool: Selection tool used in digital editing.

Megabyte: A unit of measurement for digital files, 1024 kilobytes.

Megapixel: A million pixels.

Memory card: A small removable storage device used in digital cameras to save captured images.

Minimum aperture: Smallest lens opening.

Mode (digital image): The tonal and color space of the captured or scanned image.

N

Noise: Electronic interference producing speckles in the image.

O

Opacity: The degree of non-transparency.

Opaque: Not transmitting light.

Optimize: The process of fine-tuning the file size and display quality of an image.

Out-of-gamut: Beyond the scope of colors that a particular device can create, reproduce or display.

P

Pixel: The smallest square picture element in a digital image.

Pixellated: An image where the pixels are visible to the human eye and curved or diagonal lines appear jagged or stepped.

Primary colors: The three colors of light (red, green and blue).

R

RAM: *Random access memory. The computer's short-term or working memory.*

Reflector: *A surface used to reflect light in order to fill shadows.*

Resample: *To alter the total number of pixels describing a digital image.*

Resolution: *This term can be applied to optical resolution (how sharply the image was captured), screen resolution (the number of pixels being displayed by your monitor, e.g. 1024 x 768), printer resolution (dots per inch or dpi) or **image** resolution (pixels per inch or ppi).*

RGB: *Red, green and blue. The three primary colors used to display images on a color monitor.*

Rubber Stamp: *Another name for the Clone Stamp tool used for replicating pixels.*

S

Sample: *To select a color value for analysis or use.*

Saturation (color): *Intensity or richness of color hue.*

Save As: *An option that allows the user to create a duplicate of a digital file with an alternative name or in a different location.*

Scale: *A ratio of size.*

Scratch disk: *Portion of the hard disk allocated to software such as Elements to be used as a working space.*

Screen redraws: *Time taken to render information being depicted on the monitor as changes are being made through the application software.*

Sharp: *In focus; not blurred.*

Sliders: *A sliding control to adjust settings such as color, tone, opacity, etc.*

Stamp Visible: *The action of copying the visible elements from a number of layers and pasting them onto a new layer.*

System software: *Computer operating program, e.g. Windows or Mac OS.*

T

TIFF: *Tagged Image File Format. Popular image file format for desktop publishing applications.*

Tone: *A tint of color or shade of gray.*

Transparent: *Allowing light to pass through.*

U

Unsharp Mask: *A filter used to sharpen images.*

W

Workflow: *Series of repeatable steps required to achieve a particular result within a digital imaging environment.*

Z

Zoom tool: *A tool used for magnifying a digital image on the monitor.*

Shortcuts (PC)

 Printable PDF file on DVD

Action   Keyboard shortcut

Navigate and view

Fit image on screen	Ctrl + 0
View image at 100% (Actual Pixels)	Alt + Ctrl + 0
Zoom tool (magnify)	Ctrl + Spacebar + click image or Ctrl + +
Zoom tool (reduce)	Alt + Spacebar + click image or Ctrl + -
Show/hide rulers	Shift + Ctrl + R
Hide panels	Tab key

File commands

Open	Ctrl + O
Close	Ctrl + W
Save	Ctrl + S
Save As	Ctrl + Shift + S
Undo	Ctrl + Z
Redo	Ctrl + Y

Selections

Add to selection	Hold Shift key and select again
Subtract from selection	Hold Alt key and select again
Copy	Ctrl + C
Cut	Ctrl + X
Paste	Ctrl + V
Paste into selection	Ctrl + Shift + V
Free Transform	Ctrl + T
Distort image in Free Transform	Hold Ctrl key + move handle
Feather	Alt + Ctrl + D
Select All	Ctrl + A
Deselect	Ctrl + D
Reselect	Shift + Ctrl + D
Inverse selection	Shift + Ctrl + I

Painting

Set default foreground and background colors	D
Switch between foreground and background colors	X
Enlarge brush size (with Paint tool selected)	]
Reduce brush size (with Paint tool selected)	[
Make brush softer	[+ Shift
Make brush harder	] + Shift
Change opacity of brush in 10% increments (with Paint tool selected)	Press number keys 0–9
Fill with foreground color	Alt + Backspace
Fill with background color	Ctrl + Backspace

Image adjustments

Levels	Ctrl + L
Hue/Saturation	Ctrl + U
Group layer	Ctrl + G

Layers and masks

Add new layer	Shift + Ctrl + N
Load selection from layer mask	Ctrl + click thumbnail
Change opacity of active layer in 10% increments	Press number keys 0–9
Add layer mask – Hide All	Alt + click Add Layer Mask icon
Move layer down/up	Ctrl + [or]
Stamp visible	Ctrl + Alt + Shift + E
Disable/enable layer mask	Shift + click layer mask thumbnail
View layer mask only	Alt + click layer mask thumbnail
View layer mask and image	Alt + Shift + click layer mask thumbnail
Blend modes	Alt + Shift + F, N, S, M, O, Y (Soft Light, Normal, Screen, Multiply, Overlay, Luminosity)

Crop

Commit crop	Enter key
Cancel crop	Esc key
Constrain proportions of crop marquee	Hold Shift key
Turn off magnetic guides when cropping	Hold Alt + Shift keys + drag handle

Shortcuts (Mac) *DVD* Printable PDF file on DVD

Action	Keyboard shortcut
Navigate and view	
Fit image on screen	Command + 0
View image at 100% (Actual Pixels)	Option + Command + 0
Zoom tool (magnify)	Command + Spacebar + click image or Ctrl + +
Zoom tool (reduce)	Option + Spacebar + click image or Command + -
Show/hide rulers	Shift + Command + R
Hide panels	Tab key
File commands	
Open	Command + O
Close	Command + W
Save	Command + S
Save As	Command + Shift + S
Undo	Command + Z
Redo	Command + Y
Selections	
Add to selection	Hold Shift key and select again
Subtract from selection	Hold Option key and select again
Copy	Command + C
Cut	Command + X
Paste	Command + V
Paste into selection	Command + Shift + V
Free Transform	Command + T
Distort image in Free Transform	Hold Command key + move handle
Feather	Option + Command + D
Select All	Command + A
Deselect	Command + D
Reselect	Shift + Command + D
Inverse selection	Shift + Command + I

Painting

Set default foreground and background colors	D
Switch between foreground and background colors	X
Enlarge brush size (with Paint tool selected)	]
Reduce brush size (with Paint tool selected)	[
Make brush softer	[+ Shift
Make brush harder	] + Shift
Change opacity of brush in 10% increments (with Paint tool selected)	Press number keys 0–9
Fill with foreground color	Option + Backspace
Fill with background color	Command + Backspace

Image adjustments

Levels	Command + L
Hue/Saturation	Command + U
Group layer	Command + G

Layers and masks

Add new layer	Shift + Command + N
Load selection from layer mask	Command + click thumbnail
Change opacity of active layer in 10% increments	Press number keys 0–9
Add layer mask – Hide All	Option + click Add Layer Mask icon
Move layer down/up	Command + [or]
Stamp visible	Command + Option + Shift + E
Disable/enable layer mask	Shift + click layer mask thumbnail
View layer mask only	Option + click layer mask thumbnail
View layer mask and image	Option + Shift + click layer mask thumbnail
Blend modes	Option + Shift + F, N, S, M, O, Y (Soft Light, Normal, Screen, Multiply, Overlay, Luminosity)

Crop

Commit crop	Enter key
Cancel crop	Esc key
Constrain proportions of crop marquee	Hold Shift key
Turn off magnetic guides when cropping	Hold Option + Shift keys + drag handle

Index